Advance Praise for
THE CULTURE TRAP

"Gary Gripp died before finishing his seminal work, a book that tied together his understanding of human cultures and life. Gary and I were online friends. Beyond the personal loss, I feared his keen perspectives would have died with him. Fortunately, Nick Brink took up the effort, assembled the chapters, and smoothed the edges to present 'THE CULTURE TRAP.'

A few human cultures lived sustainably for thousands of years in a balance with Nature. In a Darwinian twist, unsustainable cultures consistently overwhelmed their neighbors. While many seek to avoid the climate and ecological consequences obvious today, our deeply inherited cultural beliefs stop us. At core is whether we are one with or separate from Nature. 'THE CULTURE TRAP' is addressed to future generations as a warning of what beliefs need be taboo. To live sustainably, Gary introduces us to Holonic Reciprocity, and mythic stories that may help us adopt it." —**Rudy Sovinee, creator of 1wow.org**

"Gary Gripp gave the world a wonderful gift with this profound and important book about the trap in which we find ourselves, and what we should do about it." —**Derrick Jensen, author of more than 25 books, including** *Bright green Lies: How the Environmental Movement Lost its Way and What We Can Do About It* **and** *A Language Older than Words*

"My own complete commitment to the commonweal and to the cleanest air to breathe for ourselves and for our families was a 'gut instinct' for me that will not give up. Gary Gripp's journey to a life of peace and a path toward justice for all celebrates our natural world, yet brings unceasing attention to the cultural failures of corporate greed, individual narcissism, consumerism and patriarchy. We celebrate you Gary Gripp and your success in finding your '... joy and hope to craft my own lighter existence on the Earth.'" —**Nancy F Parks, 43 years of Clean Air activism for all through the Sierra Club**

THE CULTURE TRAP

Living in Loyalty to the Whole

GARY GRIPP

Epigraph Books
Rhinebeck, New York

The Culture Trap: Living in Loyalty to the Whole © 2021 by Nicholas Brink

All rights reserved. No part of this book may be used or reproduced in any manner without the consent of the publisher except in critical articles or reviews. Contact the publisher for information.

Paperback ISBN 978-1-954744-34-9
eBook ISBN 978-1-954744-35-6

Library of Congress Control Number 2021917106

Book design by Colin Rolfe
Front cover image of Sahalie Falls by Jillian Taylor

Epigraph Books
22 East Market Street, Suite 304
Rhinebeck, NY 12572
(845) 876-4861
epigraphps.com

CONTENTS

Acknowledgments vii
Foreword: Nicholas E. Brink, Ph.D. ix

PART I: THE CULTURE TRAP

Chapter 1: What you Need to Know 3
Chapter 2: Your Future World 6
Chapter 3: The Theft of Our World 9
Chapter 4: Some Prehistory 16
Chapter 5: A Turning Point 23
Chapter 6: On the Farm 31
Chapter 7: The Normalcy Bias 38
Chapter 8: Why Domestication? 44
Chapter 9: Life on the Lake 50
Chapter 10: A Second Twisted Turning 57
Chapter 11: Unrestrained Exploitation 66
Chapter 12: Imbibing Belief 77
Chapter 13: At Mother's Knee 85
Chapter 14: Global Climate Crisis 91
Chapter 15: Failing Ecosystem 97
Chapter 16: Loss of the Web of Life 105

Chapter 17: The Indigenous Worldview 120
Chapter 18: Three Faces of Culture 128
Chapter 19: Living in the Gift 141
Chapter 20: Law of Holonic Reciprocity 150
Chapter 21: Failing Morally 158
Chapter 22: The Foundation of a New Story 166
Chapter 23: The Technology Trap 176
Chapter 24: Education in Culture 187
Chapter 25: Land Management Fatality 200
Chapter 26: The Science-Nature Separation 212
Chapter 27: Corporate Race to Extinction 225
Chapter 28: Love Your Piece of Land 233

PART II: THE SOPHIA MYTH AND OTHER ESSAYS

Chapter 29: The Sophia Myth 247
   Introduction to Four Essays on the Sophia Myth
   Part 1: A New Story to Live By
   Part 2: From Fragments to a Nearly Integrated Whole
   Part 3: A Fallible Goddess versus the Almighty Yahweh
   Part 4: Myth, Truth, and Meaning
Chapter 30: The Tree, The Human and Morality 305
Chapter 31: Indigenous Folks and Us 309
Chapter 32: An Ideology that is Morally, Socially
and Ecologically Bankrupt 311
Chapter 33: The Most Dangerous Animal on Earth . . . 332
Chapter 34: Whose Woods These Are, I Thought I Knew . . 343
Chapter 35: The Most Dangerous Social Institutions . . . 356
Chapter 36: Biosystems, Power Systems, and People . . . 368
Chapter 37: Raw Capitalism: An Overview 379
Chapter 38: Once Was Wannabe 387

Bibliography 405

ACKNOWLEDGMENTS

I WRITE THESE acknowledgements for Gary after his passing. First, two members of his family provided essays and important support in this publication venture, Mark Gripp, Gary's son who is in possession of Gary's computer, and Pat Thornton Gripp, Gary's partner, who often spent time listening to his essays and gave him creative feedback. Pat and Mark have offered continued support in bringing together these essays in *The Culture Trap*.

Gary sent his essays to many people, seeking feedback and support from them. When I would receive an essay it often contained names of others, and I would Friend them on Facebook. Thus, over thirty of Gary's 309 Facebook friends have become my friends too. One of these lists included five other names: Rudy Sovinee, Susan Avery, Dave Warren, Steven Earl Salmony, and Suz Elle Steen. All are now my Facebook friends. Other familiar names from Gary's essays who have become my Facebook friends include Erica Velis, Ann Baird, Skye Daniels, Steve Mann, Carmine Leo, Gerhard Dekker, Jared Tyler, Carmelia Jamison, Dan Hanrahan, Derrick Jensen, Erik Michaels, Geoff Pearce, James Day, Jenny Lisak, Suzy Skye, Ted Howard, Martha Peterson, David Casey, Lynne Blahnik, Paul

Shaffer, Tina Mccafferty, Joram Echeles, Michael Dunkley, John Beaulieu, Bill Everett, Peter Cohen, Owen Troy, and John Higson. I have messaged his over three hundred Facebook friends, have told them of this project and I have received enthusiastic feedback from over twenty of them, including Arthur Sevestre, Geoff Pearce, Bob Colgan, Nina Parker, and Jan Wyllie not mentioned above. In addition to the above mentioned I am sure I have missed many names of others who were important to Gary in his writing. Gary would have wanted to thank all who have given him support and for their continued support in the production of this book.

NICHOLAS BRINK

NICHOLAS E. BRINK, PH.D.

FOREWORD

I FIRST WANT to acknowledge the Esopus Lenape, the First Nation people who tended and cared for the land where we now live in the Hudson Valley of New York.

In 2007, Toni Gripp Brink in her search for relatives connected with Gary Gripp, a cousin she vaguely remembered from her early childhood, seventy-some years ago. He was living in Oregon beside the McKenzie River, and we had the opportunity to visit him at his home in McKenzie Bridge in 2014. Again, it is important to acknowledge and remember The First Nation people who cared for the land and the McKenzie River where Gary lived. These people were the Molalla and the Kalapuya.

Upon arriving for this visit the first thing he did was take us on a tour of his vegetable garden, something of central importance in his life. Another activity of importance to him was his daily walks along the river or on a trail through an old growth forest. Also, coming from deep within him was his daily writing, writing that explored his personal beliefs about the culture, what was happening in the world around him, and the meaning of life.

Discovering that I too am a writer, Gary in 2013 sent me one of his essays that I found most relevant to my thinking and writing. This began a regular correspondence. As Toni observed, Gary and I "were on the same page" in our interests, observations, and concerns about life and the apparent demise of civilization as we know it. By the end of 2014 I had collected 25 of his essays, which he brought together as a book, first titled *Unlearning the Big Lie*. With my success in finding a publisher for my books, Gary looked to me to help him publish his. But as he accumulated more knowledge and wisdom, he continued writing, revising, adding chapters, and editing it until his death on December 5th, 2018. To quote Gary from a Facebook post a year earlier, December 12, 2017: "My life only makes sense to me if I manage to complete the book I started two years ago and am working on right now. It is meant to be the summation of a lifetime's worth of living, reading, thinking, and paying attention to things. If I fail to complete the book before I die, I fail myself and my mission at the very deepest level." All the while he read and discussed his writing and revisions with his longtime partner, Pat Gripp.

These essays and Gary's manuscript sat on my bookshelf for several years until I turned to them with the thought of following through on Gary's dream of publication. I contacted Mark, Gary's son, and Pat, his partner, sharing with them my plan on how to go about this project. As a result of these conversations, Mark sent me from Gary's computer his most recent manuscript, now titled *The Culture Trap: Living in Loyalty to the Whole*. Pat, with whom Gary regularly reviewed his writing, has volunteered her help and encouragement for this project.

As I continue with this Foreword I want to explain the meaning of a number of words and concepts as used by Gary, first

FOREWORD

The Culture Trap. Gary sees three different meanings for the word culture: culture as the creative beauty found in artistic expression, second, the superficial description of the culture in which we live; and third, deep culture, the deep automatic beliefs that we hold within ourselves. These deep cultural beliefs are likely so automatic that we may not be aware of them, thus we are trapped within them, *The Culture Trap*. One of these deep cultural beliefs is the belief that we have a right to take from the Earth, an Earth that is inert or dead, taking from her anything that we might consider a benefit to us without reciprocity. He uses the word theft to describe this taking, a cultural theft that he considers on the path to our suicide. On the other hand, the deep cultural beliefs of the hunter-gatherers, a group that he sometimes calls our wild ancestors, lived and live with the belief that the Earth is alive and provides for us, provisions that he refers to as her gifts. Gary's writing brings to our awareness the deep cultural beliefs of the theft culture, beliefs that many of us are seeking to break free of in our attempt to move forward towards the ways of our wild ancestors. Yet, we continue to live within this suicidal culture of theft, thus I use the pronoun we in the description of our current lives.

At the age of nine, Gary lived on a remote lake in northern California where he regularly took walks in the deep woods. On one occasion he stopped at a tangle of brush where a vision of a beautiful river came to him. Years later after moving to Oregon, this vision came alive when he saw the McKenzie River, the river pictured on the cover of this book. Thanks to his loving extended family, Gary's ashes have been scattered on the McKenzie River. Such visions as Gary's were and are part of the lives of the hunter-gatherers, our wild ancestors and are very much part of my life in my practice and teaching of ecstatic trance. Visions began Gary's and my parallel journeys to find the answers for healing the Earth from impending destruction. Our journeys have taken us by different signposts but eventually to the same destination, that our salvation can be found in the lifeways and worldview of the indigenous people of the world.

Gary's book, *The Culture Trap*, is addressed to those few who Gary believes might survive the extinction of life on Earth as we know it. The book was written to provide these survivors with the history of what has brought about this impending destruction/extinction, while beseeching them to live in unison with the wisdom and knowledge of all life that may have survived with them. He asks those who might remain with the "civilized" or theft culture who put themselves above all other life to carefully examine these beliefs as Gary does in this book. Gary believes, as I do, the history leading to our demise began about 10,000 years ago with the beginning of agriculture, the beginning of the human attempt to control all that is of the Earth, control that is promoted by the Judeo-Christian belief that we have been given "dominion over the Earth." This belief voiced in Genesis gives us permission to steal from the Earth for our own wealth. It considers everything of the Earth below the humans in the evolutionary process as inert, dead, or meaningless.

For the many millennia before the beginning of agriculture, humans lived in unison with the Earth, believing that everything of the Earth is interdependent and important for their survival. Gary offers ten precepts to describe this life way of the hunting and gathering people:

1. The Earth is our mother; care for her.
2. Honor all your relations.
3. Open your heart and soul to the Great Spirit.
4. All life is sacred; treat all beings with respect.
5. Take from the Earth what is needed and nothing more.

6. Do what needs to be done for the good of all.
7. Give constant thanks to the Great Spirit for each new day.
8. Speak the truth; but only of the good in others.
9. Follow the rhythms of nature; rise and retire with the sun.
10. Enjoy life's journey but leave no tracks.

Gary proceeds chapter by chapter describing how we have become separated from the Earth, a separation that is defended again by the Judeo-Christian scripture in Genesis of when Adam and Eve gained the knowledge of good and evil. This duality of good and evil, of us versus them, separates us from the hunter-gatherer's unity with the Earth, knowledge that forced Adam and Eve out of paradise.

Gary's personal story of living on the lake in northern California and on a farm in Oregon shows how his life countered the life of the thieves of nature. The deep cultural beliefs that separate us from all other life and substances of Earth have made us into the thieves of nature. These cultural beliefs are not those held by our wild ancestors. They knew that everything of the Earth, including humans, is conscious, alive and dependent upon each other, an interdependency that sustains everything of the Earth. Living in this world of interdependency created the paradise known to our hunter and gathering ancestors. The hunter-gatherers did not take from the Earth more than they needed at the moment, and gave back to the Earth in their respect for it.

Felicitas Goodman, the anthropologist who researched ecstatic trance and began the Cuyamungue Institute where I became a certified instructor of ecstatic trance, wrote in her book *Ecstasy, Ritual and Alternate Reality* (pp. 17-18), words that describe the world of our wild ancestors:

In a very real way, the hunters and gatherers open the first chapter of our human history. And fittingly, this dawning was as close to paradise as humans have ever been able to achieve. The men did the hunting and scavenging, working for about three hours a week, and the women took care of daily sustenance by gathering vegetal food and small animals. It was such a harmonious existence, such a successful adaptation, that it did not materially alter for many thousands of years. This view is not romanticizing matters. Those hunter-gatherer societies that have survived into the present still pursue the same lifestyle, and we are quite familiar with it from contemporary anthropological observation. Despite the unavoidable privations of human existence, despite occasional hunger, illness, and other trials, what makes their lifeway so enviable is the fact that knowing every nook and cranny of their home territory and all that grows and lives in it, the bands make their regular rounds and take only what they need. By modern calculations, that amounts to only about 10 percent of the yield, easily recoverable under undisturbed conditions. They live a life of total balance, because they do not aspire to control their habitat, they are part of it.

These words may surprise the thieving culture who believes that the life of the hunter-gatherers was marginal at best, but the research of Marshall Sahlins in his book, *Stone Age Economics,* supports Felicitas Goodman's picture of this life. Our wild ancestors lived off the Gifts provided by our Mother Earth. They were not the Thieves as are the corporations, sciences, religious institutions, and educational systems that live with the deep cultural belief that all is there for the taking and promote the belief that this Theft is progress. My book, *Trance Journeys of the Hunter-Gatherers,* describes how ecstatic trance opens the door to listening to the spirits of the Earth and of our ancestors, trance experiences that bring us together in unison with the spirits of the Earth.

FOREWORD

These deep cultural beliefs of Theft trap us on our suicidal journey into the world of our demise on Earth. But where are we going on this journey? Gary makes the case that we will not be able to escape from this trap, that it is too late to change. Because of our large numbers, a population that covers all livable areas of the Earth, we cannot return to the hunter-gatherer culture of living off what our Mother Earth provides. There is no longer the Wild Earth that provides. We now depend upon corporate farms to provide enough for this population. Also, our cultural beliefs are so ingrained that to change these beliefs is beyond comprehension.

Yet I have experienced a large and growing number of people who recognize the suicidal nature of these beliefs of deep culture, people who support or have organic and regenerative farms, people who are leading the way into the New Age in many different ways. This New Age described by Jean Gebser is the Era of Time-Free-Transparency, the era when we return to the spiritual ways of the hunter-gatherers by learning to again listen to the spirits of the ancestors and the Earth. According to Gebser, the transition between each of the past four eras of consciousness has occurred in violence. His first and second eras were of the hunter-gatherers, the first when all listened to the spirits, and the second when the tribe depended upon the listening of the shaman. The third era was the Mythic Era of recorded myths with which we are familiar. The fourth era, the Era of Rationality, is the era from which we are in the process of leaving, the era of our suicidal journey. Though Gebser has hope for our survival in our return to *Our Ever-Present Origin*, the title of his book, this hope appears very thin if not impossible because of the depth of our suicidal culture as portrayed by Gary. I continue to hope there is a chance for the sustainable survival of humans. Gary's vivid description of where we are going is undeniable, yet I am strongly committed to live my life in ways to reverse this journey, as unlikely as it may seem. Gary, in the way he was living, was also on the path for this reversal. Considering the ten precepts by which our wild ancestors lived, we can live most of them now, though we are unable to live off what our Great Mother provides while leaving enough for her gifts to naturally regenerate. Only number 5, "Take from the Earth what is needed and nothing more," is the problem, but even then we as individuals could live by it. In bringing the Earth back to health, our organic and regenerative gardening and rebuilding the soil with composting is a beginning. With our numbers we cannot live by gathering, but we can begin to build on our knowledge of foraging. With the growing numbers of like-minded people, we can do our best to live by these precepts.

In moving to the Hudson Valley of New York, Toni and I have connected with several groups. One is the Hudson Valley Herb Alliance, and another is the Rondout Valley Permaculture group, both leading us in the right direction. In leaving the Penns Valley of Pennsylvania we left behind several important groups, The Penns Valley Conservation Association which has been rebuilding the riparian buffers along the local streams; the Pennsylvania Association for Sustainable Agriculture of several thousand members who are finding ways to live sustainably on their small organic and regenerative farms; and the Pennsylvania Certificated Organic, the certification agency for Pennsylvania and surrounding states. Being part of these organizations has given me hope that our journey into the New Age is on the right track.

Though planting gardens was not part of the way of life of the earliest hunter- gatherers, they did over time learn the way of planting and began having gardens to supplement their wild ways of living. With their gardens they continued to venerate the Earth and live within the ten precepts. We have learned much over the millennia, knowledge that will remain with us and provide us with greater understanding of the indigenous ways of how to live sustainably. For one, our current knowledge shows us the way to avoid the destruction of the Earth as imposed by the ways of the monocultural agriculturists by composting and building permacultures that are an early attempt to emulate Wild Nature. This requires much smaller family gardens, a growing trend among those of us who are relearning the wild ways of living.

Gary believes, as I do, our population needs to be drastically reduced, and the direction we are going with natural catastrophes, pandemics, droughts, and potential starvation lead the way. Whether we are the deep culture thieves or those who respect the gifts our Earth provides, Gary's words are important for us to hear. He offers a deeper historical perspective of where our journey is taking us, a story that is eye opening to new thoughts of what we must do to survive. Gary's friend Derrick Jensen in his popular book *Bright Green Lies* also takes us on this journey of vividly describing the thieving nature of our Green Movement. How can we survive the predicted and observed catastrophes, pandemics, droughts, and starvation that are ahead of us? We can find ways to avoid the results of the natural catastrophes by where and how we live. Yes, forest fires are a threat to Oregon, but our wild ancestors knew the importance of these fires and how to use them as Gary describes. For floods, we can move to higher ground. Our wild ancestors lived by water, but their dwellings were easily moved to higher ground. For pandemics, I believe more virulent ones are on their way, but healing can be found by listening to the spirits of the plant life available to us. Then by working together in community and not far from a source of water, we can grow what we need to survive.

We are experiencing a number of ways of what this coming

life could be like. We have periodic power failures when we have no running water because our electric water pump shuts down, we have no heat, and we are unable to recharge our electric car. Though these power failures are short lived, again our thinking begins, thinking that prepares us for the future. We might wish that we lived closer to a source of water and had an indoor fireplace, but we can haul water up from the river and build an outdoor fire with the wood from the dead Ash that surrounds us. During the COVID epidemic we have been frequently on the internet Zooming with others, one group being Neetopk Keetopk, Algonquin words that mean "My Friends, Your Friends." This community of friends is seeking the ways of the Esopus, the earlier residents of this land upon which we live before our invasion. But again without electricity Zooming will not be available to us.

With the desperation of the people coming out from the city there will likely be violence as predicted by Gebser, violence from those who are hanging onto their thieving ways in their fear of change, but I believe that we are better situated to survive, living by the ten precepts as our wild ancestors lived. *The Culture Trap* provides considerable information on the ways of the hunter-gatherers to give us some direction. On our daily walks we are meeting our new neighbors and discovering new secrets of nature that have been hidden from us like the active beaver dam shown to us by a neighbor. Those living the Big Lie, the thieves of the Earth, do not understand how to live and are much more vulnerable to demise, thus I have hope that those of us who listen to the words of Gary are better prepared to follow the new ways. We will make mistakes but I believe many of us are moving in a healthier direction. Hopefully those who are living by the deeper cultural beliefs of the ten precepts have reached sufficient numbers that we are the beginning of the return to the ways of our wild ancestors.

FOREWORD

Beyond *The Culture Trap* with its 29 chapters I found among Gary's essays parts two, three and four of the Sophia Myth. Finding these essays very enlightening, I asked Mark if he could find part one of this series. He did find it along with an introduction to this four-part series. He also sent me eight additional essays that Gary apparently wrote later before his death in December of 2018. These writings, the four-part Sophia Myth and the eight additional essays, are important in exploring the thinking of Gary, so they have become Part II of this book.

In Gary's mind, the much-preferred culture to the culture in which we are trapped is that of the Indigenous Americans with their deep respect for our Great Earth Mother. The Gnostic Sophia Myth shows that the Gnostics also had this deep respect for the Living Earth. Science has been unable to measure or discover the physiological basis of consciousness, but the story of the Gnostic deities that exist in the Pleroma at the center of the Milky Way offers a mythic explanation. These deities are pure consciousness and are the creators through their dreaming state of consciousness. The pair of co-creator deities or Aeons, Sophia and Thelete, dreamt the Anthropos into existence and threw him into the outer reaches of the Milky Way galaxy. Sophia, being young, curious, and impetuous, ventured out to the border of the galaxy and from there plunged in a frightful fall downward into the swirling stardust that would form Earth. There she merged with the particles to become one with the Earth, becoming the consciousness of our Great Earth Mother. In my love for the myths of the ancient cultures of the world, Sophia now resonates within me. This Gnostic myth continues, attacking the Demiurge that is an imposter or false god that arose from a different source to become the Judeo-Christian God.

The remaining eight essays look into what has happened

historically over the last couple hundred years with the development of the corporation and the insidious nature of these power-seeking institutions. I have learned much from these essays that are so well researched by Gary, research that brings to light his profound understanding of the history of our Thieving Culture. Gary, dying in December of 2018, saw the Trump administration rise to power, and his essays well explain the nature of Trump's demented power, though Gary never mentions Trump or the Republican Administration by name.

Upon further questioning Mark uncovered and sent me another set of eleven of Gary's essays. Most of these were duplicates of what Mark had already sent me, though one essay in particular is especially important and an appropriate conclusion to the book, Gary's journey into the world of the Native Americans. From my personal communications with Gary I am very aware of the resonance he felt in reading and studying the ways of the Native Americans. In this concluding chapter he describes his personal journey into the Native American ways, a journey that is uplifting and hopeful, a positive way of ending the book.

I totally concur with Gary's beliefs in where our Thieving Culture is taking us, a harbinger of the demise of our culture as we know it. Our only hope is found in the ways of the indigenous Americans and the indigenous tribes of the world that offer us new yet ancient deep cultural stories we can live by. Gary, Thank You.

NICHOLAS E. BRINK, PH.D., Author of a number of books including, *The Power of Ecstatic Trance; The Trance Journeys of the Hunter-Gatherers; Ecstatic Soul Retrieval,* and *Loki's Children.*

PART I

The Culture Trap

CHAPTER 1

WHAT YOU NEED TO KNOW.

I DON'T KNOW what kind of story you will have been told about the damaged world we left you, but I am guessing that what it leaves out is what you most need to know. Even in my own time, the stories we are telling ourselves lack depth of analysis and are shaped to serve the shallow interests of the few. So I feel I have reason to worry, because I grew up in a world that told itself lies--lies we did our best to live-- and we ruined the world in the process.

Ours is a complicated story, yours and mine, and while many may grasp parts of the story with great clarity, very few know the back story, or how to sort truth from lie, and see the epic of civilization as a unified whole. Don't misunderstand me: I make no claims to omniscience, or to owning the One True Story. There is no One True Story, except as a kind of abstract ideal to work toward, and that is the best I can offer. But I do have a story to tell, and I am hoping you will find it has relevance for you.

The human being lives by story. In a very real and existential way, we live **in** story, and often in several stories at once.

This comes, I think, from being a cultural animal. Instead of living by inborn instinct like the rest of the animals, we are the recipients of a novel innovation in the evolutionary history of the world. We are a highly social animal, a grouping animal that lives according to myths, memes, ideas, values, and perceptions that are passed on from person to person, generation to generation, in a process called acculturation. We learn how to think and feel about the world we live in by the influence of those around us, and most of what we pick up in this way is seldom registered by our conscious mind.

As an evolutionary adaptation in the face of rapid environmental change, culture would seem to have the advantage over genetically transmitted instinctual behaviors, because (theoretically, at least) culture can respond to rapid changes much faster, thereby giving humans an adaptive edge. All well and good as long as the stories of a people's culture are a good fit to the actual world that those people live in. But here is the rub. The culture that you and I share--the culture of civilization--is maladaptive in the extreme, making us misfits in an ecological world.

The Earth and its Community of Life are made up of systems within systems within systems, and what makes these systems ecological is their relationship, one to another. All these systems share the quality of interdependence, and cannot exist apart from this highly complex network of reciprocity: of taking and giving back. This is the way of the world, but the culture of civilization has denied this reality for thousands of years, and has constructed an elaborate story that is anti-ecological, and for a very long time now our people have been living in a story that is a lie. I have come to see through this lie, and its many elaborations, and I don't know what to do with this knowledge but to try to pass it on, in the rather remote hope that seeing our situation for what it is will allow

WHAT YOU NEED TO KNOW.

you, or someone, to break free from the group-think of our renegade culture, and find a new and better story to live in-- one that is compatible with an ecological world.

CHAPTER 2

YOUR FUTURE WORLD

YOU AND I have never met, and likely never will. That is because I am an old man now and you have yet to be born. You may be my great granddaughter or grandson, or possibly the children of one of these. I am thinking of a range between twenty and forty years from right now, knowing that you will be living in extremely tough times. I like thinking of you as a close relative, because that might establish a bond between us, but sharing genetics is less relevant to either of us than sharing a particular attitude toward life and the world, maybe sharing similar sensibilities.

I am imagining you as an individual very much like myself: naturally inquisitive with a powerful urge to understand yourself in relation to the world around you, but living in darkly opaque times. The world you have inherited from the people of my generation is broken, but I am guessing you are unclear about how it got to be this way. This is where I think I can be some help to you, because I have made a lifelong project out of asking just exactly that question: How did things get to be this way? And this question can be applied to any subject that might interest you. If you ask how the Universe got to be this way-- that will take you into intellectual disciplines like astrophysical cosmology, or possibly cosmological mythology. If your interest is in how our own planet Earth got to be this way—that will take you into fields like geomorphology. If you are interested in the relationship between the evolving planet's geology and chemistry and how these interacted with an emerging biological presence to create a world of wondrous complexity and diversity—well, you have got a fairly large project ahead of you. My point is that at all these scales, the question is the same: How did things get to be this way? Implied in any possible answer to this central human question is a sense of historical perspective--that is: understanding events and conditions as sequential, one thing following another, with some sort of cause and effect relationship also implied, even if that relationship is not always obvious.

My own deepest interest, at least since the age of twenty, has been to understand my own people and their relationship to Nature. It has always been a puzzle to me why the people of my culture seemed so intent on destroying the very world that gives us life. For the longest time I couldn't make any sense of it--and still don't at the deepest gut level. But after many years of looking into this question, I do at least have some sort of intellectual understanding of this conundrum. And this is what I want to share with you. My hope is that if the story I am about to tell makes sense to you, you will take it to heart, and will see the wisdom in not repeating our mistakes. But I also have to tell this story for my own sake, because writing things down has always been my way of discovering how I see the world. The act of writing seems to draw out of my unconscious mind an unarticulated understanding, and, by putting this into words, to clarify that understanding to my conscious mind. For me, now, near the end of my life, this will be a summing up—one last attempt to make sense of the world. And, because I have always felt a strong sense of responsibility to give something back for all that has been given to me, this will also satisfy my felt need for reciprocity.

CHAPTER 3

THE THEFT OF OUR WORLD

YOU MAY BE just as curious about me and my world as I am about you and yours. The better to help you start to develop your own historical perspective and to place yourself and your surroundings in context, I am going to tell you about where I live, and give you some idea of its condition as of 2018.

I live on the North American continent in a country that at this time is still calling itself the United States—though as a people we are far from united. My state of Oregon is on the west coast, and, because I live on the west side of the Cascade Mountains, our weather is moderated by the maritime influence of the Pacific Ocean. This means that our summers, when it seldom rains, are not bake-oven hot, but usually fairly comfortable, and our winters don't get too awfully cold, and almost never reach zero. What we get in abundance here, fall, winter, and spring, is lots and lots of rain. And this is probably one reason why the state of Oregon is not so overcrowded the way California, to our south, is. Lots of people seem to shy away from rain, especially when it comes with day after day of dark gray skies. But let me tell you, the summers here are glorious, and where I live in the foothills of the Cascades is a popular tourist destination.

How I ended up in this place is a little unusual. When I was eight, nine, and ten, and living with my family on a remote lake in northern California, I spent a lot of time alone, either out on the lake or deep in the woods. On this special day I am going to tell you about, I was nine and in the very densest part of the woods, my movement stopped by tangles of shrubs and vines. I can remember just standing there when suddenly the picture of a river appears in my head—a vividly detailed picture of an especially beautiful river. I had never seen this river before, and I had no idea why I was seeing it now in my visual imagination. Nor did the picture come with any sort of message: no parting of the clouds; no voice from on high telling me what this river was supposed to mean to me; just an unforgettable picture of a river that was its own unique shade of blue-green, with its whitewater rapids showing a paler, phosphorescent shade of this same blue-green.

Four years later, when I was living in Ashland, in southern Oregon, I would sign up for a summer church camp, which turned out to be a couple hundred miles to the north. Shortly before arriving at White Branch Youth Camp I would pass the McKenzie River and immediately recognize it as the river of my waking dream. So, there it was: an actual river, and not just some invention of my unconscious mind. But what of it? If this coincidence was supposed to mean anything, I had no idea what, so I just let it go—for about twenty years, while I put in my time in high school, then the army, then five different colleges and universities—until I was ready to settle down. And when I finally did decide to sink in roots, I did it here on the banks of this river, where I have spent the second half of my life.

For the last nine years I have been living on two acres that

THE THEFT OF OUR WORLD

belong to my son, acting as a kind of caretaker, landscape designer and planter, and dedicated gardener. I live in a twenty-nine-foot trailer that was new some twenty-five years ago. I should say that trailer living is not considered prestigious in this part of the world, but it works for me, and since my trailer is paid for, and I pay no rent here, it works for me financially, too. These days, my sole income comes from a government program called Social Security, which provides me with enough to get by on, but not much more. By your time—maybe somewhere between 2040 and 2060—I doubt that you will be living under a functioning national government, and therefore social programs like this one will no longer exist. But you should know that there was a time when the nation-state appeared to be a vibrant and viable form of social, economic, and political organization. As I hope to show you along the way, the nation-state is but one phase of human social evolution. Many now think of it as a more or less permanent pinnacle, but it is neither of these. It is just one phase among many.

As for these two acres I live on, they have suffered unconscionable abuse. Once old growth forest, the first big trees were felled here with ax and crosscut saw, about a hundred years ago. Then, twenty years ago, they came in with chainsaws and a Caterpillar tractor, took the standing trees down, bulldozed the root-wads, loaded them in a dump-truck, and hauled them off—along with most of the topsoil. What topsoil wasn't removed was left to blow and wash away, which it predictably did. What my son and I have been doing for the past twelve years is trying to restore this industrially ravaged land to some kind of biological integrity. We have planted a couple dozen fruit and nut trees, a hundred or so blueberry bushes, and forty or so rhododendron bushes, along with other native flora. And I have carved out, by hand, a diverse kitchen garden which covers about twenty-five hundred square feet—which in spring, summer, and fall comes pretty close to being a full-time job.

When I am out in the garden, down on my hands and knees, weeding with my hand plow or just pulling them up by the roots, I stop now and then and look around, noticing all the bird and insect activity in my immediate area. Even though I am wearing a wide-brim hat, I feel the sun on my cheek, and now and them a slight breeze, as I glance up at the mountains to the north and then over at those to my south. This is when I know why I had that vision of a river, now more than sixty years ago. I am exactly where I want to be, doing exactly what I want to be doing. And how many people ever get to say that? My guess is you wouldn't be among the fortunate few. Mind you, I am not telling you about the felicities of my world to make you feel bad, but to provide you with some context and perspective. And believe me, the world I inherited, though far more intact than yours, was, and is, far from pristine, or even fully functional.

To give you a deeper look at the landscape I live in, I am going to take you along on my daily hike. I am privileged to walk for an hour every day in old growth forest, two different hikes in separate locations. One is along the beautiful McKenzie River, and even though it is just a beauty strip, a linear fragment of the old growth forests that once defined this mountain and river landscape, there are still trees six- and seven- and eight- foot through, and two hundred feet tall. My other old growth grove is situated on a mountainside, and the trail switches back and forth across a finger ridge, and puts you in sight of a flow of water that follows the folds in the land. There are particular trees on both of these hikes that are remarkable individuals. On this steeper hike I know of two yew wood trees that are three feet in diameter. This is a rarity even for this once-excellent yew wood habitat, and these particular yews show character traits, in their folds and branching, that mark them as absolutely unique individuals. Yews are shade-loving and slow growing trees of the lower and middle canopy, and these two have been standing where they are since before Columbus.

On my hike by the river there is one old Western Red Cedar (we also have incense cedars) who must have a particularly strong will to live. It is about seven feet in diameter measuring the longest way across its somewhat oval shape. Fire has hollowed it out at its base and has burned a conically shaped "room" out of its center that is well above man-height. Its top was long ago broken out and it has formed three stovepipe branches out its sides, now growing upwards as leaders, and these are more than two feet thick at their base, and they, too, are asymmetrically oval. One of these stovepipe branches was long ago ripped away by a glancing blow from another falling tree, leaving behind a silvery scar. Despite its deformities and many scars, this tree has its own tenacious beauty.

A forest is more than just trees, and a healthy natural forest has species diversity and a multi-layered canopy, as well as diversity in its undergrowth. These two groves are mostly Douglas firs with some hemlocks and cedars mixed in, along with big leaf maple and dogwood, a few alders and chinquapin, and of course yew. The understory is rich in Oregon grape, salal, sword fern, rhododendron, and vine maple, with the entire forest floor, including down trees and nurse logs, being covered in bright chartreuse-green feather moss. In spring and summer a succession of flowering plants decorate the forest floor with blooms ranging from wood sorrel white to Oregon grape yellow to Calypso orchid magenta.

Both of these groves show some stumps from selective logging long ago, mostly grown over with feather moss; otherwise, these are relatively whole, intact ecosystems. When I walk in them I feel relatively whole and intact myself. I have to drive four miles to get to either of these daily walks of mine, and I go to the trouble to get to these places because they make me feel differently than the nearby second growth "forest" I can walk to right out my door. This second growth stand was clear-cut, then replanted, more than sixty years ago. Douglas fir trees planted ten feet apart do not a forest make, even when they get to be in the sixteen to twenty inch class, as these trees are. This is an even-aged monocultural stand with very little understory diversity, the ground cover consisting of Oregon Grape and little else. When I walk in it, I don't get the same feeling of wholeness and biological integrity I find in old growth, and my sense of well-being is diminished to just the extent that this human-planted "crop" of trees fails to be authentically what Nature means by Forest.

Coming out from these sanctuaries of near-primal forest, I am exposed to a disturbing number of clear-cuts. When I look at a mountainside that has been stripped of its trees, leaving only logging slash and naked soil behind, I feel like my own skin has been ripped off, leaving only sensitive flesh behind, and with the pain I feel a gaping void of emptiness. This feeling of emptiness and compromised wholeness has happened to me over and over again through years and decades of being exposed to brokenness, and my feeling of inconsolable loss, smoldering anger, and unresolved grief has never lessened or abated.

Someone once said, "You become what you behold," and I believe there is truth in this. If all you see around you is the brokenness, ugliness, and wrongness of the human-made cityscape or paved-over suburbs, how are you supposed to feel like a whole human being? Cities are, of course, a relatively new innovation in human history. And it is not just cities that are absent of the necessary trees. Many a farm-scape has gone the

THE THEFT OF OUR WORLD

way of industrial agribusiness and gotten rid of wind-rows and fence-rows, dragging the plow right down to the creeks, leaving nothing of the primordial world behind. We humans have a long-term relationship to trees—much longer than all these experiments in unsustainability-- and this gets to the heart of my point. We are who we are only in context. We are not isolated, autonomous beings. The human heart is not separate from the body that contains, enfolds, and nurtures it. When we lose our vital connection to the wholeness of a living world, we lose an essential part of our innate humanity, and, losing ourselves, we lose our way.

Whatever is left of the natural world for you to inherit, I know it isn't enough, because it has been robbed of so much of its essence, leaving you robbed of much of yours. As I have been saying, and will continue saying, it is extremely important for you, and those who may follow you, to understand your situation in context, the better for you to rebuild your world in the right direction. To that end, you need to understand some of your deep past.

CHAPTER 4

SOME PREHISTORY

WHEN I SPEAK of the historical perspective I of course mean to include what we know of pre-history. But don't get the idea that the long view I am promoting here is easy to come by. It isn't. The long arc of history is something you have to deliberately seek out for yourself, and in this way go against what your culture wants you to know. We who call ourselves civilized know for an absolute fact that civilization is the highest and best way that humans have ever found to organize themselves and their world. Any evidence to the contrary must be suppressed, and if it somehow escapes whatever violence is required to remove it from awareness, it is vehemently denigrated and denied. While this general pattern persists within society at large, in the last thirty years or so certain academic disciplines related to the study of cultures other than our own have turned up bits of information that, if systematically pursued, start to paint a picture rather unbecoming to this civilization that is so intent upon preserving its illusions about itself.

What is so amazing is that this militant and thoroughgoing

SOME PREHISTORY

will toward self-delusion has enjoyed tremendous success (at least by its own standards) for several thousands of years, and has transformed the world in the process. But that world is now unraveling, and among those who bear witness to this reality there is much confusion as to what is actually going on. This is because their conditioning and education has all been within the bubble of self-delusion, and they haven't learned yet to swim against the currents of culture that tell them how and what to think. I have been swimming against those currents most of my life, and so what I offer to you is very far from the official version of what is causing the breakdown of the living world. If you require group consensus before you can accept something as self-evident fact, what I have to say won't be of much use to you. If, as I fervently hope, you are an independent critical thinker, please give provisional credence to what I have to say, and see if it doesn't ultimately accord with what you know about the world, and make better sense of it than the stories that led us to empire, and then to empire failed.

So, let's begin our history lesson back in the days when all humans lived by hunting wild animals and gathering wild plants, and we ourselves were wild, and the world was inhabited, and enchanted by, spirit beings. What paleoanthropologists call "anatomically modern humans" began to appear in Africa about 200,000 years ago, and though we don't know much about their lives they evidently made their way in the world, with little change, for hundreds of human generations. Then something happened that transformed the human into his "behaviorally modern" form. One theory has it that with the eruption of super-volcano Mt. Toba some 75,000 years ago on the island of Sumatra the number of our common ancestors was reduced to just a few thousand—a population bottleneck--due to six years of volcanic-winter conditions all over the planet. In this time period, something happened to the human brain to change anatomically modern humans into behaviorally modern humans—people just like us. The essence of that change was to become aware of being aware, along with the capacity for abstract thought. Exactly what it was that changed us, and how it affected our evolution, is open to speculation. But whatever happened, these newly transformed humans began finding their way out of a climactically harsh Africa in a succession of migrations stretching over a period of some twenty thousand years. It is from this dispersal that the continents, and many islands, got peopled by people like us.

We cannot know the precise conditions of the living systems into which our distant ancestors journeyed and settled, but I think it is fair to suppose that many ecosystems were behaving at near-optimum performance levels. Or, put another way, 3.8 billion years of evolutionary history had created impressive complexity and diversity, as well as a deep resilience against cataclysmic events, and though there had been such events, like the fallout from the super-volcano, and intermittent extremes of climate change, there were no overly dominant species (like us) to throw ecosystems severely out of balance. When suitable human habitats were found, I imagine them to be rich in biodiversity and natural beauty, a place where humans could thrive as part of a thriving natural landscape.

What I am trying to get at here is something ephemeral and subtle, and it has to do with the relationship between the human and the natural world—a relationship requiring that Nature be valued for what it is, and not transformed into something else-- in order for this vital relationship to prosper. By respecting the integrity of all living beings and Mother Earth's own agenda the integrity of the human is also preserved.

Before the monotheism that characterizes organized religion today, there was place-based spirituality. And just as the world of humans managed to develop more than five

SOME PREHISTORY

thousand distinct languages, there were probably, at one time or another, that many and more spiritual traditions or bodies of spiritual practice. I take it that every one of these was influenced by interactions between a particular group of people and their immediate physical surroundings. Our Western scientific worldview would deny these people the spirit world they (collectively, and pretty much unanimously) believed animated, or was somehow associated with, those same individuated physical surroundings—dells and glens, rivers and mountains, groves of trees and individual trees, rocks and caves and enchanted grottos. Many indigenous peoples are on record as stating that the plants, the animals, the rocks and trees, interact with them and let the people know how to live in their particular place. If the people pay attention to these voices, and cultivate the appropriate attitudes of humility and respect; if they perform all of the prescribed rituals, and live by local and Universal Laws, then they get to go on living in that place.

Spiritual practice in this context is at once an individual and a group affair. The group holds a body of moral strictures, rituals, and stories in common, and ceremony is undertaken as a group, informed by shared beliefs. The individual participates in the common mythos, but also has his own relationship to the world of spirit. This, I would say, is the archetype of the spiritual life of humans, and it endured through millennia. For that reason, it became embedded in our collective unconscious. This is the kind of spiritual experience we are hard-wired to expect, and in which those before us likely found deep and full satisfaction. But since our particular culture came on the scene (and with it the rise of monotheism) this is not the spiritual experience now open to us.

It is not open to us for many reasons, not least of which is the systematic erasure of the particularities of place as the civilized peoples of the world displaced the indigenous aboriginals, overrunning their territory and transforming it into something else. When a cathedral-like dell in the woods is felled and bulldozed, it would seem that the spirits who once inhabited that place would be driven off. The culture of civilization tells us that no such spirits exist, or ever have existed. According to one major civilized tradition, there is only one spirit being, except that that one is actually three. Wherever this particular proselytizing religion has gone in the world to convert all to its One True Truth, it has been intolerant of the Natives' beliefs in the many spirits of their place, and has taken violent measures to suppress both the beliefs and the believers.

When science came to rule the world (its roots in physics, chemistry, and mathematics) it came with a prejudicial disposition against anything that couldn't be weighed, measured, or computed. Science's divorce from religion became final about the time of the Newtonian-Cartesian synthesis. From then on any mention of invisible realms or anything smacking of mysticism or spirituality became categorically taboo. Along with the taboo came an attitude of scorn and disdain that is routinely passed on from generation to generation of the scientifically inclined. This attitude (and the ideology that feeds it) pretty much precludes arriving at new knowledge about invisible Earthly realms through scientific inquiry, as all who try are labeled as quacks and not authentic scientists.

In such a climate as this, mention of spirits residing in particular places is, at the very least, suspect. How do I know that spirits inhabit places, and that attentive humans can converse with those spirits? In truth, I don't know that as pure provable fact. I have spent a lot of time in wild Nature, and I have had any number of good feelings arise from that contact—feelings of appreciation, joy, exhilaration, awe, and others less easy to

SOME PREHISTORY

name. I have also had two visionary experiences in Nature, both at the age of nine: one that told me what I would do with my life, and one that told me where I would live. Told me, I say, but not like a voice whispering in my ear. In the case of my life's work it was more a feeling-sense and Gestalt than anything else. In the case of where I would live, it was simply a clear mental picture of a river. Both came to me when I was alone and in wild Nature, at a time and place where I might be receptive to them.

What I do know for sure is that many an indigenous person has gone on record as declaring the place where he and his people live is inhabited by spirits that "speak" to individuals within the band or tribe, and convey all kinds of information useful to the individual, or to the group as a whole. Often the information received will pertain to how the people should relate to their chosen place. *Black Elk Speaks* and *Lame Deer Seeker of Visions* are only the most prominent of hundreds of narratives wherein people embedded in the land tell of their communion with spirit beings of their particular place.

What the juggernaut of civilization has visited upon these peoples and their lands is complete or partial erasure. In the process, this destructive force has removed not only for them, but for all the rest of us, a vital human connection to Nature. Where in this world can a human now go that hasn't been transformed from its original enchanted, spirit-animated, physical perfection (as accrued over millennia of geomorphology and biological evolution) into something not itself? When you pave paradise and put up a parking lot, something gets lost in translation, not lost just in terms of beauty to ugliness, but lost in terms of human identity and potential. The human being cannot be wholly herself without an ongoing connection to, and conversation with, the natural world. And in a world where there is not much Nature left--to be itself, as itself--there are not many human beings who can be themselves, and all they could or should be.

For several years now I have been trying to come to terms with what has been lost to the human condition as a result of our aberrant culture. I call this phenomenon the fall within the rise of civilization. There are so many powers once fully available to humans that have withered within us and atrophied, including acute sensitivities to our physical world (and also to the invisible dimensions) that are now all but denied to us. In a world made over by humans--for humans--our humanity diminishes, and so does the joy of life that once was our birthright. We have become as spiritual orphans, because spirit has been taken out of our world. Without spirit, and the means of renewing our connection to this world and to the Cosmos at large, we lose ourselves in a world robbed of its meaning. For this I blame civilization, whose goal and purpose seems be the destruction of all that is valuable and good in this world. If you doubt this, just look at our history, and where it has brought us. And consider also where it is taking us—right off the edge and into the void—and by us I mean the entire Community of Life, our Larger Self, the Gaian Whole.

CHAPTER 5

A TURNING POINT

IN SKETCHING THE history of our spiritual condition as a people, I have skipped right over the turning point that has ultimately led to this condition. That turning point, known variously as the Neolithic Revolution, the Agricultural Revolution, and the Beginning of Civilization, marks a momentous change in the way people came to believe, behave, and make a living from the land—which makes it also a momentous cultural revolution. It is important to understand exactly what happened in these early days of civilization because these changes would come to have profound implications for all life on planet Earth.

When our wild ancestors were hunter-gatherers, they lived in groups of twenty to thirty individuals and they shared equitably what they plucked, dug, and hunted. They were mobile, following the ripening of fruits, nuts, and berries as well as the bulbs, corms, and roots they relied upon. Being attuned to the migrations of the birds and animals they favored, and knowing just where and when their preferred plants were ready for the taking, most such groups followed a seasonal pattern of moving from camp to camp within a territory they claimed as their own. When climactic and other environmental conditions were stable, a richly endowed territory might serve a group for many human generations, the people becoming one with the land, learning what it had to teach them about living in balance with their particular Community of Life. The teachings of the land about itself became the people's traditional ecological knowledge, and it was kept alive through story, ritual, and cultural meme, passed from one generation to the next. In this way the people belonged to their chosen place, believing, at the same time, that their place had also chosen them. The people and the land were engaged in a dance of mutually beneficial exchange, and as long as the people gave back to the land as good as they got, observing the Law of Reciprocity, both people and land prospered.

With the advent of pastoralism and the cultivation of crops this ancient way of life was supplanted by an altogether different relationship between the people and the land they inhabited. Living in the old way, the idea that a human being, or group of human beings, could own sacred Mother Earth was absurd in the extreme. If the people were respectful and observant of the Law of Reciprocity, they might be fortunate enough to belong to a place, this being a sought-after condition which conferred many benefits. But reversing the equation of who belongs to whom was unthinkable— revolutionary beyond all reason.

But the privatization of the commons was a necessary condition for agriculture to flourish, and indeed agriculture and private property have historically always gone hand in hand, the two being co-dependent as well as co-evolutionary. In those early days, when the Indigenous Worldview was dominant, "ownership" of land and crop was necessitated by the near-universal values of the sharing economy, where any surplus beyond what an individual and his family might immediately need was considered common property of the group, and legitimately available to each and all. Under these conditions any would-be farmer must lose all incentive to go to all of the work of planting, weeding, and watering a crop only to have the proceeds of his labor "shared" by his group at harvest time. A revolution in values, beliefs, and cultural institutions was necessary to make farming a going concern, and this would require the growing dominance of a particular personality type.

Within any population of humans there seem always to have been a range of personality types, and this form of diversity has no doubt contributed to the fitness of human groups throughout the ages. One recognizable type is what might be called the aggrandizer, and this personality may manifest in a number of different ways: as self-proclaimed "leader," as bully and dominator, or as accumulator of power and its tokens. Within the egalitarian framework of hunter-gatherer society, such individuals were kept in check by group peer pressure and other culturally sanctioned leveling mechanisms. Within this kind of social order, the people so enjoyed being an equal-among-equals that they took great pains to protect themselves from would-be tyrants.

Given this long tradition of egalitarianism and sharing as background, it can't have been easy for pioneering agriculturalists operating as loners. But at some point a number of non-sharing, aggrandizer individuals must have formed their own group of cultivators, who, as neighbors, cooperated in helping each other protect their crops from those of the "sharing" persuasion. Following some such pattern, the planting, tending, and harvesting of grains and other foodstuff managed to get a foothold in certain prime locations, and though this was a land-use revolution, it was also, necessarily, a cultural revolution.

The cultural institution of private property was a revolutionary discontinuity with the human past. The concept that any part of Mother Earth could belong to--be the private property of--a human being was such a reversal of the natural order of things that it could only be maintained by force of violence, and the perpetual threat of violence. It would be difficult to overestimate the far-reaching implications of this seemingly simple revolution in land tenure. Indeed, Western civilization--with its long history of wars of conquest, its campaigns of oppression, slavery, and colonialism--could never have unfolded the way it did without the enabling cultural institutions of agriculture and private property.

Working synergistically, private property and agriculture initiated changes in cultural practice and belief that would transform the human condition, even as transformed ("civilized") humans would come to transform the living world. One of the first principles of systems thinking, as well as of ecology, is that you can never do just one thing. This is because everything is connected to everything else—systems connected to systems, one interpenetrating another, in an interdependent network of systems, where notions of linear cause-and-effect almost never apply. Even using the latest scientific knowledge and techniques, grasping how systems interrelate with one another is far from obvious, and sometimes discernible only in retrospect, if at all. What follows is my own synthesis, derived from three decades of intensive research, but offered only as my very best guess at how things got to be the way they are--and with the caveat that however detailed my analysis, it is bound to be an oversimplification of dynamic, complex, adaptive systems as they influence and impinge upon each-others' inner-directed agendas. If you can picture trying to sort out a ball of writhing snakes in an attempt to identify and name each one individually, you begin to get a graphic hint of the difficulty—but here goes, anyway.

That some creatures must die in order for others to live is a universal condition of life on Earth. While evidently a necessary condition, this hard reality makes violence and bloodshed an everyday part of staying alive. At the same time, all life forms are held to be sacred, as is the Earth and Sun that make life possible---this according to the Indigenous Worldview. How to deal with this paradox is a question that has been answered in different ways by different cultures for as long as humans have pondered the terms of our tenure here. The guidelines for an honorable harvest, practiced by many indigenous peoples all over the world, and far back in time, is, it seems to me, their attempt to make the best of a hard situation. If you have to kill to stay alive, at least you can do so in an ethical and respectful way.

When we went from hunter to herder our relationship to our fellow creatures within the Community of Life was turned upside down, as was our relationship with Mother Earth. As hunters, we lived in natural ecosystems rich in diversity, and as a top predator we were dependent upon the healthy balance of that ecosystem. We were beholden to the good graces of Mother Nature for our very lives, and Mother Earth, our own planetary manifestation of Mother Nature, was the source of all that was good in the world, and was regarded, therefore, as sacred. She was also a power and a personality you wanted to stay on the good side of, and so our wild ancestors sought to live their lives in the ways she seemed to prescribe, while also investing much ceremonial activity into placating this being who had the power to crush or make miserable those who displeased her. And not only was Mother Nature an intelligent, sentient, willful being with her own agenda and agency, everything in the world was seen this way; not just certain animals, but all animals, all plants, rocks, rivers, mountains, coves, and dells—everything. One of the words used to describe this way of understanding the world is animism—a word often spoken in disparagement of a backward and primitive people who lack the enlightenment of a contemporary civilized education. For me, the word animism has no such connotation, and when I use that word I do not mean for it to have any such pejorative associations.

Hunting (like fishing) is one of those activities where success or failure may depend upon any number of unknown variables, and persons who engage in such chancy activities tend to build up a set of beliefs around the sources of their successes or failures. Most tribal people who depend upon hunting as a mainstay of their lives believe that their chosen prey have something like a guardian spirit who, like Mother Nature herself, must be kept in a generous mood. Incurring the displeasure of the guardian spirit of a group's prime prey species can bring down much suffering and bad ju-ju upon the people. Knowing this, most such groups engaged in elaborate rituals around the killing, butchering, distribution, and disposal of leftovers of their chosen animal, and they followed strict (yet flexible) guidelines in everyday practice. These include: taking no more than you need, and using all that you take; always ask permission before a kill, and always give thanks afterwards; never take the first or the last of anything; be respectful of the animal that is giving its life so that the people may live; share equitably what has been given; know the ways of the ones who take care of you so that you may take care of them; because the relationship between predator and prey is all about reciprocity, be sure to give back as good as you get—and this includes taking care of the habitat which sustains those who sustain you; do all this with an attitude of respect and gratitude.

A TURNING POINT

Within the Indigenous Worldview, all beings, all spirits, all "things," have their own internally guided destiny to fulfill. This includes the land itself, which, in its variability and local individuality, naturally becomes what it is best suited to become. Likewise, every species within the Community of Life—both plant and animal—has its own particular place and purpose within its ecosystem, ranging from the very local to the regional all the way up to the global, since everything is connected to everything else in vast networks of interdependency, and nothing stands alone in isolation from the whole. Within this big-picture view, the hunter's prey species is also seen as having its own place and purpose, and each individual within that species is understood to have its own creaturely life to live, its own destiny to fulfill. As a matter of respect and reverence for the sacredness of all life, the hunter seeks to make a clean kill which surprises the prey while in the fullness of its being, and preferably toward the end of a life lived wild and free. Killing with respect, sensitivity, and gratitude is still killing, but it is making the best of the non-negotiable conditions of life on Earth.

The violence that the hunter visits upon his prey is sudden and final, or should be, according to the hunter's code. If it isn't, there are apologies to be made to the suffering individual and to its guardian spirit. The violence committed by the herder is not limited to the time of slaughter, but extends over the entire life of the captive species, beginning with the selective breeding that begins with a wild animal living as a free agent in its natural habitat, with the intent and purpose of transforming such a creature into genetically-diminished, tractable domestic livestock. This is violence to a gene pool that has evolved, by natural selection, over thousands, millions, and even billions of years: a human usurpation of a natural process. And, it is the theft of all the pleasures of living wild and free as a natural being— selective breeding stealing this potential from all future individuals within each genetically tampered-with species, but stealing also from the ecosystem whose wholeness was compromised by the loss of one of its own. Genetic manipulation by humans is a form of playing god, of usurping the evolutionary process for our own self-interested, short-sighted ends, and we jumped into this with no concept of the far-reaching implications of our tampering—implications that directly affect you and the damaged world you have inherited. But before spelling out some of those implications I feel I should give you a little of my own background so that you don't jump to erroneous conclusions about why I am telling you all this.

CHAPTER 6

ON THE FARM

I WANT TO share with you a little about my life on the farm, and at the same time introduce you to the concept of the normalcy bias. All of us are subject to the normalcy bias, and we come by it quite naturally, simply by assuming that the world we find ourselves in is normal, natural, and typical. The world I found myself in, in mid-twentieth century America was, I now see, in many ways very far from the norm of human life, when looked at in historical context. For one thing, I was at the tail end of one phase in our people's history at a time when the small family farm was still a viable social and economic institution, as it had been (or had seemed to be) for centuries and even millennia, going back to Europe and the Fertile Crescent. By your time, a farm like the one I am going to tell you about is likely to be nothing more than a fond memory, if that.

We moved onto the farm when I was thirteen, none of us knowing the first thing about the farming way of life. My grandparents had sold their high-end home in Santa Monica, California, some thousand miles to the south, and bought these forty acres of orchard and alfalfa field four miles north of the lovely little town of Ashland, Oregon. This was a gift to their son and his family: finally, a place where we could sink in roots, and hopefully bring some stability into our lives. The house, a one-story rambling ranch style home, fronted Valley View Road, which was paved but not busy. Just south of the house was three acres of fruit and nut trees, which, I believe, the Lemleys, who lived there before us, used mostly for fresh eating and home canning. The main orchard, just on the other side of the alfalfa field, was close to twenty acres, and this was all planted in pears, to be sold at market.

I was there in the living room with grandpa and grandma and mom and dad when they were considering buying the place, and Lemley told about the high prices they had gotten for pears during the war years, and what a boon that had been for his family. It seems they had emigrated from Oklahoma in the dustbowl years of the thirties—dirt poor—but had landed here in the beautiful Rogue Valley, where pears just loved to grow. How they ended up with this place I never learned, or have forgotten, but they hung onto it, and raised a family here by dint of hard work and fortunate timing. As their successors here on the farm, we were no great shakes, lacking both experience and the proper work ethic, but now we had a home, and each of us found in this new life something meaningful.

The main orchard and the alfalfa field were relatively flat ground, but with a bit of a slant. The ground behind the house was on a steeper gradient and a bit rolling, covering about four fenced acres. The barn, big and unpainted with a huge old loft where the hay was stored, (and where I lost my virginity) was situated on the only flatish ground behind the house, at the bottom of a fairly steep run of ground. I can't remember if Bessie the cow came with the place or if we bought her at auction, but it was one of my jobs to milk her in the late afternoon; and mornings, too, if it wasn't a school day. There must have been four milking stalls built-in to the barn, with a board that swiveled from the bottom to lock her head in place. And I generally hobbled her, too, so she wouldn't kick over the milk pail in a moment of awkwardness or ill-temper. I remember the radio we had in the milk room to soothe both the milker and the milked. Its case was made of wood, laminated I think, and it had its own little shelf, about head-height, and of course that was back in the days before transistors, when radios came with tubes. We had a big green can of bag-balm that we kept on the same shelf as the radio. First you'd turn on the radio, then grab the can of bag-balm and the bucket and set yourself up on the milking stool. In the early days, before I realized it was necessary to hobble her, Bessie would keep moving just as I got situated, in what I took to be an act of resistance. I don't think she much liked my milking style in those early days, either, and it did take me awhile to learn how to squeeze her teats in just the right way. You couldn't just squeeze; you had to squeeze and pull down at the same time. And here is where the bag-balm came in handy, kind of smoothing out the friction between her skin and mine. I also learned to lean my head into her hindquarters as I milked and this seemed to help establish a bond between us—or so it seemed to me at the time.

So, like many farm families, we had whole milk, and once in a while mom would go to the work of making our own butter. But most of the time we bought margarine—a manmade kind of butter that was then thought to be better than butter. I think it would be fair to say that for us this was a bit of a hobby farm: we made use of some of the opportunities it offered, but we never acted as if our lives depended upon it; never made farming a full-time job.

My mom, Ann, always felt a strong attraction to gardening, even though she grew up as a city girl. During the war years it became fashionable to grow a Victory Garden; the idea was that if people grew many of their own vegetables this would take pressure off the agricultural sector, which could then concentrate on feeding our troops overseas. Mom, in the early years of her marriage, threw herself into gardening—less, I think, as patriotic duty than just for the love of growing things. I can remember her Victory Garden on my grandparent's residential property in Santa Monica, and how much pride she took in it. So it wasn't surprising that she would get a garden going on the acreage here on Valley View, where we had a big garden every year, trying different vegetables to see what worked best, and which ones we would actually eat. I don't know if it was because of that garden, or not, but each one of my five siblings became passionate gardeners as adults, as I did myself. In fact, gardening is more than a passion; I think it is fair to say that, for me, gardening is an obsession that only grows stronger with each passing year, as I learn by trial and error, and also trial and success, how best to participate in this miracle of Nature that starts with a seed and ends with something good to eat.

Because we had the barn and a couple acres of sloping pasture behind the house, we decided to make use of it in the same way many of our neighbors did with their own pastureland: we went to the livestock auction and bought a couple young steers. We raised these from calves until they were big enough to butcher, then took them to the abattoir in Ashland to kill them and cut them up into steaks, roasts, and ground beef. When I was fifteen and had made a little money working odd jobs in the summer, I bought a calf of my own, as an investment. The idea was, you buy a small calf and put it out to graze in summer for as long as the grass keeps growing; then in the winter you feed it some of the alfalfa you grew, baled, and stored in the barn; sometime in spring you'd sell it back at auction and make a tidy little profit. Of course I was being subsidized by my parents in having free access to pastureland and hay, but on the other hand I did quite a bit of work around the place, including bucking two or three crops of hay in a season, which, on fifteen acres, and at about eighty to a hundred pounds per bale, is a pretty good workout. One aspect of that job I'll never forget is how little bits of hay will fall down your neck as you heave them up onto to the flatbed wagon. Especially in the heat of August, when you are sweating like a pig, all those little stickers that have fallen down inside your collar itch like crazy, in a particularly irritating way, because, with the next bale coming up to be bucked, there is no time to do anything about it.

And speaking of pigs, we had to try that, too. We picked up a little weaner pig at auction and gave him an area partly under cover of the barn and partly out in the fresh air. I don't think we understood the principles of composting at the time, but we saw our pig as a convenient garbage disposal, and it was another one of my intermittent jobs to deliver table scraps to this curly-tailed little grunter that we named Jethro. When you live in close proximity to barnyard animals, you come to realize that they are beings with their own individuated personalities, and it seems natural to give them a name to call them by. But I remember one morning with the family sitting around the breakfast table eating hashbrowns, eggs, and bacon, and dad saying: "Well, Jethro tastes pretty good, doesn't he?" And everyone just stopped in mid-bite and looked at one another. As rookies, we had made a pet of a pig we planned to eat, and now we were consuming its flesh, and feeling "funny" about. Someone got up from the table right then, saying they weren't hungry; maybe it was my sister, Sharon. I know that I kept on eating, because Jethro really did taste good. But we never raised another pig like that, and I think the reason was that we could eat anonymous meat without a second thought, but the meat of someone we knew was just too much, and left us with a gnawing sense of discomfort.

We had two bodies of water on the property: a natural creek called Butler Creek that meandered through the big orchard, and an irrigation ditch that snaked through the sloping land below the barn. Of course it was easy to tell the difference between the two: to see that one was made by Nature and the other by man. The irrigation ditch carried a lot more water than the creek, and though it was curvy as it ran through our property, because of the slope of the land, it had a uniformity about it that identified it as a human artifact. The ditch felt somehow wrong to me, but I couldn't say exactly why. It was just a vague feeling I had. Of course I had seen other irrigation ditches in various places, and so I was inclined to consider them as a normal part of the world I inhabited. This was the normalcy bias, doing what it normally does: accustoming me, or any of us, to what we find in the world around us. And for most of us this comes with the added bonus of allowing us to believe, or to assume, that because this is the way the world is at this moment in time this is also the way the world is supposed to be—that there is an inherent rightness to the world as we find it.

At the time, I had not yet heard of Manifest Destiny, and how developing the western United States as rapidly as possible was part of the power politics of nineteenth and twentieth century American life, or how that had a bearing upon every large-scale irrigation project I had seen in California and also here in Oregon. Nor was I aware that taking water from one place and channeling it to somewhere else was a cultural tradition going beyond our European roots all the way back to the Fertile Crescent. Neither did I know that irrigation gradually but inevitably ends up destroying soil fertility with the salts it leaves behind, thus making irrigated agriculture a short-term proposition that leaves behind waste and desert land where once grew amber waves of grain.

The normalcy bias has its uses, especially in psychological and sociological terms. It helps us adjust to the world around us. But it also has its limitations, because it fails to put things in their historical context. The normalcy bias tells us where we are, but not where we are in relation to what went before or what is likely to follow. It is a perspective without perspective.

CHAPTER 7

THE NORMALCY BIAS

BACK IN THE early part of the nineteenth century, Thomas Jefferson, our third president and author of our Declaration of Independence, was convinced that the small yeoman farmer was the very backbone of our democracy. As an independent operative, responsible for eking a living out of his smallholding, with all the planning and hard work it takes to make such an operation successful, the yeoman farmer was seen as embodying the highest ideals of self-governance and rectitude. During the first half of the 19th century there were many such small farmers in America, especially in the Eastern half of the country--with more to come as our people pushed their way westward, clearing ever more land as we went. This was the pioneer phase of our country's development, and was a time when the little guy, the ordinary person, had the opportunity to show what he could do. It was a man's world in those frontier times, and though women certainly player their part, theirs was mostly the supporting role of wife, mother, and drudge—with many dying of exhaustion before their time. But for those who could make a go of it, the life of the small farmer was felt to be a full and good life by the farmers themselves and also by the public at large. Indeed, in the public imagination farm life was considered to be downright idyllic, and altogether wholesome.

What is most appealing about farm life is the independence it affords (at least in theory), along with the opportunity to spend a great deal of time out of doors in an environment that has been made over, and simplified, still retaining certain elements of pristine Nature. A farmer's independence grew ever more illusory as time went on and the inequities in our economic and political systems compounded their stratifying effects, with farmers finding themselves ever more deeply in debt: to the seed companies, the implement dealers, and especially to the banks. Many a farming story has ended with the little guy in overalls being foreclosed upon, and ruined by a predatory shark in a suit.

As I was living the farm life in mid-twentieth century America, I knew nothing of the agricultural revolution that was already underway and would come to dominate the next half century and more of the agricultural scene. The so-called Green Revolution was supposedly based upon improved plant genetics and an intensification of longstanding agricultural techniques—but that intensification came with its own social and ecological costs. Agriculture became agribusiness, and with this change the small yeoman farmer was to become an endangered species. Farming ceased to be a way of life and became instead a mechanized industry, and, like any other industry, was based upon imperatives of "efficiency" and economies of scale. The watchword was: "Get big or get out."

Land holdings were consolidated and further simplified to accommodate the giant-sized farm machinery now coming into vogue. Small farmers were bought out by neighbors willing to go with the get-big program. When these overleveraged operations were beset by crop failures, market manipulations by Big Players, or by overwhelming debt, many of these medium-sized farmers also fell by the way. Corporations and Big Money interests bought up these small and medium-sized properties, consolidated them into one big property, removed barriers that might impede their giant machines—rises, depressions, any little irregularities of the landscape, and especially trees—thereby creating a monolithic farm-scape suitable for a vast expanse of whatever monocultural crop might maximize profits, whether soybeans, cotton, or corn. And not to forget all the chemical inputs now required to coax maximum return on investment: the synthetic fertilizers that find their way into creeks and rivers and create a vast dead zones in the gulf; and also the obligatory pesticides, fungicides, herbicides that poison the soil's complex ecology, wiping out most of a vibrant biology that, in simpler times made the Earth so naturally productive.

For me and my siblings, life on the farm was pretty much an idyll: a wholesome way of life that made a positive contribution to our development as young people growing toward adulthood. Given the circumstances of the time, it was as good a life as I could have hoped for, and certainly far better than life in any city could ever have been. If I were to go by nothing more than the perspective of the normalcy bias, it would be quite easy to romanticize farm life, as I experienced it, and make the assumption that farm life in general was an all-around good thing—as many people still believe today. In fact, our culture encourages us to believe that agriculture is an overall good thing, and, of course, a huge advancement over the way humans lived before the dawn of agriculture. But this is a far from accurate portrayal when you consider the actual historical facts.

The science of forensic archeology has looked at the skeletal remains of agriculturalists and hunter-gatherers who lived around the same time and place, and what they found tells a story of malnutrition and physical decline among those practicing the agricultural lifeway. The farmers, whose diet was much less diverse than their undomesticated cousins, showed a high incidence of tooth decay, a major shrinkage of their skeletal superstructure, including a ten-percent shrinkage of cranial capacity. That is, they were significantly shorter and slighter, with a reduced brain capacity, and they suffered from bad teeth.

Another significant health effect comes from those who practice animal husbandry living in close quarters with their domesticated animals: infectious disease, including smallpox, mumps, measles, influenza, and chicken pox, all of which were endemic to farm animals, and jumped hosts. When people live in close proximity to one another, as in towns and cities, what comes around tends to go around. As the geneticist Spencer Wells notes: "Ultimately, nearly every single major disease affecting modern human populations—whether bacterial, viral, parasitic, or non-communicable—has its roots in the mismatch between our biology and the world we have created since the advent of agriculture." (*Pandora's Seed*, p. 90.)

Another side effect of agriculture and early state-making was the routine practice of slaving raids. Agriculture has always required the work of many hands, especially at harvest time. As the historian James C. Scott observes: "For the early states, the taking of loot, particularly human captives, was not a mere by-product of war but a key objective. Slaving wars were systematically conducted by many of the earliest states in the Mediterranean as part of their manpower needs." (*Against the Grain: A Deep History of the Earliest States*, p. 172) Imagine yourself as a small yeoman farmer, living your life with your family, trying to make a living on a small piece of land—struggling, at times, but essentially a free and autonomous individual—when suddenly you are attacked and swept away by slavers. Not only will you never see your family again, but as a captive you will be brutalized and forced to live out your foreshortened life under the whip of slavery. This scenario was a common theme in the lives of many who lived in or near the grain-growing areas of the Old World, and this model of state-building prevailed for many centuries as the norm.

If you happened to live during this historical epoch, your normalcy bias would reflect the prevailing insecurity of your situation in life. You would know that you could live some part of your life as a free and autonomous individual only to one day be overrun by marauders and forced into slavery, your human dignity shackled and chained, your life no longer your own.

For myself, I was born into a time and place that was particularly fortunate, as such things go. It was boom times America, following our victory in World War Two: the nineteen-fifties and sixties especially saw an essentially new class of people coming into their own; we were the middle class, and we were better educated, better paid, and enjoyed more opportunities for personal growth and material prosperity than any previous American generation. For someone like me, coming of age in these decades of economic expansion, it was only natural to assume that this was simply the way the world was—and thus was formed my own normalcy bias.

I cannot know the precise conditions of the life you are living, coming two or three or four decades behind me, but I can make an informed guess, based upon some things I have learned over the last seventy-plus years. I am afraid that your life will have more in common with the yeoman farmer become slave than with the privileged life that I have enjoyed. It feels unjust to me that this should be so, especially since

THE NORMALCY BIAS

my generation grew up under the influence of the Myth of Progress, according to which each succeeding generation will have it better than their parents. But like many of the myths of our culture, this is mere wishful thinking, contradicted by material reality as well as by the large historical forces that all but determine the trajectory of our lives.

I expect you to be living in a world that is falling apart: politically, economically, ecologically, socially, and in most every other way. There is nothing I can do about the material facts of your life, and maybe I cannot help you in any other way, either. But I am hoping I can, by providing you with some historical perspective on your situation, along with some clues about how things got to be the way they are. I have always had the faith that there is something magical and transformative about coming to terms with as much truth as can be taken in and processed. Knowing may not change your material situation, but it does have the potential to affect how you think and feel about your condition in life, by making you less the victim and more the inquiring intelligence that sees through knowing eyes.

The normalcy bias assumes a world that is more or less static, with the effect of locking you in to the daily grind, by shuttering your vision of what is possible and what has gone before. The antidote to the normalcy bias is the historical perspective, and I hope you find it as liberating as I have.

CHAPTER 8

WHY DOMESTICATION?

THE DOMESTICATION AND cultivation of plants came with so many downsides that it seems almost a wonder that the practice ever got a foothold among our wild ancestors. Certainly the life of an agriculturalist required more time and physical labor than earning one's living by hunting and gathering. And just as certainly, the nutritional value of cultivated crops was inferior to what might be procured within natural ecosystems. And, too, the settled lifestyle, living in cramped, smoky quarters where there was no good way to dispose of accumulating wastes, cannot have seemed like an improvement over the nomadism of those following the migrations of birds and mammals and the seasonal ripening of the land. All these considerations have led historians and paleoanthropologists to puzzle over the whys and wherefores of this dramatic shift in lifeway. I have my own theories about this, as will become evident, but I will here drop a hint in a single word: Power.

The institution of private property dramatically changed the social structure within those communities that came to adopt agriculture as their main source of livelihood. The transformation of the egalitarian social order found among immediate-return hunter-gatherers, to the hierarchy, patriarchy, and totalitarianism that came to later characterize civilization, was not the revolution of a day, a century, or even a millennium. And, even before agriculture, certain groups of hunter-gatherers (called delayed-return hunter-gatherers) were already edging toward inequality by practicing the preservation and storage of food. At whatever point food ceased to be totally communal, but was guarded and hoarded by particular individuals, and dispensed at their pleasure, a new power dynamic began creeping in. It is likely that those groups who chose agriculture as a way of life were of this delayed-return variety, where egalitarianism had already been eroded. And in those early days it was not an all-or-nothing situation: hunting for meat and gathering of fruits and berries continued to round out the diet of the early adopters of agriculture, whose cultivated crops provided limited nutritional value.

As time went on and land under cultivation expanded, the hunting and gathering grounds diminished accordingly, and people became more reliant on what they could grow, and the animals they could herd and confine. This tendency toward expansion was built into agriculture from the very start, and initiated a self-reinforcing positive feedback loop that started small but has grown so overwhelmingly immense that in my own time land dedicated to agriculture now dominates the globe. Several factors are involved in this growth imperative of agriculture. One of these involves the relationship between food and population. It seems to be a principle of population dynamics that when you expand the food supply, humans tend to produce more offspring, so as not to let the food go to waste. As the population expands, so does the need for more living space, along with more agricultural land to provide for these new mouths to feed. More food leads to more people;

more people leads to expanded food production, which leads to more people. And so the cycle goes.

Another factor affecting the will-toward-expansion is what happens to soils under cultivation. As crops are planted and harvested, the soil's fertility is depleted. In swidden (or slash-and-burn) agriculture, as practiced in the tropics, the soil's fertility is usually played out in just two or three years-- and the people then move on, leaving waste land behind. In more temperate regions, soil exhaustion takes longer--especially if the soil is amended with animal manure or other fertilizer— but eventually the soil's fertility is lost, or poisoned by the accumulation of salts from irrigation. Much soil loss is due to the breaking of the ground when it is tilled, which leaves the unprotected soil vulnerable to being washed away by rains and blown away by winds (as in the American Dustbowl of the 1930s). When looked at in historical perspective, it becomes obvious that agriculture has always depended upon the mining of topsoil, mining being an activity that depletes a resource faster than it can regenerate. In my time, in America, topsoil is eroded at the average rate of three tons per acre per year, while topsoil builds at the rate of one inch per 500--1000 years— making agriculture a short-term boom and a long-term bust.

The imperative for expanding agricultural operations in order to exploit uncompromised topsoil, and the need for more living space for a fast-growing population, comes with an accompanying imperative for violence. If, in the earliest days of agriculture there was still some land unoccupied by humans, violence was required to transform a natural ecosystem into cropland. Forests had to be felled, and root-wads burned, displacing all the inhabitants of the former forest. This is a form of violence, and a loss, that the people of our culture almost never consider. Among the more mobile animals, being displaced from one's natural habitat means trying to compete for habitat and something to eat with others of its kind in territory already occupied and filled to its own carrying capacity. For the less mobile animals and forest plants death comers even more quickly. And it is not only random individuals of various species that are destroyed in this way, but a whole suite of reciprocal relationships among the species, and the synergistic functioning of the ecosystem as a whole. And something else is lost, too, something few of the people of our culture ever bother to consider, and that is the violence committed upon Mother Earth herself. In the natural world, specific ecosystems tend to evolve exactly where they are best-suited to be. Often, it is not just a case of evolution, but of co-evolution, with plants and animals co-evolving to be well-matched to one another and to their geo-physical and bio-physical environment. Clearing land for agriculture without regard to what is being erased from the world is an act not only of violence, but of flagrant disrespect of Mother Earth and her 3.8-billion-year Project of Life—and, I would say, a defilement of the sacred.

At some point in pre-history pretty much all available territory where people could make a living had been claimed, and the agriculturalist's growth imperative bumped up against territory that was already claimed by others—and that meant conflict: human on human violence.

Under the new regime of private property, once land started producing agricultural surpluses, those foodstuffs had to be stored and guarded. The person who claimed ownership of the land and the crops it produced now had to protect his investment with hired guards. When it became time to expand into new territory, these guards easily morphed into soldiers to go up against those who were defending their territory against invasion. And thus began the structural violence that has been a hallmark of civilization ever since: the institution of ongoing war. This is not to say that Paleolithic hunters never got into violent disputes over hunting grounds; but these were limited skirmishes with few fatalities—not "civilized" warfare at all. Partly, this is a matter of scale. When everyone was living in small, scattered, mobile groups, there was simply no incentive to risk one's own small group in an all-out conflict with another band. Warfare might occasionally be the outcome of chance encounters, but war as an institution made no survival sense. Groups that are mobile work best at a scale of twenty to thirty individuals. When a group becomes unwieldy in size, or dissention arises, some part of the group goes off on its own, and thus maintains a group size that is optimal for the hunting and gathering lifeway. In other words, there are no imperial designs built into nomadism , as there are in built into serial sedentism, and the claim to private "ownership" of land.

The structural violence inherent in the synergistic combination of agriculture and private property is of course not limited to the destruction of other species, the dismantling of ecosystems, and rise of militarism—ordinary citizens of agricultural communities also suffer under this regime. The new social order, based upon the ownership and non-ownership of land and other property, establishes a hierarchy unknown among immediate-return hunter-gatherers--and this stratification only intensifies as the disparity between classes of people widens. When those who have wealth, privilege, and power lord it over those who do not, a new authoritarianism creeps into the relations among agrarian peoples; and when history takes a sexist turn, patriarchy bursts on the scene. In this new way of life, the rich exploit and dominate the poor, while men of all classes dominate and exploit women.

There is more to this story of power and domination: a story of how climatological trauma led to social trauma, which in turn was enshrined in culture--but that revelation will have to wait its turn.

WHY DOMESTICATION?

Meanwhile, I hope you can appreciate that my understanding of how things got to be this way was not easily come by, and certainly is not the mainstream view of the genesis of patriarchy, war, classism, sexism, and a world where the rich parasitize the poor. The dominant narrative will tell you that agriculture is the greatest thing that ever happened to humans, and that civilization is the highest and best form of social organization in the history of the world. Developing a counter-narrative within this context of cultural self-congratulation and anthropocentrism has required a disciplined course of self-directed research, and, I would have to say, a particular kind of personality and way of apprehending the world. There is so much more I want to share with you about what led up to the broken world you have inherited, but I feel that I should first give you some sense about how my particular worldview was shaped by early childhood experience.

CHAPTER 9

LIFE ON THE LAKE

BEFORE I TELL you about those formative years I spent on the lake, and how they shaped the way I came to see the world, I want to briefly go back to my earliest memories of growing up in a house with competing narratives. My first clear memory is kind of an odd one: I was four and sitting on my bed when for some reason I became hyper-aware of myself as a person distinct from everyone else around me. My very small bedroom, sometimes referred to as the sleeping porch, was between the huge bedroom where my grandparents slept and the slightly smaller one occupied by my parents. This placement was symbolic of my being caught in the middle between two antagonists, in the form of my mother and my grandmother.

Gretchen, my grandmother, was very protective of her relationship with my father, and deeply resented my mother for taking her boy away from her. She had him here under her roof, but not all to herself, as she would have preferred. So there was a competition between these two women for the affections of my father, and that was at the heart of their mutual enmity. But there was also a competition between them for my own loyalty and affection, and this is where the competing narratives came in. Gretchen never missed an opportunity to try to discredit my mother, finding fault with almost everything she did---making her seem like quite a despicable person. For her own part, my mother, Ann, would tell me about the dirty tricks that Gretchen routinely played on her, like taking and hiding some of her clothes, or a sentimentally valued ring. And more than once Gretchen sabotaged something mom was cooking, like turning up the temperature of the oven when she was baking cookies, so they'd burn and be inedible. Some of the accusations and counter accusations were petty, like these; but some were quite serious, and called into question the integrity and character of the other person.

This was my world when I was four, five, six, and seven. I was caught between two powerful authority figures, each giving me different versions of the world, each playing on my emotions, testing my instincts, requiring me to sort out for myself the relative merits of each conflicting story. The conflict between these two women would play out over decades, the dynamic changing only slightly over the years. But I bring this up because of what it did to me, and also for me. It made me question just about everything I was told, to sort through possible implications, and to seek out the underlying motives behind whatever narrative was being pedaled. And this came to include the cultural narratives I was exposed to on a daily basis. I could see that teachers, preachers, politicians, and just about everybody else were in the business of selling ideas and ways of looking at the world. Because of this early childhood experience, I became a selective and discriminating judge of story lines I was exposed to, and in this way developed the ability to "see through" culture, and how its narratives were meant to influence my view of the world.

As I would later discover, this is not a common ability. Most people are quite unaware of how they have been played by culture and made to think that all their beliefs, values, and perceptions are strictly their own. Culture, in this way, is a great deceiver, and to the extent that it has its own agenda and purposes, culture is not necessarily an ally or friend. And to the extent that culture has been cynically manipulated to serve the interests of the few, at the expense of the many, culture can be, and in many cases has become, the enemy of all life.

Probably I was born with a rudimentary disposition to be the kind of person I turned into—not a contrarian, necessarily, but someone with a sense of the world that was different from those around me. For instance, most everyone I know easily falls into the category of anthropocentrist-- being not only human-centered in their thinking, but having rather inflated, self-flattering, ideas about the status of human beings in the world. I think it is fair to say that they believe the world is all about humans, and all the other species on Earth are just here to serve our interests, and have no meaning of their own. I don't believe that at all, and one reason why is almost certainly connected with three formative years I spent in a world far from the man-made disasters we call cities.

When I was eight, nine, and ten, I lived on a remote lake in northern California. It was far enough out in the sticks that I had to walk or be driven three miles on dirt road to the school bus turn-around, which was itself fifteen miles out from the six-hundred-person town where the school was. This whole area, even today, is remote and unsettled enough to have no franchise fast food outlets whatsoever. But it was not the school or the town that had such a big effect on me; it was the lake itself, and the fact that the lake was on the Pacific Flyway, which then supported six million migratory waterfowl, as these birds cycled south and north and south again with the changing seasons. Our lake was in sight of Mt. Shasta, except

LIFE ON THE LAKE

for those times when the ducks and geese were on the fly and so filled the sky with their wing beats and raucous cries that they made the mountain disappear. There were lesser and greater Canadian honkers, and it was a delight to see them fold back their wings and stretch out their webbed feet as a squadron of them cruised in for a landing on the lake that was our front yard. The ducks would poke around in the tules and cattails, feeding on whatever they could find there. Grebes would also fly in with the ducks and geese, and for some reason we called them hell divers. There were also black-bodied white-billed coots that we called mudhens, and unlike the ducks and geese, who could rise off the water with graceful alacrity, these mudhens had to flap and flap and kind of run along the lake's surface for a good long ways before they finally achieved flight. I had the use of the family rowboat then, and had developed a slow, gentle stroke that would take me out among all these birds without much disturbing their feeding, or squabbling, or sunning themselves on the odd protruding log, or just paddling easily along, sometimes in formation and sometimes in broken ranks.

My young mind and sensibility took all this in with an excited delight. The part of me that was trying to be a hunter, wanted to exploit all of this bounty with my new .22 rifle. At least there was a voice in my ear telling me that I should be thinking in these terms. But mainly I just enjoyed being in the middle of so much Life, embodied in so many life-forms. The geese would gather in the fields across the lake and feed by the hundreds and thousands. One day when I was watching them feed and take off and land and feed some more, something happened to make all of them take off at once and fill the sky as a mass, and then break off into their own flocks and form their characteristic lopsided Vs as they headed to their next destination. When I looked back to where they had been feeding I noticed some movement. It was a goose trying to fly but unable to get off the ground. I told my mom I was going to go get that goose and bring it home, and she assented. I rowed across the lake as quickly as I could, jumped out of the boat, and ran down that goose, after much drama and noisy complaint. I stuffed it in a gunny sack, tied it off, and deposited the goose in the stern. By the time I got to our side of the lake, it had settled down a bit, and I got it to the house with only a bit of struggle. When I opened the sack in our living room, Mom looked the goose over and determined that it had been shot in the shoulder and broken its wing bone. "What should we do with it?" I asked. "What do you want to do with it?" She asked in return. I thought about how it would be good for at least a couple dinners, and how this would be my first goose, and how much the family would appreciate me for bringing fresh goose to table. Sitting in our small living room, so composed, the bird seemed very large, and not just large, but stately, its eyes alert but not alarmed. What would I do with it? Shoot it in the head with my .22? Take an axe to its neck? Looking at it without the excitement of the chase I began to realize that this goose was its own being, just like I was my own being, and I just didn't have it in me to take this being's life. Mom helped me get it back in the bag, and I rowed it back to where I had found it, and turned it loose. It occurred to me that a coyote might end up having goose dinner that night, but that was out of my control. I had gone to a bit of trouble to catch that goose and bring it home and take it back again, but I now knew something I hadn't known before. In just the same way that all dogs are the same, and yet each is an individual; and just as all people are the same, and yet each is an individual; so too with geese, who are all the same, and yet each has its own essence and will to live and even its own sense of dignity. I saw that in the living room of our house when I was nine when a wild creature had

LIFE ON THE LAKE

been brought into an alien enclosure and showed me something of itself.

As fall turned into winter only a few ducks and geese stayed on at our lake. Then in the spring they came back by the tens of thousands, on their way north. Next fall they came back again, and I then began to see that there was a pattern here, a cycle, and that this was part of something much bigger than me or my family, and bigger even than all human beings. This was Nature, and Nature was the source of all this abundant life around me, as well as my own life, and that of my family, and of all humanity. Nature was the source of all Life, and Life was good, and Nature was good because Nature was the source of Life.

The Korean War was going on back then—1950, '51 and '52—and this last little bit of the last frontier was a rarity in the world even then. The experience I had then is now available to almost no one. In the year nineteen hundred, the Pacific Flyway supported 12 million migratory waterfowl. In 1950 it was six million. Today it is just about a million. There is a pattern and trajectory here. In 1950 there were about 150 million people in America. Now we have more than doubled that number. There is a pattern and trajectory here, too.

I got a taste for life in all its abundance when there was still a little abundance left. It was a remnant then, and now only a remnant of a remnant remains. Before my European ancestors arrived on this continent half a millennium ago, North America was the very picture of natural abundance. Life was thriving here; ecosystems were intact; there was integrity, stability, and beauty within the biotic community. Nature was whole. From my perspective, this is what it is all about. The meaning of Life is Life fully expressed. It is Life in dynamic balance, in all its complexity, diversity, and overflowing abundance. If you were to ask me for my best vision of the future, it would be a continuation of this 3.8-billion-year evolutionary Project of Life—and that could be with, or without, the human being, depending on who we turn out to be.

CHAPTER 10

A SECOND TWISTED TURNING

IN TRYING TO make sense of the dynamics behind the radical transformation of the human character over the last eight or ten thousand years, as we went from hunter-gatherers to pastoral-agriculturalists, and then on to the vicious people of war and empire we would later develop into, it has always seemed that something was missing from the equation, some crucial explanatory detail. The lure of power and greed, as these became associated first with large pastoral estates and later with the rise of the State, has provided a partial and necessary motive force, but has seemed lacking in sufficiency. There just had to be something more; yet scholarship on the subject has, until recently, had little convincing to offer. Now it is clear that that "something more" can be summed up in the word "trauma," or, more accurately, trauma compounded by more trauma.

We know that something happened to change the human psyche somewhere between 75,000 and forty thousand years ago: something that made us aware of being aware while also disposing us to think symbolically. This psychic transformation can be seen perhaps most dramatically in cave paintings, such as those discovered in southern France, which display a mind and sensibility indistinguishable from our own.

With the rise of settled pastoralism and agriculture, a formerly suppressed personality type came ever more into dominance: the aggrandizer, the self-important Big Shot who saw himself as better than those around him. Psychologist Steve Taylor calls this an "ego explosion," a phenomenon he traces back to the Middle East and central Asia, and about 6,000 years back in time. He goes on to make this rather provocative claim: "The Ego Explosion is the most momentous event in the history of the human race. The last 6,000 years of history can only be understood in terms of it. All the different kinds of social and psychic pathology we've looked at—war, patriarchy, social stratification, materialism, the desire for status and power, sexual repression, environmental destruction, as well as the inner discontent and disharmony which afflict us—all these can be traced back to the intensified sense of ego which came into existence in the deserts of the Middle East and central Asia 6,000 years ago. (*The Fall: The Insanity of the Ego in Human History,* p. 124) What Taylor seems to be talking about here is more than a smattering of aggrandizer personalities going off the rails; what he is suggesting instead is a pathological ego trip affecting all of society. But how does something like that come to be?

According to James DeMeo, a researcher combining the disciplines of psychology and historical geography, the pathology began with severe and enduring drought, famine, and starvation, due to the drying out and desertification of a once-prosperous homeland. For those who survived, there was the additional trauma of losing family and being displaced from their home. Extreme and deepening climate change set something in motion within the survivors, but it took something else to transfer the trauma to others; it took culture.

A SECOND TWISTED TURNING

DeMeo divides culture into two basic types: what he calls unarmored matrist and armored patrist. Matrist culture is egalitarian, non-violent, with permissive child-rearing practices and a permissive pleasure-approving attitude toward adolescent sexual activity. Human pleasure is welcomed and institutionalized; spontaneity is valued, with few to no codes or taboos. Nature is revered.

Armored patrist culture is characterized by parental domination of children, with a pattern of traumatizing infants and painful initiation of youngsters. There is a restrictive, anxious attitude toward sexuality, genital mutilations are common, as are female virginity taboos; adolescent lovemaking is severely censured. Women are held to be of inferior status and limits put on their freedom. Family structure is hierarchical, authoritarian, often violent and sadistic. Asceticism, avoidance of pleasure and seeking of pain are common. Attitude toward Nature is inhibited and fearful.

According to DeMeo, matrist culture is the default human condition. "The origins of patrism, defined and equated with patriarchal authoritarian or armored human culture, was originally rooted in the process of ancient desertification, specifically that which began in the Arabian and central Asian portions of Sarahasia. Famine, starvation, and mass migrations related to land abandonment severely traumatized the originally peaceful and sex-positive inhabitants of those lands, including a distinct turning away from original matrism toward patristic forms of behavior. Once established within human cultures by new social institutions, armored patrism spread out beyond the borders of Sarahasia by the new trauma-inflicting social institutions, thereby recreating the older environmental traumas in each new generation." (*Saharasia: The 4000 BCE Origins of Child Abuse, Sex-Repression, Warfare, and Social Violence in the Deserts of the Old World*, p. 389)

According to this view, the physical and psychological trauma of fighting for survival in a land of plenty gone suddenly and terminally dry is what set in motion a social and cultural contagion that is with us still. The conditions of famine, starvation, social turmoil, and land abandonment were the sources of the original trauma that turned the people from unarmored matrist to armored patrist. Once these armored characteristics get established within a society they become institutionalized and are passed on culturally and socially from generation to generation. The mechanism for this transformation of a people was never fully spelled out in Taylor's story of *The Fall*; In *Sharasia* it is, and it is based on the psychological and social insights of Willhelm Reich and his sex-economic viewpoint.

"Sex-economic theory—which provides a dynamic and scientifically testable alternative to mechanistic genetic determinism for the passing on of behavior traits from one generation to the next—rests upon the existence of a spontaneously honest, loving, social and peaceful core to human nature, characterized by strong bonds of both sexual and romantic love between males and females, including adolescents and the unmarried. As such, it demands some <u>outside force</u>, some powerful and widespread anxiety-provoking trauma, to destroy a peaceful and loving social group and drive it toward pleasure-anxiety and social violence. Whatever this outside force is, or was, it would also be required to initiate generalized changes within the sphere of sexual behavior and genital function, to create chronic sexual frustrations and undischarged emotional-energetic tension—the 'fuel' of pleasure-anxiety, armoring, and sadistic aggression which is turned back into the social group, organized into social institutions and 'traditions,' for the socially-approved attack upon and repression of sexual functions and pleasurable activity in the next generation. Once the armor is formed and generally exists culture-wide, it becomes a force for its own self-perpetuation, this time wholly from <u>within</u> the culture. After the outside force has worked its traumatic damage, social structure would change, and institutionalization of trauma would occur."(pp 44-5)

The "institutionalization of trauma" is an abstract way of talking about something that is highly palpable, and felt both emotionally and physically in people's actual lives. DeMeo continues: "Newborn infants, mothers, and children would then be attacked and repressed by ritual traditions, by distorted and damaged social institutions which would rationalize a thousand different methods for the denial of pleasure and infliction of pain, implanting new barriers of fear, compulsion, and anxiety into male-female relations. Outside forces would then no longer be necessary to recreate the trauma in subsequent generations. People thereafter would then become their own traumatic oppressors, and would hence only 'feel comfortable' with neighbors and leaders who would likewise support the continuation of the same harsh and repressive ways of living. The softer individual with a new idea or new ways of living would then be the odd person, the 'heretic' or 'provocateur' who—by virtue of their unbearable softness—would be a constant reminder of what had been lost, and what was missing from the lives of the majority. Likewise, the emotionally-soft and fluid cultural group would be viewed with much suspicion and anger by the more hardened social group. Of necessity, as a means to control within-group anxiety (family, school, professional group, village, or nation) the softer persons or groups would, through some convoluted and illogical rationalization, be compulsively attacked, driven out or even totally destroyed by the more hardened and rigidly armored individuals." (p. 45)

The psychological, social, and cultural dynamics involved in DeMeo's explanation of how a people become transformed from unarmored matrists into armored patrists rings true to me, satisfying my best understanding about how we humans—as the complex social and cultural animals that we are—behave in groups over time. Indeed, I find this way of understanding the human plight infinitely superior to the glib proclamations of the scientific materialists who reduce all these complexities down to a genetically controlled biological determinism free of nuance.

When abrupt climate change hit the people of the Middle East and Central Asia some 6,000 years ago, it came as a shock to their agricultural and pastoral way of life; as conditions worsened and became more widespread, shock devolved into unrelieved trauma. Although DeMeo never uses this term to describe their condition, what these people suffered would seem to be a form of post-traumatic shock disorder--and what happens to the individual human personality and to group dynamics under PTSD is not a pretty thing to behold, then as now.

The book, *Saharasia*, provides the reader with historical maps based upon exhaustively compiled data about climate and movements of peoples, as well as social trends, going back some 6,000 years. These graphic aids are particularly valuable to someone like me who has puzzled over the great transformation of human culture that took place between our wild hunter-gatherer ancestors and our own agricultural civilization—a transformation that amounts to a near reversal of foundational beliefs and values. Just when this overturning of worldview took place, where, and under what conditions, has remained vague for me, despite specifically seeking answers to these questions. Now that vagueness has given way to a clarifying, if rudimentary, grasp of the where, the when, and the how—thanks to the exhaustive evidence supplied by DeMeo in this book.

Armored patristic culture can be thought of as a social

A SECOND TWISTED TURNING

pathology that infects the whole of society. In the case of Western culture, as chronicled by our own historians over the last three thousand years, this institutionalization of trauma—expressed as patriarchy, slavery, war, and empire--is perhaps best understood as a kind of mass psychosis. An exceptionally clear example of a patrist culture overrunning and displacing a matrist culture can be seen in the history of the last five hundred years on the continents of South and North America. This is a case not only of one people (white people) brutally inflicting trauma upon another--in the form of torture, imprisonment, slavery, and genocide—but of forcing an alien lifeway upon the remaining survivors. This was accomplished in large part by ecocide: by erasing much of the land's natural complexity, with its long history of supporting the hunter-gatherer way of life, by land clearance, along with the deliberate wiping out of key species, such as the buffalo and many runs of salmon. From among the matrist peoples who suffered these abuses at the hands of the settler-colonists emerged an explaining story, and with the story came a word to describe the monster and its monstrous behavior: wetiko.

The term, wetiko, eludes narrow definition, but Jack Forbes, who brought the concept of wetiko to a wider audience in his book *Columbus and Other Cannibals*, points in the right direction when he says: "The *wetiko* psychosis is a sickness of the spirit that takes people down an ugly path with no heart." (p. 188) This spiritual sickness is characterized by an inflated sense of self-importance accompanied by a lack of conscience, personal integrity, or compassion for others. When wetiko afflicts an individual, it looks very like sociopathy or psychopathy. When it possesses an entire society it looks very like civilization, empire, and capitalism—and is considered normal, because it is the norm. As I am fond of stating, because it is true: the culture of civilization is based on lies, theft, and deadly violence. This is because all known civilizations have been empires, and all empires are based upon the rapacious exploitation and plunder of peoples and places, without mercy or remorse. The European conquest of the Native peoples of this land—our American genocide—employed the full spectrum of wetiko behaviors, including lies, theft, and deadly violence, as well as every manner of treachery, betrayal, and bloody atrocity imaginable to a sick collective mind. This bit of history was wetiko on a rather grand scale, but readily rationalized and normalized as "Manifest Destiny."

As I am also fond of saying, because it is true: "our culture is nothing if not a self-promoting, self-aggrandizing propaganda machine." Accordingly, we are the best, most righteous people who have ever lived, and whatever we might do in the world will always be justified by our special status as an exceptional people. And if you don't believe us, just ask.

What is at work here, in the movement from hunter-gatherer to agriculturalist, as well as from unarmored matrist to armored patrist, is a radical change in allegiance. Among the "primitive" peoples of the world, living in small bands, the primary allegiance of the individual was necessarily to the group. This made survival sense, since the lone isolated individual has a very low fitness level, whereas the group, with its various synergies, is much more viable as a unit of fitness. "All for one and one for all" is a longstanding survival strategy with a proven record of success. But the equation changed with the ego explosion and the rise of civilization. In accordance with the self-absorbed narcissism that characterized this extreme shift in emphasis, the individual supplanted the group as the unit of chief concern. Selfishness and self-glorification (far from being scorned and suppressed, as formerly among the egalitarian peoples of the world) now became the approved social norm, the social ideal. The American Dream--especially in its wealth-glorifying neoliberal iteration, where the culturally approved goal is to become a millionaire or billionaire--is merely an intensification of a pattern established 6,000 years ago in the deserts of Saharasia, then codified in the books of Genesis and Exodus, some 2500 years ago. With divine permission to take "dominion" over all the creatures of the Earth, as well as the Earth itself, wealth creation at the expense of the planet's ecological integrity became the institutionalized norm of civilization—and now the Big Lie has gone global in scope. When reality asserts itself, it, too, will be global in scope.

CHAPTER 11

UNRESTRAINED EXPLOITATION

I LIVE IN a world where unrestrained exploitation of natural resources is the global norm. And because it is the norm, the normalcy bias disposes most everyone to believe that this is a perfectly acceptable way to live in the world; that things are just as they should be. But this is a lie and a delusion, and is based upon even deeper cultural falsities. And though it is true that our people have "successfully" lived these lies for six thousand years, it is also true that reality ultimately asserts itself, and that this sort of self-deception comes with a price. Unfortunately, rewards and punishments are distributed unevenly and without justice. The prime exploiters tend to reap most of the benefits, while others, including future generations, are lopsidedly left with the unhappy consequences. This is part of why living a lie succeeds. The lessons of truth never reach those most in need of learning, and so the delusion lives on.

Bucking the normalcy bias, I want here to explore the proposition that certain things which the people of our culture have identified as "resources," put here for human use, are no such thing. What we call "renewable resources" are gifts

UNRESTRAINED EXPLOITATION

of Nature, and their use is permitted to humans, as long as they are in fact renewed. The forests of the British Isles and of Europe have been cut down for human use, but not renewed. When a renewable resource is used in this way, it is mining the resource for one-time use, and, I would say, is in violation of an ancient human compact with Nature--the ultimate source of our lives. It is allowable to live off the interest of Earth's solar budget and to partake of Nature's emergent abundance. It is not permissible to live off the principal; that constitutes mining, and is theft.

Our wild ancestors, who well understood and practiced the principles of ecology, knew not to be too greedy or improvident with Nature's bounty. If you take too much of any resource you depend upon (say salmon or bison) you may deplete its population beyond its ability to regenerate and reconstitute itself. No doubt these lessons were learned the hard way, and then passed on to future generations through cultural stories and traditions. In this way, each hunter-gatherer group developed its own set of ethical guidelines about how to deal with the "resources" of their chosen ecosystem, with an eye toward maintaining ecosystem balance and resilience. This was, of course, in their own self-interest; that is to say, in the medium- and long-term self-interest of the group, as a collective. The incentives toward moderation would have included an attachment to a particular landscape and the group desire to maintain a long-term presence in their chosen territory. Thinking several generations ahead in this way, the people learned to live lightly on the land.

Another hedge against greed was built into the nomadic lifeway of our immediate-return hunter-gatherer ancestors. If something was too burdensome to carry from one camp to another there was a very strong incentive not to value or acquire it in the first place. "Travel light, and take from the land no more than you need" was the order of the day. Groups of this kind, comprised of twenty to thirty individuals, were staunch egalitarians, and jealously guarded their freedom from would-be bosses and bullies. On the one hand, their first loyalty was to the group, not to themselves; but on the other, individuality and personal freedom were paramount values in their lives. This way of life necessarily produced many remarkable individuals, and, it would seem, rather fully self-actualized human beings. The incentives were there to be all that a person could be, and a fully-actualized human was of high value not only to themselves, but to the group.

The transition from immediate-return hunter gatherer to settled agriculturalist constitutes an immense shift in lifeway. But the transformation may not always have been quite that abrupt. An intermediate step between the two may have moderated for some the extremity of the change; that step is the delayed-return hunter-gatherer lifeway. Delayed-return means that foodstuff is stored and dispensed by a particular person or group, giving this person (or persons) power over others, thus undermining the egalitarian impulse and establishing a rudimentary hierarchy. Delayed-return societies, such as the Northwest Coast fishing tribes, tended to live in established communities, where the acquisition of material goods was less discouraged than among their mobile cousins. Here, in nascent form, are conditions that might soften the transition to the settled, stratified agricultural way of life-- although there is no historical record of salmon people voluntarily becoming a grain and livestock people. As long as there were fish to catch (or bison to hunt), why would they?

Our agricultural ancestors got their first taste of wholesale theft with their initial clearance of land for the planting of grain. When you steal the habitat of other creatures you also steal their lives, but this form of ecocide is only the beginning

UNRESTRAINED EXPLOITATION

of the thieving (mining) way of life. After two or three years of working the soil, most of its nutrients have been exhausted, and soil nutrition must be imported from elsewhere, which is yet another form of theft. If cropland is watered by means of irrigation, then water is also stolen from somewhere, and someone, else. The breaking and turning of the soil, as is required when planting annual crops, exposes the loosened soil to the wind and rain, which erodes the topsoil at a rate that exponentially exceeds its rate of regeneration. And this is yet another form of mining that steals from the future (and other species) for the short-term gains of the few.

Once embarked on the thieving, non-egalitarian way of life, it was an easy slide into other such practices of injustice and unsustainability. Next came the mining and smelting of metals, leading inevitably into an arms race among competing groups for a superior arsenal of weapons—an arms race that continues to this day. In addition to renewable resources (which now seldom get renewed), the people of our culture have identified another part of the living planet to be used by humans, which they call "non-renewable resources." These include fossil fuels such as coal, oil, and natural gas; metals such as iron, copper, nickel, silver, and gold; various other elements, including the rare earths, and any number of miscellaneous compounds. All of these are integral to the Earth, are under the Earth's skin, and can be accessed only by ripping into the Earth itself. Inevitably, it is a violent process, whether accomplished directly by humans using sharp prying tools or giant machines that gouge out the Earth, tons of flesh at a time. Few, if any, of these non-renewables come to the surface in pure form. They come with a lot of the rest of the Earth, referred to as "overburden" or "spoils," which is treated as waste. In the case of mountaintop removal, everything that is not coal is bulldozed toward lower ground, including into creeks and rivers. In any mining process, much of what is brought up to the surface of the Earth (along with the sought-after treasure) is toxic to life. As long as it was buried, its life- and health-threatening properties were no problem. But, once above-ground these poisons are released into the biosphere to work their ongoing harm, and the harm has not only been cumulative, but cumulative at an ever-increasing rate.

This is thanks largely to the discovery and exploitation of fossil fuels and the invention of machines to make use of this remarkably abundant yet finite source of power. In the way that one thing leads to another, the Age of Science led to the Age of Industry and Technology, all of which went into hyper-drive with the unrestrained exploitation of fossil fuels. From the perspective of Western civilization, the way this all unfolded appears to have a certain inevitability about it—as if there really were no other way things might have gone. But this is likely not the case in any absolute sense. That is, just because something exists beneath the surface of the Earth—whether iron, or gold, or oil—does not automatically mean that it must be brought up and put to use. This is a choice: not so much at the level of the individual or community, but at the level of culture. Ours is a culture that couldn't say no to this kind of temptation, but other cultures have said no, and continue to say no, for reasons of their own.

The Mayan shaman, Martin Prechtel, speaks for a group of people who are the survivors of a failed civilization. Their ancestors knew the glories of imperial power, and also the humility of social collapse. Presumably, they have learned something from this experience, and it has changed their worldview. I think it fair to say that they became less materialistic and more spiritual in outlook, perhaps reclaiming some part of the worldview of their indigenous, animistic, ancestors. In any case, these modern Mayans hold the belief that the Earth

UNRESTRAINED EXPLOITATION

is sacred, and is home to an entire panoply of spirits. The way Prechtel explains it, what is beneath the Earth's crust belongs to the Earth, and to take what belongs to the Earth is either theft or a borrowing. If it is a borrowing, then it will require a great deal of ritual activity to pay off the spiritual debt even for the humblest of withdrawals from Earth's storehouse.

In an interview with Derrick Jensen, Prechtel goes into great detail about the ritual requirements incurred when taking from the Earth just enough to make a single knife. Prechtel says: "A knife, for instance, is a very minimal, almost primitive tool to people in modern industrial society. But for the Mayan people, the spiritual debt that must be paid for the creation of such a tool is great. To start with, the person who is going to make the knife has to build a fire hot enough to produce coals. To pay for that he's got to give a sacrificial gift to give to the fuel, to the fire."

Jensen asks, "Like what?"

"Ideally, the gift should be something made by hand, which is the one thing humans have that spirits don't."

He continues: "Once the fire is hot enough, the knife maker must smelt the iron ore out of the rock. The part that's left over, which gets thrown away in Western culture, is the most holy part in shamanic rituals. What's left over represents the debt, the hollowness that's been carved out of the universe by human ingenuity, and so must be refilled with human ingenuity. A ritual gift equal to the amount that was removed from the other world has to be put back to make up for the wound caused to the divine. Human ingenuity is a wonderful thing but only so long as it's used to feed the deities that give us the ability to perform such extravagant feats in the first place.

"So just to get the iron, the shaman has to pay for the ore, the fire, the wind and so on—not in dollars and cents but in ritual activity equal to what's been given."

"All these ritual gifts make the knife enormously 'expensive,' and make the process quite involved and time-consuming. The need for ritual makes some things too spiritually expensive to bother with. That's why the Mayans didn't invent space shuttles or shopping malls or backhoes. They live the way they do not because it's a romantic way to live—it's not; it's enormously hard—but because it works." (*Dreams*, pp. 238-39)

The concept of spiritual debt is consistent with a worldview that regards the Earth, the Cosmos, and all of life to be sacred, and therefore to be treated with the utmost reverence and conscientious respect. This is the Indigenous Worldview, based in the knowledge and belief that everything that exists is in some way inhabited by Spirit, or is Spirit. When this understanding of life and the world is not only believed but is practiced in daily life by a group or a people, it is called animism. This is how people lived in the world for untold human and hominid generations, and this was their default worldview. Then, just a few millennia ago a dramatic reversal took place—the desacralization of Earth and of all the life thereon.

This desacralization began with a lie born of trauma some six thousand years ago in the deserts of Saharasia. I call it the Big Lie, because it is foundational to many of our cultural institutions--thereby begetting more lies. The Big Lie, which is anti-ecological at its core, states that the human is separate from, and above, all the creatures of the Earth, as well as the Earth itself. It is a lie because everything is connected to everything else in networks of interdependence, and nothing is, or ever could be, separate and independent from everything else. This obvious fact of life was well understood by our wild ancestors and was fully integrated into their way of life. To completely reverse this longstanding view of the world must have required an enormous amount of bad feeling—feeling born from an overwhelming sense of betrayal. The founders of our culture of civilization had once been flourishing pastoralists in a land of plenty, when everything was abruptly taken from them by a grudging Mother Nature, as she withheld the life-giving rains, reducing herds and families to a few straggling survivors. Resentful and bitter at the loss, un-reconciled and irreconcilable, these survivors of abrupt climate change trauma took their revenge on Mother Nature by casting her in the role of adversary, on the one hand, and as desacralized storehouse of goodies, on the other.

We have seen how the trauma of losing quality of life, a way of life, and the lives of loved ones, can transform a people—at first, due to an outside force, such as abrupt climate change, but subsequently the trauma becomes internalized, by way of cultural tradition, and thereby passed on to future generations. Over the last six thousand years, traditions born of trauma have fed the culture of Western civilization, and these traditions have come down to us today, not diluted by time but intensified, elaborated, magnified unto extremity. What began with the rise of a patriarchal class, based upon pastoral agriculture, private property, and the accumulation of wealth- -measured in cattle and sheep, and other tokens of social superiority—was to become an enduring theme of our culture, and perhaps especially so after being codified in the biblical books of Genesis and Exodus. In Genesis, in the voice of Abraham's servant, we are told: "And the Lord hath blessed my master greatly; and he hath given him flocks, and herds, and silver, and gold, and manservants and maidservants, and camels and asses." (Genesis 24:35) Here we are to suppose that Abraham is a highly worthy individual, much favored by a God who showers him with these material and reputational rewards as tokens of his worthiness and virtue. The creation of wealth, along with its various tokens, is not only sanctified and underwritten by God, but is here set up as a social ideal to be emulated by the faithful.

It is a social order built upon the presumption of inequality among humans, as determined by the peremptory favoritism of a mercurial deity; an authoritarian social order that favors a steep hierarchy among individuals, in which women are subordinate to men and slaves grovel in fear before a powerful master. Men of property are favored above all others in a class system that tends to lock people into a rigidly defined role within society, based upon one's status at birth. Born into slavery, few escape the tyranny of its bonds. Born to privilege, the fortunate just naturally assume their own superiority to those beneath them in the social order. And so the system bangs on, structured from the start to perpetuate stratification and social strife: with the oppressed many working on behalf of the privileged few.

The very concept of wealth creation knows no bounds or limits; but this is not a good match for a finite, ecological planet—which is the kind we live on. Way back when, "Take all you can take" was the order of the day. It still is, only now we have the means to exploit unto utter exhaustion whatever is left. Being suicidal as well as Gaia-cidal, this is not a situation with a long-term future.

The unrestrained exploitation of fellow-humans mirrors the unrestrained exploitation of natural resources. Just as the invention of extractive technologies have been used to maximize the exploitation of natural resources (adding an exponential factor to that endeavor), so too have our social engineers been busy creating laws and policies that favor the very rich over everyone else. This has been going on for a long time, beginning in America with the writing of our constitution, with the granting of special dispensation to white male property owners, and to commerce. But it is really only in the last forty to fifty years that class warfare has become so tellingly overt, and so extreme in its manifestation—especially here in America, but also globally.

As of the early part of the 21st century, income and wealth inequality have become recognized as a serious social, economic, and political problem. Economists, political scientists, and other professional "experts" see dangers in the widening wealth and income gap. Globally, the world's eight richest individuals own as much as the combined wealth of half the human race. In America, 1% of the population owns 40% of the nation's wealth. The bottom 80% own 7%. There are lots of numbers like these which show the ever-widening crevasse between the haves and the have-nots. Elsewhere, I will explore some of the far-reaching implications of these trajectories. For now, I just want to underline the point that the unrestrained exploitations of people, places, other species, and the Earth itself are all pieces at the heart of it all is the Big Lie of Separation—and that lie is only about 6,000 years old.

One other point worth noting is what happens to a group, a society, or a people when they abandon the principle of "all for one and one for all" and put in its place the principle of all against all. One promotes the long-term welfare of the group, while the other, in advancing the individual as the unit of central importance, promotes a cynical social disunity and lack of trust among competitors in a zero-sum game in which there is no "us." This is, of course, just one of many manifestations of the Big Lie of Separation, but this one is likely to prove lethal to the survival of our kind. If we cannot come together as a group, in an act of collective will—as we evidently cannot-- then chaos and entropy are going to have their way with us, picking us off one by alienated one. At the heart of all this dysfunction and delusion is our culture of civilization—as should presently become self-evident.

CHAPTER 12

IMBIBING BELIEF

TO TRULY UNDERSTAND your own situation, within the context of the history of your own people, you must also understand your own culture. But, as it turns out, culture is something almost no one understands. And of course this means that very few people have much of a clue about who they are (in socio-historical context), or any sense of historical cause and effect, and how one thing leads to another leads to another. The first thing to understand about culture is that its most vital functions are invisible, and, being invisible, must be inferred by their effects. But it is more complicated even than this, because culture is not just one thing (having at least three distinct faces) and cannot be understood apart from the human psychology it interacts with.

Many people are not even aware that they are cultural animals, and have no idea that much of the identity that they claim as their own has been imparted to them by culture. This is not ordinarily a problem among peoples with a wholesome culture: they imbibe the directives of their culture, behave as they are expected to, and perhaps live full and interesting lives, never realizing the centrality of culture in everything they have done. For people such as these—and by now there are vanishingly few left in the world—ignorance of culture is no particular deficit. But our situation is different, and ignorance of what culture is and how it works shows every prospect of being fatal, because culture is central to everything we do.

The way that culture enters our lives and penetrates our being seems innocent enough--especially since much of it comes from those we respect, like, and trust. The values, perceptions, and beliefs of our people are passed on to us--mostly without conscious thought or effort--by parents, relatives, friends, and teachers, either by word of mouth or by example. Our cultural conditioning happens in the course of our daily interactions with those in our in-group, as they impart, and we pick up, how best to meet the expectations of society. This is how culture works for us: shaping our individual beliefs to harmonize with the belief system of our group, so that we and it make a good match. The dynamic is the same, whether the culture itself is healthy or sick, life-affirming or life-destroying. And this raises the question about whether it is better to be well-adjusted to a pathological society, and of course share in the larger pathology, or to be a life-affirming misfit among the wetiko unwell.

This question raises the further question about how much choice we have in the matter of conforming, or not conforming, to our culture. From my own experience, I would say that the younger we are, the fewer our choices. Later in life, some of us may reject the main thrust of our cultural conditioning, and embark on the lifelong project of decolonizing our minds and constructing a belief system and worldview consistent with our own deepest instincts. This can be done, and has been done, but it is a massive undertaking, and its successes are always partial. This is because culture starts working on us from day one of our lives, and never lets go. Also, those first few years of cultural conditioning have made a deep impression on us long before we are capable of developing the critical intelligence to question what we have taken in.

I want to tell you about my first day in the world, by way of showing how perceptions, presumptions, attitudes, and beliefs are shaped by forces over which we have no control—and how these early influences mold us all in ways we barely understand.

When I came into the world in 1942, childbirth had already been wrested from the hands of mid-wives, who usually performed their supportive role in the home of the mother-to-be. Accordingly, I was born in a hospital in a fairly large city and was delivered into the hands of a male doctor, who might have used steel forceps to help pull me out of the womb. Like all hospitals in the West, this one had all the flat surfaces and hard edges that signify the kind of institutional sterility we have come to expect of such places. I believe they allowed my mother to hold me in her arms for a few minutes before they whisked me away in a kind of basket to a room full of other newborns. After giving me time to cry myself out (and not before, so as not to "spoil" me), I was eventually given a bottle of something called formula to suck on, while my mother lay in her hospital bed squeezing out some of her breast milk into a waste container, to drain away some of the pressure. According to the doctrine of the day, formula (a product of industrialized chemistry) was supposed to be better for me than my own mother's milk. Separated from the touch of the one who had carried me inside her body for nine months, offered a chemical concoction by a stranger in uniform, isolated inside my small cage in a roomful of equally isolated infants, I got my first taste of what my life would be in industrialized institutional America around the middle of the twentieth century.

This theme of isolation would be reinforced again and again throughout my toddlerhood, as I was put behind bars in a crib at night, locked into my high chair at mealtimes, then put behind bars again in my playpen when no one had time for me during the day. All this prisoner-hood was for my own protection, of course. And what it told me was that I was not a member in good standing with the group, and would be excluded from the group at the convenience of whoever was in authority.

These were standard child-rearing practices of the time, and were consistent pretty much throughout the Western world. What this taught me was that I, like everyone else, was an isolated individual with a rather tenuous connection to the group as a whole. What the evolutionary experience of my species implanted in me was the expectation of belonging to a group of people, and to a place, that I would embrace as my own. When the world I was born into failed to provide me with the experience of belonging, who could I blame but myself? Surely it was some deficiency of mine that caused me to be treated like the outsider I have always been.

Now, if I had been born into a tribe in the Amazon jungle, my introduction to humanity and the world would have been quite different. After I had been held and suckled by my mother, the women in our small band would gather round and talk to me, passing me from one to another, admiring and welcoming me. Within a few days, there would be a ceremony involving all of the people in our band, all focused on welcoming me into the group, and into their jungle world. All this touching and talking to me would likely have given me a sense that the world I had entered was warm, soft, and welcoming—and was the very place where I belonged.

Until I expressed a readiness to walk on my own two feet, I would be carried around by my mother, held by an arm and a hip, or in a kind of sling. From this vantage point, and in the warmth of my mother's touch, I would partake of the life of our people, observing the physical acts of daily life as well as the facial expressions and tones of voice of particular people as they interacted with each other. While not being the center of attention myself, I would be in the middle of it all—just like I belonged there.

The author of *The Continuum Concept*, Jean Liedoff, spent two and a half years living among just such tribal peoples--called the Yequana and Sanema--and was astounded to see how much happier and well-adjusted these people were than those of her own culture. In trying to understand what lay beneath these differences, she noticed a pattern that amounts to a principle. The tribal peoples trust to instinct and believe in the innate sociality of the human being, whereas civilized people do not. "*The assumption of innate sociality* is at direst odds with the fairly universal civilized belief that a child's impulses need to be curbed in order to make him social....If there is anything fundamentally foreign to *us* in continuum societies like the Yequana, it is this assumption of innate sociality. It is by starting from this assumption and its implications that the seemingly unbridgeable gap between their strange behavior, with resultant high well-being, and our own careful calculations, with enormously lower degrees of well-being, becomes intelligible." (pp. 84-5) Do we trust our own instinctive human nature, or do we not? If we don't, then we substitute something far less satisfactory in its place: mistrust of who and what we are.

James DeMeo, drawing on the work of Willhelm Reich, speaks of indigenous cultures such as the Yequana as being *matrist* in orientation: they trust their own instincts and the rightness of the world, while embracing Nature and Life itself. *Patrist* cultures like our own mistrust instinct, glorifying reason as the sole path to knowledge, while seeking to dominate Nature, rather than harmonizing with it—which is consistent with our general bio-phobia: our culturally induced antipathy to the ecological and organic nature of the living world.

Even among the civilized, instinct may not be completely overridden by culture—especially among those who are imperfectly acculturated and whose inborn instincts remain strong. Historically, every hundred or two hundred years our culture will produce a reaction against the absurdities and limitations of our left-brain-dominant way of being in the world, in the form of a Romantic movement, which emphasizes intuition, instinct, and feeling over rationality and reductionism. Wordsworth and Coleridge sparked such a mini-revolution in Great Britain, while Goethe and Schiller led the movement on the Continent. Later, Whitman, Emerson, and Thoreau would articulate the same impulse in America. But whatever course corrections might have been accomplished by these explorations into our deeper nature were soon overwhelmed by the foundational ideologies of our trauma-based culture. And so we have remained, as we began, as a people mistrustful of the world and of our own nature as humans.

The society I was born into, or any society, is first and foremost a collection of human beings. Until quite recently, most societies have evolved to be homogenous—both ethnically and culturally—and more or less distinct from other groups. Occasionally, the categories of society and culture will merge or blur into one another, but generally they are two different things. One is a population of flesh and blood beings; the other is an intricate and comprehensive program that serves as a guidance system for these beings. That culture can work as a guidance system for a society depends upon our nature as a grouping animal. Like birds who fly in flocks, fish who swim in schools, elk who graze in herds, or wolves who hunt in packs, the human evolved to live, and make a living, in groups. For most of our hominid past, we were mobile hunter-gatherers, most often living in groups of twenty to thirty individuals—some part of which would be extended family. Like the flocking, schooling, and herding animals, the human has what must be characterized as a "group mind." Because of this natural group affinity, most people feel most comfortable when their worldview, values, and feelings, are mirrored by those around them; they likewise tend to feel discomfort when they stand as an isolate from the group. And this is especially true when it comes to the foundational beliefs of a culture—what I call deep culture.

If everyone in your group believes the world is flat, but you are quite sure it is round, and you insist upon this, you are likely to endure a great deal of ridicule, at best, and possibly something much worse. This is because the foundational beliefs of deep culture are central to a people's story of the world, and once you start questioning the underlying assumptions of the story the whole narrative is in danger of unraveling.

An interesting and curious aspect of our being a cultural animal is the way humans live by story—and not only **by** story, but how we live **within,** or inhabit, story. A society's foundational stories are referred to by anthropologists as Myth. Myth in this sense isn't a judgment on the veracity of a story; for one thing, no such judgment could be culturally unbiased. Instead, Myth is meant to suggest a category of story that is archetypal, and resonates with the human psyche at a deep, unconscious level. Such myths offer a template or pattern to be emulated by individuals, and by the group as a whole. Myth tells a people who they are, what is valuable, and how they should live. Living by story gives us humans our direction in life, and also a sense of meaning and purpose, which, in the other animals is accomplished by genetically programmed instinct. In our case, however, instinct is overridden and overwritten by culture. And this is why understanding culture is so important: it is central to our individual and collective lives, and yet its workings go unnoticed and unacknowledged by even highly educated people. This is partly because culture works in secretive and surreptitious ways, and partly because our educational system is incentivized to ignore culture's deepest influences, as are most of our institutions. The status quo depends upon it.

CHAPTER 13

AT MOTHER'S KNEE

AS A NEWBORN, I got my first taste of material and behavioral culture within the institution of the hospital. The physical hospital that enclosed me was (and is) a manifestation of a cultural institution. That is to say, the concept of a hospital preceded this particular physical embodiment of the hospital. The concept that doctors are a necessary part of giving birth, and that the hospital is the preferred venue for this biological event, was part of the conventional wisdom of the day—and as such, part of the culture. My mother, who grew up in this culture, believed, as most people did, that doctors were trained experts who know what was best for people's health. Thus she accepted these conditions for giving birth, and both her experiences and mine were determined by the choice that wasn't really a choice. If she had opposed this by-then usual way of bringing a baby into the world, she would have felt opposition all around her, not least from my father's mother. My point is that there are conventional ways of doing things—cultural norms--and though conventions come into fashion then go out again, to be replaced by something else, at any given time in a society there are what have been called best accepted practices, or, simply, "the way we do things here"—and most people conform to these conventions of the day.

These are aspects of what I call commonplace culture, and they serve the daily routines of life as well as meeting common emergencies. These are a society's conventional solutions to everyday problems: one size fits all. When enough people, or strategically placed people, find a common practice unsatisfactory--and have something better to replace it with--the society moves on with this slight shift in cultural practice, and few look back with regret. Fifty years after this first hospital experience, home births and the reinstatement of midwives began to come into fashion. Sometimes the father is even allowed to be present as his wife gave birth to their child—a practice hitherto taboo. In general, this kind of cultural change goes by the name of progress—and progress is held in high esteem by almost everyone. Indeed, the belief in progress runs both deep and wide among our people, and that is because progress is either one of the founding myths of Western culture, or is built upon one of the founding myths, depending upon the analytical tools you use to sort this distinction out. In either case, progress is a cultural meme imbibed by almost everyone exposed to the idea: which brings me back to acculturation--the process by which we absorb our culture.

As a new arrival, I am naturally curious about this world I've been born into, and attentively observe everything around me, including the interactions of family members and others they interact with, noticing facial expressions, body language, and the tones of voice they use with one another, as well as how people react to me. Growing into toddlerhood, I am able to explore further and find out what is permissible, and what is not, among these people who call themselves my family. Some things I am told directly, but most I overhear or observe from a little distance, my diminutive presence mostly unnoticed. When my father is gone all day, and I'm home alone with my mom, I learn that men have jobs where they earn money, and this money makes it possible to have a house, a car, and food on the table. It seems this thing called money is a pretty good idea, especially as without it there might not be much to eat, and I really like to eat. I also like the time at home with my mom, who plays and snuggles with me, and talks to me just like I was a regular person, and not in that tone of voice some other people (like my grandmother) use to let me know that I am a person of low status--just a baby.

Like a sponge, I absorb everything I am exposed to, including the language of those I hear speaking. I don't know this then, but language is a major carrier of culture, and not just in its vocabulary, but in the way it is formed, and how that in turn shapes how we perceive and think about the world. In English, sentences (defined as complete thoughts) are formed in the pattern of subject-verb-object. And this reflects--and in many ways determines--how we see ourselves and the world around us. Subjects act upon objects, and it early-on becomes obvious that subjects are more important than objects. That is, the presumption of hierarchy is built into the very syntax and grammar of our language. When Dick gives his dog, Spot, a bone, the presumed superiority of the human over the dog is not only built into the human-centeredness of our culture, and into the power relationship of "master" to dog, but hierarchical power relationships inherent in the way our language is structured—subject-verb-object--which subliminally reinforces a worldview in which superior subjects (humans) act upon (dominate) inferior (sub-human) objects. We take this syntax for granted, but most non-Indo-European languages operate on quite different principles.

Certain rules of grammar in English serve to further

subordinate beings other than humans into the category of object, denying them any kind of personhood or subjectivity. For instance, my dog, Sheena, whom I know to be a unique individual possessed of intelligence, sentience, interiority, and volition, must, according to the rules of grammar, be referred to as a "that" (a thing) rather than a "who" or "whom" with a subjective identity. It is improper to say "the dog who rejected the offered bone." Instead, the "correct" construction is supposed to be, "the dog that...." And these are just two instances among thousands where our everyday language directs us in how to think about the world, and our place in it.

Okay, now I am a preschooler who has absorbed the general way in which our language works, along with a pretty fair vocabulary. I am still hanging out mostly with my mom, and I continually ask her questions about things I see around me and don't quite understand. Say she takes me to the zoo, and I ask why this tiger keeps pacing in his cage, or why that monkey looks so unhappy. I think my mother's answer would be one with several sides to it. First she would tell me that the tiger and monkey were far away from home. The tiger was used to hunting in a large territory where it was free to roam wherever it felt like. Same with monkeys, who like to spend most of their time hanging out in trees with other monkeys. Being caged like this was making these wild creatures a little bit crazy and very unhappy.

But, on the other hand, these zoos existed for a reason. For one thing, as an American I would likely never get a chance to see such magnificent creatures if it weren't for this zoo. And many wild creatures, including this tiger, were being pushed to extinction—due not only to habitat loss but also to over-hunting and poaching to sell parts of tigers on the black market. Having such animals in zoos like this was sort of a hedge against extinction, even if many wild creatures refused to breed in captivity. I think my mom would also mention how she felt about seeing these animals in this condition. While she hated to see them unhappy, she was still thrilled to see in the flesh creatures of such exotic beauty and presence, and, because we lived in a city, there were few opportunities to experience animals other than squirrels, rats, and mice, the occasional birds that flew through, and sidewalk pigeons. And this is probably where she would leave it, allowing me to sort through all these ambiguities for myself.

(That is one thing I have always appreciated about my mom: she would give me good information then let me do my own thinking, feeling, and deciding. In this way, she was more *matrist* than *patrist*: trusting my capacity to respond morally and thoughtfully to the world around me--out of my own best inborn instincts, honed by our kind over untold generations.)

This is literally taking in culture at mother's knee, and this has been the common experience of most humans throughout history. One may also take in culture at father's knee, and often this will have a particularly masculine edge to it. When people live together in extended families (a rarity now in America) grandparents, aunts, uncles, and others will also impart their own particular take on cultural expectations. When people lived in small bands, any group member might contribute to the cultural education of the young. Nowadays, in the age of universal mass education, the classroom teacher takes on the role of cultural mentor, or, in some cases, cultural drillmaster. Most schools also have sports programs, and these tend to greatly reinforce the regimentation and authoritarian structure of the classroom—imprinting on young people the importance of following rules, doing exactly as their coach or teacher instructs them, and accepting their place in the hierarchy—with the expectation of working their way toward the top.

THE CULTURE TRAP

Certain games, like basketball, teach lessons about the kind of fierce competition they will encounter in the world of market capitalism that awaits them. Grab the ball away from your opponent, run it down the court and put in the basket, or pass it to a team member to put it in. Get in your opponent's face, do all you can to physically intimidate them, maybe accidentally bumping or tripping them, to let them know that you are going to fight for the prize. If a foul is called on you, it's no big deal; your coach, your teammates, and your fans in the bleachers will cheer you on for your display of partisan aggression. And, ironically enough, the lessons learned in school sports will endure far longer than much of what is "taught" in the classroom.

Social mores, norms, and expectations are imbibed by the cultural animal from infancy to old age. This is cultural conditioning (or programming), and most of the acculturation process takes place subliminally, below the level of consciousness. This is why so many people don't know what culture is, or how it has had its way with them. The process remains subterranean and surreptitious: out of sight and out of mind. When most speak of culture, this is not what they are talking about. Mostly, they are talking about the artifacts of culture, not the process. Nor are they aware of the agenda behind the process—but I think it highly important that you understand what is happening here, and begin to "see through" culture and how it works.

CHAPTER 14

GLOBAL CLIMATE CRISIS

LET ME TELL you why I worry so about the world you will inherit, and how this damaged legacy will shrivel your prospects for a good life. As I write this it is 2016, the majority of the world finally seems to be waking up to climate change, even if most are still in the early stages of acceptance. An international Climate Summit was recently convened in Paris, where 196 countries made promises to each other about curtailing carbon emissions, with an agreement to meet again in five years to talk about more carbon reductions. The preceding four Climate Summits all failed to get meaningful commitments from the biggest polluters, including not only China but the world's very worst planetary citizen, my own country of America. Thanks in part to the extraction, processing, and burning of fossil fuels, combined with a rich endowment of natural resources and what some like to call the entrepreneurial spirit, America became a global economic power in the last half of the twentieth century. In the process, we created a class of people known variously as robber barons, the one-percent, or the power-elite, and these super-rich individuals are in fact this nation's plutocracy. Known to own politicians and buy whatever laws and policies they so desire--which, just by coincidence, happen to add value to their own vast holdings—these plutocrats effectively call the shots. Among these are not a few Oil Barons, who over the years have purchased a rather large chorus of climate change deniers in both houses of Congress, while also employing the corporate media to raise doubts about human-generated climate change. This is something that climate change activists have long suspected, but recent damning evidence shows that oil companies, led by Exxon-Mobile, knew more than thirty years ago that their products were causing climate disruption. Not only did they bury this information, produced by their own scientists, they colluded with other oil companies to run a campaign of climate denial and disinformation.

I am not offering this as an excuse for our climate paralysis, nor would I put all the blame on criminally irresponsible oil companies. Few of us ordinary citizens--even among those wise to the media-promoted smokescreen--have been eager to make the changes in our lives that halting or slowing climate chaos clearly requires. I just want you to recognize that in the three or so decades since global warming first appeared on our radar screen, actions were being taken to prevent the kind of scientific and societal consensus that would be necessary for concerted climate action. Now, with this delay, at least a degree and a half (Celsius) temperature rise is already baked in, and couldn't be stopped if all anthropogenic greenhouse gasses were to cease tomorrow. So you will doubtlessly be living in a much warmer world than any creature alive in my own time would find comfortably tolerable—and I cannot tell you how sorry I am for what we are putting you through, and for how much we have taken from you.

If the news has been slow to get out about dangerously high

carbon emissions, when it comes to the much more potent greenhouse gas, methane, there has been an information blackout. Anthropogenic methane has three main culprits: methane leaks from natural gas extraction, methane release from paddy-grown rice, and enormous amounts of methane escaping into the atmosphere from livestock, and most of all cattle. The beef industry is not only huge, but immensely powerful politically; and Big Beef, like Big Oil, have for years run disingenuous public relations campaigns to promote their product. And it gets worse, because as Big Beef expands to meet global market demand, they destroy intact rainforest and other ecologically vital ecosystems, reducing complex biodiversity to biologically simplified grazing land, or to vast swaths of genetically modified soybeans, all to feed more and more of these human-tended monsters of methane pollution. But here again, it is not just the evil corporations or their manipulative marketing campaigns that are to blame—though they are far from innocent. Western civilization has an extensive history as a beef eating people, and this longstanding cultural influence has been magnified many times over here in the Western Hemisphere, where a thinly peopled and lightly used continent has, over the last century or two, given graziers *carte blanche* to run cattle pretty much wherever they please. Under these windfall conditions, the cattle industry has exploded into a mega-industry. Demand has followed supply and North Americans now raise and eat massive quantities of beef—which we regard as perfectly normal, and a sacred human right.

Up until a short time ago I would have said this was a culturally ingrained habit, which, like other habits, was amenable to change. Recent conversations with a number of intelligent individuals who are also heavy beefeaters convince me that these otherwise reasonable people have fallen under the spell of an addiction. They are adamant: they are not giving up beef, nor do they find the methane pollution of cattle anything to worry about. Indeed, some of them believe that the answer to the climate crisis is more cattle, but with carefully monitored rotational grazing. From all I can tell, neither the cattle industry nor those who depend upon it for their daily fix of beef, are yet ready to consider changing their ways for a little thing like climate change.

The growing of rice for human consumption has long been a practice in Asia, and this staple crop has fueled a population explosion over several centuries. Now that these people are here and integrated into the global economy the prospect of cutting back on rice production seems highly unlikely. So, no help here.

As for methane release from natural gas extraction, Big Oil may eventually be required to take greater care at the wellhead, but methane escape is all but inescapable, and this source of anthropogenic methane pollution will cease only when the energy return on investment (EROI) makes further extraction uneconomical. The market will set the agenda, either by working well, by cheating (by 'externalizing' true costs), or by failing altogether.

But methane pollution directly attributable to humans is only part of the story that no one wants to talk about, or in any way confront. A relatively small amount of background methane escapes into the atmosphere from naturally occurring methane chimneys, where subterranean methane pockets are exposed by changes in the Earth's crust (as, for instance, by seismic activity) which effectively removes the 'lid' that held the gasses in place. Sub-surface methane deposits remain effectively contained so long as the uppermost layers of the crust remain intact. When that uppermost layer is ice, snow, and permafrost, and this 'lid' is melted away by rising global temperatures, large amounts of this climate-wrecking gas will be released. These releases will inevitably add to global warming, which will in turn speed up melting and more methane release, in a self-reinforcing positive feedback loop of ever-worsening climate chaos. Certain independent scientists believe that somewhere in this scenario of runaway climate forcing a tipping-point will have been reached, and beyond that point there will be no going back to the old regime that was the interglacial norm for more than twelve thousand years. The Earth will be in a new phase, and it will be distinctly unfriendly to Life--and that will be that for who-knows-how-many thousands or millions of years until the Earth reaches some new (totally unpredictable) tipping point, and ushers in a fresh phase in its evolutionary history.

Even though many reputable climate scientists agree that this is a scenario that is likely to occur in the lifetimes of many alive in the world today, the International Panel on Climate Change (convened by the United Nations and considered the global arbiter of climate science) has chosen to focus on carbon dioxide pollution and to more or less ignore methane. There are several billion of social, political, and economic reasons why almost no one is willing to confront the full seriousness of what our way of life is doing the climate of this once-thriving planet. The changes required of us, and the urgency with which they are demanded, is far more than anyone wants to contemplate. If only we had begun an orderly transition some thirty years ago...but forget that: we didn't. Even now as we seem about to shift into crisis management mode, it is obvious to the well-informed that whatever we do is going to be too little too late.

I want for you to know that there were a few of us who thought beyond our own present comforts, and would have happily made some sacrifices to insure that you and other of our descendants had a shot at a good life--if only these were shared sacrifices that we all participated in as a collective. This is how humans have operated for as long as we have been cultural animals: as a group that shares equitably, in good times and in bad. But we seem to have lost that ability in modern times, and at some point I want to explore with you the reasons why. But for now I have what I'm afraid is going to be some more bad news for you, and for this ruined world we have bequeathed you.

CHAPTER 15

FAILING ECOSYSTEMS

AS IF A hellishly hot Earth were not enough to endure, I am afraid that global warming is going to unleash a cascade of ecological failures that devastate the living world. The first rule of ecology is that you can never do just one thing, and the reason for this is that everything is connected to everything else.

Within just the last few years a number of environmental anomalies have occurred in various parts of the world, and I believe these hint at much worse to come. Just this month (January) it rained at the North Pole at the same time it was snowing in Atlanta, Georgia. Meteorologists point to a 'lazy' jet stream for this and other such anomalies. The jet stream is a high-altitude current that pushes weather fronts in an easterly direction; its course is generally sinuous, but going steeply south, and pulling the polar vortex down with it, is not its typical behavior. Why this is happening now is not fully understood, but is believed to be associated with the melting of Arctic sea ice in a warming world.

In recent years the phrase, 'the new normal' has gained a

worrisome currency among those who follow environmental trends--and the trends, they just keep a'trending.

Brazil, with its rainforests and many rivers, is known as the water capital of the world, and yet Sao Paulo, the economic center of the nation and home to 20 million is suffering its deepest drought in eighty years. Although a simple cause and effect relationship cannot be established here, because complex natural systems involve multiple interacting factors, where cause and effect intermingle—yet there remains one drought-causing suspect that stands out from all others, and that is the ongoing deforestation of the Amazonian Rainforest.

It is pretty well understood that large expanses of forest make their own weather. In addition to this, forested land also attracts marine weather from out at sea and pulls it in over the land by process known as the biotic pump. This is how the hydrological cycle works: rain falls upon the forest, and what is not absorbed by the trees and a very thin layer of soil flows through a network of rivers, back out to the ocean, where it evaporates and forms rain-bearing clouds, which are pulled back over the land, where they repeat the cycle all over again. Remove enough trees, and this life-nurturing cycle falters or fails.

Off the coast of my home state of Oregon, the Pacific Ocean is exhibiting at least two environmental anomalies. One is a dead zone that has appeared each summer and fall since 2002, and, oddly enough, its source seems to be quite different from more typical oceanic dead zones, such as the one off the coast of Louisiana. That immense region of low-oxygen (hypoxic) waters is known to be caused by agricultural runoff, consisting of nitrogen-rich chemical fertilizers and domestic animal wastes which drain into the Mississippi River and are deposited into the waters of the Gulf Coast, where they feed massive algal blooms. After the algae dies, it falls to the ocean floor, where it is fed upon by cyanobacteria, which proliferate and deplete the dissolved oxygen required by fish and other marine life. The Dead Zone off the coast of Oregon is not caused by agricultural runoff but by too much wind. Upwelling of nutrient-rich water, brought up from the ocean's depths, is driven by wind, making these nutrients available to marine life all up and down the food chain. So wind is a good thing for marine life, but so too are lulls in the wind, because these allow demand to catch up with supply. With an oversupply of phytoplankton brought up by ceaseless upwelling, along with an undersupply of (overfished) fish to feed on them, massive quantities of dead phytoplankton fall to the ocean floor, where they are consumed by cyanobacteria, which in turn deplete these waters of their life-giving dissolved oxygen. Hard-driven ceaseless winds appear to be behind the Dead Zone(s) off the coast of Oregon and Washington--but why the near-constant winds that drive this dynamic? So far, the best scientific guess is that rising temperatures on the land are attracting stronger and more constant winds from out at sea, making marine upwelling too much of a good thing.

Since the fall of 2013, another sort of Dead Zone has taken over the North Pacific Ocean, extending from the Gulf of Alaska to the waters off Baja California; it is called 'the blob,' and it has expanded from 300 miles wide by 300 long, to 500 miles wide by 2000 miles long, running to depths of 200 feet. Likened to a smaller and more northerly El Nino, the blob--which can be as much as 7 degrees Fahrenheit warmer than normal--is thought to be responsible for anomalous West Coast weather, as well as for the sudden die-off of sea birds, sardines, and seal pups. This warmer water of the blob is too warm for the native nutrient-rich phytoplankton of the North Pacific, but amenable to a poorer quality tropical variety--and this (starvation) may be the leading reason behind the mass die-off of tens of thousands of Cassin's auklets in recent months. In the last year and a half sea stars have died by the tens of millions, and though the proximate cause has been identified as a particular known virus, it is still unknown exactly what change in ocean conditions favored this epidemic spread of the virus. The blob is on the list of suspects, but with so many different factors affecting ocean health, or ill-health, isolating single-factor causes is seldom possible.

Science has known for nearly a century that the Pacific Ocean has alternating warm and cold spells, spanning several years or even decades at a time--a maritime cycle that goes by the name: Pacific Decadal Oscillation (PDO). Operating on shorter turnaround times than PDO, and originating further to the south, El Nino (the warm phase) and La Nina (the cool), also follow an alternating pattern of warm and cool spells, which tend to have dramatic effects on continental and even global weather, as trade winds push warm water westward toward Asia, then reverse and push cooler water eastward toward South America in the equatorial Pacific. Neither of these cyclical drivers of oceanic and atmospheric conditions seems to be linked with the blob. The worry is that the blob, far from cyclical in nature, is instead a harbinger of an ever-warming ocean: an ocean where population collapses like the ones we are seeing today will seem as nothing, but will be magnified many times over as pollution, acidification, and warming combine to produce cascades of ecosystem failure, throughout the food chain, and likely starting at its base--with phytoplankton, zooplankton, krill, and the like--which could go into steep decline, or be wiped out entirely, by a compounding of insults to this oceanic system which is vital to all life on Earth, not least of all because these tiny marine creatures provide half of the oxygen we breathe.

The terrestrial half of the oxygen we breathe comes mostly

from trees, and trees are not doing very well right now. Deforestation at the hands of humans and their chainsaws is a huge problem globally. An observant Frenchman from a previous century once quipped: 'Forests precede civilization; deserts follow.' This pattern continues, but now at an ever-accelerating pace. Globally, forests continue to fall to make way for short-term mining, grazing, or agricultural operations--until the former forest has been exhausted and is left as useless wasteland. This form of forest destruction is direct, predictable, and theoretically reversible. If humans are directly responsible for laying waste to vast swaths of forest, presumably we could slow this process down, halt it completely, or even reverse the process by planting trees instead of cutting them down. Theoretically, humans could take this situation in hand and make Earth a more Life-friendly planet. But even if we could somehow muster the collective will to reverse this form of deforestation, such (theoretical) control is not even remotely available to us in the face of what is happening to forests in a warming world.

Every forest biome on Earth is suffering the effects of climate stress. The boreal forests to the north, the tropical forests to the south, and the temperate forests of the mid-latitudes are all in trouble. In the Pacific Northwest, where I live, pine forests are dying from several different pests and diseases. In the high country of the Washington and Oregon Cascades, white bark pines are being taken out by white pine blister rust. This is also happening in places like Glacier and Yellowstone National Parks, in the Rockies, where Grizzly bears depend on the nutrient-dense nuts of this pine to fatten them up for a long winter of hibernation. The Pinon Pine of the American southwest is being reduced to a remnant of its historical range, affecting wildlife all up and down the food chain-- in this case by the ips beetle. Ponderosa and lodgepole pines are under attack all over the Northwest, with the worst of the damage occurring in British Columbia, where thousands of square miles of green pine forest have been turned first red (with dead needles) then gray (when the needles finally fall). All of the western states have been affected by the mountain pine beetle, perhaps none more severely than the pine forests of the Colorado Rockies.

These rusts and beetles are not new to the forests of the West. They have always played a part in naturally culling older or weaker trees, making way for fresh growth. What is new is the scale at which these invasions occur, and what has made them possible: namely, climate change. Drought—either as a reflection of natural weather cycles or of a one-way warming trend—puts a burden of stress on trees, and the longer drought continues the weaker and more susceptible the trees become. That is one factor. Longer summers (adding to the duration of stress) and shorter winters, (in which to begin a recovery) further weaken the trees. Pollution from an industrial society only adds insult to a forest (or, in most cases, a remnant of forest) already under siege. But what makes pests like the mountain pine beetle the epidemic threat that they have now become is the warming of winters in their range. To kill the pupae and larvae deposited under the bark of living trees, a temperature of minus forty degrees is required to persist for at least two days and nights. Even at those temperatures some will survive if they find themselves below the snow line and the thermal protection it provides. In recent years, temperatures this cold have been rare. In the last hundred years of record keeping the average low temperature in the American West has risen by 1.8 degrees Fahrenheit, and that warming trend is on course to continue—which means the death of a lot more trees.

If a Less than two-degree temperature rise over the course of a century can cause this much ecological damage, it pains me to think what is in store for the bake-oven biosphere you will inherit.

A warming planet with longer, hotter summers also means a lot more trees are going to die by wildfire. As Ecosystem Earth loses more and more of this keystone species, we may learn—after it is too late—just how vital forests actually are to all Life on Earth.

Indeed, we don't know very much at all about how Ecosystem Earth actually works, including its dynamic macro-systems, like the marine and atmospheric currents that drive exchanges of heat, energy and nutrients around the globe: macro-currents like the Jet Stream, the Gulf Stream, the trade winds, oceanic gyres, and similar phenomena that serve as our planet's circulatory system. The thermohaline circulation, (sometimes known as the Great Ocean Conveyor Belt) delivers warm tropical water northward and cold Arctic water southward, creating conditions friendly to life along the way. The warm surface current known as the Gulf Stream heads north from the Straits of Florida, moving immense amounts of water in a single oceanic river until it reaches the fortieth parallel, where it splits into two separate currents, only for those two to split again, distributing warm water to the North American and European Arctic as well as to the west coasts of Africa and Europe. As the warm water loses heat through evaporative cooling in northern waters it also becomes more saline. Both the warmth and extra salt increase this water's density, causing it to sink—or rather to plunge at speed—to the ocean's floor, where it forms a powerful bottom current which speeds back south toward the tropics. The 'chimney' where this biggest of all waterfalls plunges some four thousand feet from surface to ocean floor is a powerful driver of this thermohaline circulation. But all is not well with this system. It has slowed by as much as thirty percent in the last fifty years, and the reason—again—seems to be climate change. The melting of Arctic sea ice dilutes salinity, which in turn slows down the 'pump' that drives this part of Earth's circulatory system. The worry is that should this trend continue or accelerate, Europe could be plunged into an Ice Age. Under those conditions, growing food could become problematical, as could a lot of other things we now take for granted.

My point in all this is: that we humans are surrounded--and supported-- by systems that we do not fully understand; that these systems are connected to other systems that are likewise poorly understood; and that the non-linear interactions of these systems are beyond our comprehension or our control. As we watch systems begin to fail, it finally dawns on us that they are finely-tuned and operate within close tolerances. Over nearly four billion years of evolutionary history, these systems have acquired an impressive robustness and resilience in the face of sudden change and stochastic event. Resilience accrues slowly over time, a combination of biological diversity, ecological complexity, and functional redundancy. Our way of life has been built upon reversing this process, mining and exploiting unto near-exhaustion more than three billion years of accrued resilience, and we have done it in less than three thousand. All of which goes to show the fatal mismatch between an ecological planet and our own anti-ecological worldview.

CHAPTER 16

LOSS OF THE WEB OF LIFE

BECAUSE EVERYTHING IS interconnected, all the way up and all the way down-- from the tiniest quark to the most sprawling of galaxies--nothing really ever happens in isolation or without some effect on the Whole. Here on Earth we live in the in-between zone, where the tiniest of beings are invisible to us and the vastness of the Universe is beyond our ken. For the longest time, even Mother Earth herself was far too vast to explore in any depth, and all our knowledge of her was local, particular, highly individuated; and whatever knowledge we had of the Whole came to us not empirically but through some inner sense or intuition. Only in recent years has science begun to understand that the world is organized as systems within systems within larger systems still, as if nesting one within another within another, somewhat like Russian dolls. Of particular relevance to humans, and to all the other creatures who call Earth home, is our large self-organizing planetary system, often referred to as Gaia. The key thing to understand about Gaia is that while there are mechanical, geological, and chemical elements to the Gaian system, it is essentially run **by**

living organisms **for** living organisms. That is, the Earth is a self-regulating homeostatic system that is finely tuned to optimize conditions favorable to life, and each of the Earth's various life-forms makes its own contributions to these life-nurturing conditions. As life-forms ourselves, we humans have a vested interest in the optimum functioning of this life-promoting Gaian system. And yet we (who believe ourselves to be the smartest creature of them all) often prioritize myopically self-centered interests which run counter to the welfare of the Whole--oblivious to our stake in a fully functional Gaia.

Now numbering more than seven billion, we humans have set in motion what has come to be recognized as the sixth great extinction of Life on Earth. This is the only mass extinction caused by a single Earthly species, and we are extirpating these creatures at the rate of about 140,000 species a year. This process appears to have begun at the end of the last Ice Age, when some of Earth's largest mammals were wiped out by overhunting (with maybe a nudge from abrupt climate change), in what has been called the great megafauna overkill. Today, we are continuing in this same tradition—wiping out the last remnants of Earth's more charismatic megafauna—largely through habitat destruction, but also due to a particular kind of illegal hunting we call poaching: not primarily for the meat of these creatures but for certain coveted body parts: the tusks of elephants for the carving of trinkets; the tusks of rhinos and the bladders of tigers for their supposed aphrodisiac qualities; endangered sea turtles hunted for the decorative quality of their shells; gorillas gunned down for body-part souvenirs, while snow leopards and most of the big cats are valued not only for their gorgeous pelts but for their internal organs, used in Chinese medicine. As it happens, these and many of the other large endangered mammals are keystone species, which means they serve vital functions within their ecosystems.

LOSS OF THE WEB OF LIFE

With one or more of these keystone species absent from their natural habitat, and no longer filling their special niche, the ecosystem is thrown out of balance, and other species suffer because of it—as does the Whole.

We humans tend to admire and identify with large apex predators like ourselves--the lions, tigers, and wolves, say--though our admiration may be tempered by certain other feelings. We sense in these creatures qualities of character and spirit that we value, and perhaps covet for ourselves: the raw power emanating from big cats on the hunt; the affection and cooperation displayed among pack and herd animals like wolves and elephants; the joy-of-life on view among cavorting dolphins, or the exuberant play of otters; the cosmic connection to Mystery we suspect beneath the panther's dark visage. These inspire in us a whole range of creaturely fellow-feelings, from envy and fear to affection and respect. All the primates, from monkeys to apes to chimpanzees, impress us with a sense of family resemblance. All the mammals, in fact, seem less foreign to us than, say, the reptiles, amphibians, and fish. We are warm-blooded and they are not. Even gophers, squirrels, and mice are more like us than those things which have feathers, fins, or scales. Yet, no matter how much we may identify with particular species, most of us remain reluctant to acknowledge our deep kinship with these other living creatures of the Earth, even though we all share the same evolutionary history and much of the same DNA. As a culture, we have tended to see ourselves as not only at the very top of the pyramid of Life but as qualitatively different from the rest. We may be able to grant to those creatures directly below us in the hierarchy a certain stature, and may be troubled at the prospect of their loss. At the same time, we are likely to see the plants and the 'lower' animals as unimportant, and discount their erasure from the

Earth Community as insignificant. But such a view is more than mistaken; it is dead wrong.

The web of life is vast (as well as vastly complex), yet no part of this web is insignificant to the Whole. For instance, at the base of both terrestrial and aquatic foods chains are plants; these are the primary producers that convert the energy of sunlight into biomass by means of photosynthesis, and without them there can be no food chain--and no us. Phytoplankton consists of a group of tiny uncharismatic aquatic plants and algae, which are the primary producers of the marine food chain, and the key nutrient source for many a secondary consumer, including zooplankton. Also quite small and unimportant-looking, zooplankton is the food of choice for many of the ocean's fishes, so if something were to threaten either the plant or animal form of plankton—say a warming acidifying ocean-- the entire marine food chain would be under threat. When the base of the food chain is decimated or compromised, that loss ripples through the entire food web in a series of chain-reactions called trophic cascades—something like a line of dominoes falling, but less linear. And, because the oceanic ecosystem does not exist in a self-contained vacuum, many terrestrial species would also suffer, including those humans whose diet depends upon seafood. Also, since phytoplankton produce half the world's oxygen, their loss would be felt by every living, breathing being on Earth.

Being small and unglamorous does not translate as insignificant within the Gaian System of Life. Indeed, a vital part of this System is so tiny as to be invisible; I'm thinking especially of the microorganisms that give life to the soil, and also those that inhabit the skin and innards of humans.

All Life on Earth is built upon a foundation of single-celled prokaryotes. For the first three billion years of Life's 3.8-billion-year evolutionary history, bacteria (prokaryotes) is all there was. Even now these single celled organisms, invisible to the naked eye, constitute half of Earth's living biomass—and they are everywhere. Bacteria live in the air, the water, the soil, as well as inside and on the surface of every living being, including us. Indeed, the human body is so 'colonized' by bacteria that we are far more 'them' than 'us'—in terms of cells, ten times more bacterial than human. This raises some interesting metaphysical questions about our human identities, but of more immediate relevance is the fact that we cannot live without them. And this dependence upon microbes is true not only of us, but of most living beings on the planet.

Because we cannot see them, these miniscule creatures of the world have, until quite recently, been ignored by science. Now that microbiologists have begun looking into the larger functions of bacteria, including those in our own gut, there is cause for concern about extinctions even at this level of Life on Earth.

Among the one hundred trillion bacteria typically found on and within the human being, the overwhelming majority are either harmless or beneficial. Science has only begun to explore the various ways in which these communities of organisms (our microbiome) serve to keep us alive and healthy. What has been learned so far is that a healthy microbiome helps regulate many of our bodily functions, bolsters our immune system, and aids us in getting full nutritional value from our foods. Soluble fiber is essential to human health, but we are unable to digest fiber on our own. Fortunately, the 'good' (probiotic) bacteria in our guts perform this function for us. Fiber is broken down by fermentation, producing short-chain fatty-acids like butyrate and acetate in the process, and these in turn stimulate the anti-inflammatory arm of the immune system. This is one of the reasons why consuming enough fiber in our everyday diet is so important to our health. But there is a problem here, because the typical modern diet is long on fats, sugars, and protein, but short on dietary fiber. When the microbiome of young villagers in Burkina Faso, Africa (whose diet consists mostly of millet and sorghum) was compared to that of children from Florence, Italy (who ate a lot of the refined and processed foods typical of the Western diet), the gut bacteria of the villagers proved to be much more diverse, indicating a healthier microbiome.

Just as biodiversity in marine and terrestrial ecosystems is an indicator of ecosystem health, so it is with the ecosystem of our own bodies. When particular strains or types of microbiota go missing within the microgenome of the gut, more is lost than simple variety. The cooperative and reciprocal relationships that function synergistically when biotic communities are intact lose many of the bonds that knit them together when community members disappear. The depletion of the microbiome is furthered by a number of behavioral factors, including the use of antibiotics or anti-bacterial hand wipes and soaps, but the number-one culprit is the Western diet—burgers and fries, soda and chips, and all the other highly processed foods that have been stripped of their fiber as well as their wholesome nutrition.

The by-products of fermentation in the colon--the short-chain fatty-acids, which are so vital to the human immune system—are produced by microbes that specialize in breaking down fiber. Deprived of a sufficiency of fiber to keep them going, these beneficial microbes either die out entirely or are reduced to remnant populations. In the latter case, a change in diet to fiber-rich 'microbiota-accessible carbohydrates' may restore healthy populations of probiotic microorganisms. But once these beneficial beings have been wiped out entirely, they are gone for good—along with their benefits to human health.

Just as the ecosystem of the human body can be depleted

of essential constituents within its microbiome, so, too, can the microbiome of the soil. Good, rich, friable soil is the ideal growing medium for most species of plants, including natural ecosystems like forests and grasslands, and unnatural ones like my own kitchen garden. The number of microorganisms within a single gram of healthy soil ranges into the billions, and the number to be found in my fairly extensive garden beds is beyond reckoning or imagining. When it comes to soil health, quantity of organisms is not necessarily the key issue. Rather—and this is true of all ecosystems—it is the relationships among organisms, and their proportionality, that determines optimum ecosystem health, with symbiosis and synergy working their magic within a community of cooperation. Over millions of years of evolutionary history, the living soils of a living Earth have developed into resilient systems that nurture the green growing things of the world: the primary producers that transform sunlight into food for the rest of us. Unfortunately, most of Earth's soil-based ecosystems have been transformed by humans into degraded and diminished versions of Nature's own evolved creations, having extremely deleterious effects on the soil's microbiome.

While there are a number of human innovations responsible for this ecosystem loss--including the poisoning of soil with industrial and mining wastes, and paving over it to build highways, cities, and shopping malls--the human activity most destructive of the soil's microbiotic integrity is agriculture. This was true even in the earliest days of domestication, because, when natural ecosystems were usurped for agricultural use, biodiversity was sacrificed to an oversimplified monoculture, extirpating species large and small. Natural ecosystems tend to be mostly-closed systems that recycle nutrients, energy, and water, building new life on what has gone before, to the point of being more or less self-sustaining. When such bio-diverse systems are commandeered for agricultural use they become mostly-open systems requiring high inputs of outside fertility, energy, and water. Grasslands, forests, and other natural biomes develop ecosystem health through the complex interactions of a biodiverse community of organisms. As ecosystems become more complex over time, a redundancy of organisms performing similar systemic functions builds resilience into the whole, which serves as a hedge against sudden, violent, stochastic events like wildfire, tornado, or flood. In the absence of such events, these mostly closed natural ecosystems maintain their integrity by avoiding loss to the system—and most especially the loss of soil to the processes of erosion. Precious, slow-building topsoil in such systems tends to be held in place by the Earth's own 'skin'—including the small shallow-rooted earth hugging plants, in combination with deep-rooted larger ones, overlain by an organic layer of litter and plant residue--all helping to hold topsoil in place.

And of course it is precisely on this score that agriculture fails so miserably. The unnatural system that is agriculture requires 'breaking' the ground and turning the soil, thereby exposing it to erosion. What the sodbusters did in the American Midwest was transform a rich, self-perpetuating natural ecosystem of tall-grass or short grass prairie into naked topsoil vulnerable to being blown away by wind and washed away by rain—which they accomplished by ripping off the Earth's protective skin. Whatever natural fertility remained in these native soils was soon used up by the crops these pioneer sodbusters planted, necessitating that additional fertilizer be brought in from outside the system. The twin Achilles Heels of inevitable erosion and ever-diminishing soil fertility tell part of the story of why agriculture has always been inherently unsustainable, even at its most benign subsistence stage. Horticulture at any scale, including kitchen gardens like my own, constitutes mining:

mining topsoil unto depletion while also mining soil fertility unto exhaustion. When you add oil to agriculture its inherent unsustainability goes into exponential overdrive.

When agriculture became agribusiness, as it did in America following World War Two, mass extinctions of creatures large and small was all but guaranteed. When farms were modest in size—say, 160 acres or less—they tended to be diversified: in terms of crops, but also in terms physical structure. The riparian areas around creeks, fence rows, and wind breaks, as well as woodpiles, ponds, kitchen gardens, and ground left fallow, provided habitat for all kinds of critters, like song birds, foxes, rabbits, snakes, hawks, and deer. These fragments of ecosystems were not what they had been before sod-busting transformed this prairie landscape, but they were something, and they helped sustain a remnant community of interdependent life forms.

When farming became mechanized on an industrial scale and transformed into agribusiness, what little remained of fragmentary ecosystem health got plowed under. The words of one Secretary of Agriculture tell the first part of the story: 'Get big or get out' was the word from above, and that became the name of the game. Many small- to moderate-sized farms were bought out by the Big Boys, concentrating large acreages in the hands of a few. A subsequent Secretary of Agriculture offered this further counsel to farmers: 'Plant fencerow to fencerow.' Invoking economies of scale and machine logic, this bit of advice makes perfect business sense. The big new machines of agriculture like long straight lines and acreages measured in the thousands, and of course working land at this scale fairly sings the word 'efficiency'—which was then, and still is, a concept highly revered in business circles. So, in line with this logic, windrows and fencerows were bulldozed, along with many a kitchen garden, pond, and farmhouse—and now, for miles on end, the naked earth was opened to the tender ministrations of the machine, as well as to the wind and the rain.

That is the machine side of modern agribusiness; there is also a chemical side, where synthetic fertilizers and a dizzying array of poisons are meant to substitute for a functional ecosystem. In an interesting irony, manufacturing plants that made bombs during wartime were now turning a tidy profit using these same industrial techniques to make chemical fertilizer. Other corporate giants, who had also done well in wartime, were now turning out a variety of pesticides, herbicides, and fungicides, meant to erase any- and every-thing living that was not the desired crop itself--which brings us back to the microbiome of the soil.

'As above, so below,' goes the old saw, and it is certainly true that what happens aboveground is mirrored in what happens below. Remove all biodiversity for miles on end, turn the soil over with giant machines, douse it with chemical fertilizers and poisons meant to kill an array of plants, animals, and fungi, and what do you get? You get soil that is mostly no longer alive in an ecosystem that is mostly dysfunctional. As the dysfunction deepens, more chemicals—and now genetic engineering--are required to keep the land limping along. With each dousing of chemicals the microbiome of the soil becomes more impoverished, while the excess of such applications drain into creeks and tributaries, a chemical stew especially rich in nitrogen making its toxic way into the Mississippi River and out into the Gulf of Mexico, where it creates an immense hypoxic dead zone.

Why so much death? What is going on here?

If extinction is forever and creatures of all sizes are being put out of business by humans at an ever more alarming rate, what are the causes behind this ecological catastrophe? Setting aside

LOSS OF THE WEB OF LIFE

the Upper Paleolithic megafauna overkill (which likely implicates both technology and something in the human character and/or culture) one common denominator in all subsequent extinctions is agriculture. Overhunting can throw an ecosystem, and ecosystem relationships, severely out of balance. But if a species is not wiped out entirely within its range, it at least has a chance to recover in a case where hunting is deliberately curtailed for purposes of species conservation. But when a species has lost its habitat, and all the inter-species relationships that went with the territory it once called home, there is nowhere to go and no way to make a living. And this exactly what happens when a natural ecosystem is transformed by humans into agricultural land. The killing is not as direct as it is in hunting, but it just as final. More land converted to agriculture means that more food can be grown, and more food inevitably leads to more people. More people creates demand for more food (and lots of other stuff), which leads to more habitat loss, which leads to more extinctions. Agriculture and the overpopulation of humans create a self-reinforcing positive feedback loop, and this is an extremely negative dynamic for most of the other living creatures on Earth.

This dynamic between people and agriculture went ballistic once oil entered the equation. If not for oil, a quadrupling of our population in the last hundred years would not have been possible, though oil didn't accomplish this all by itself. Just about a hundred years ago two scientists developed what became known as the Haber-Bosch Process, which transformed atmospheric nitrogen into liquid ammonia, which could in turn be made into explosives (with the addition of nitric acid), or into synthetic fertilizer in the form of anhydrous ammonia, ammonium nitrate, and urea—contributing to a seven-fold increase in the world's food supply and a four-fold increase in the human population. This process is ongoing, with one hundred million tons of nitrogen annually removed from the atmosphere and turned into synthetic fertilizer. The founders of the so-called Green Revolution developed hybrid strains of rice, soybeans, and maize which were more productive than traditional varieties, but worked their 'magic' only with heavy inputs of this same synthetic fertilizer, along with the importation of water via irrigation canals. Soon, these capital-intensive inputs would be joined by another expensive dependence: the array of poisons now evidently required for this system to work.

And it did work, in the same way that a square peg can be made, by force, to fit into a round hole; or, more literally, in the same way that biology and ecology can be reduced to mathematics, physics, and chemistry, and forced upon the land. This sort of works, insofar as crops are planted, grown and harvested using these methods--but it works only with much violence to living beings. For instance, synthetic fertilizers deplete soil of organic matter and trace elements, cause salinization and suppress micorrhizae, while frequently turning symbiotic bacteria into competitors. Micorrhizal fungi act as a far-reaching extension of a plant's own root system, contributing to its overall health and viability. Micorrhizae form this symbiotic relationship with most terrestrial plants in an underground hyphal network connecting individual plants together and distributing water, carbon, and nutrients among them in a communal sharing process. But tilling the soil physically breaks up these sharing networks, while a heavy use of fertilizers and fungicides chemically inhibits these mutually beneficial interactions between fungal networks and plants. The fatal error of this particular reductionism is its failure to acknowledge soil's fundamentally organic nature and to respect its upper layers as a valid and complex ecosystem unto itself, with its own evolved synergies of cooperation. It appears that the violence toward Life inherent in the war-making technology behind industrial agriculture has found a new 'theatre of war' in which to operate, imposing a corrosive machine mentality upon humans while poisoning the living Earth and taking profit from the land by force.

Violence by its very nature invites trouble, and the mass extinction of Earthly species is more than trouble enough. Amid all the extinctions now going down—whether in the soil, among creatures on land and sea, or in our own guts—are certain shared commonalities, including what I would describe as institutional violence. Violence born of passion at the level of the individual is something that can be stirred up in most any of us. If we are human and animated with life we have experienced this within ourselves, and we understand it in others. Structural violence may well excite and direct an individual's passions, but it originates in culture, where it tends to be carried (surreptitiously) beneath the surface. The structural violence I have in mind has more than one cause, but its historical roots go back at least as far as the early days of agriculture, when humans began crossing a moral line by claiming land common to all living beings as uniquely their own, thereby breaking a longstanding sacred bond with Mother Earth. Once committed to living in loyalty to the Whole, agricultural humans were opting to live only for themselves.

This supremely anti-ecological move, emulated and elaborated over time, was a turning point in the history of the Earth. The human-driven extinctions we see today--even down to our own gut bacteria--is the inevitable consequence of this radical change in land use and lifeway. On the heels of this changed relationship to the Earth came radical swerves in belief, value, and ideology, putting humans ahead of all else. Without the culturally sanctioned structural violence initiated in that first theft of someone else's ecosystem (or rather, many someone else's), with that initial act of theft magnified exponentially over time, we humans would never have found ourselves crowding out our fellow Earthlings—many to the point of no return. Of course, the Industrial Revolution intensified this push toward ecological imbalance; then the cheap, portable, energy contained in oil came along and supercharged the process, followed by the Green Revolution, which propelled the process right off the rails.

This same structural violence has carried over into the Western industrialized food system, whereby Big Food supplies us with Fast Food, Junk Food, and Faux Food, while starving us of the Real Food we and our microbiomes require for optimum health.

Losing species to extinction represents a loss of complexity, biodiversity, and ecosystem function within the biotic community—and this loss is, on any humanly relevant time scale, permanent. What we don't know now is how much can be lost before all is lost. I have seen the loss of species on Spaceship Earth likened to the loss of rivets on an aircraft in flight. Rivets keep popping off, and at some point a sufficient number will have been lost that a wing or some other vital part will tear off and the craft go spiraling into freefall. The Earth and its creatures are not machines, nor are their relationships to one another machine-like. They are organic and their relationships are complex, mostly non-linear, and wholly interdependent. Nevertheless, this metaphor offers a graphic illustration of what a continued loss of constituent parts must inevitably mean to the Whole: system failure.

At the outset of this dismal recital of what we humans have inflicted upon the Gaian System of Life I mentioned that I was worried about your prospects in the world we leave behind. Of course you will be feeling firsthand the full brunt of this legacy, but I thought you might be interested in how things got to be

LOSS OF THE WEB OF LIFE

this way, as well as what we knew, and didn't know, in the second decade of the twenty first century. But enough of gloom and doom: Let's look in a different direction.

CHAPTER 17

THE INDIGENOUS WORLDVIEW

IF THE COSMOS is intelligent and evolutionary in nature, as I believe it is, then learning is central to its ever-expansive being. Learning from experience requires memory and a way to evaluate successes and mistakes, then make improvements. So I am thinking there is something like memory fields to keep track of things. My assumption is that it is more about the Whole than about any particular part of the Whole (including us wondrous humans). The big question for me is: how are we valued by Central Intelligence (or perhaps Dispersed Intelligence). Are we mere expendable instruments to be used for the purposes of the Whole, then tossed aside? Or are we highly valued beings who will always have a place at the table of intelligence, with perhaps other missions to perform as we ourselves evolve? In either case, I think we should consider ourselves damn fortunate just to be alive and to participate in an evolutionary experiment as interesting as this one. In other words, I think we should get over the infantile belief that everything is all about us, and desist from trying to cheat our presumed (but unknowable) fate.

THE INDIGENOUS WORLDVIEW

The word "culture" gets thrown around as if there were common agreement about what culture actually is, as if the term needs no further definition or qualification. This is very far from the actual case, because culture is a creature with many facets and faces, and it works its way with us on many different fronts. Culture is most commonly thought of as involving the arts and humanities, including the artifacts of "high culture," such as novels, symphonies, paintings, philosophy, and the like. This is the aspect of culture recognized and approved by most everyone as their cultural inheritance, representing the glory of our civilization. People display enormous pride in this form of our cultural legacy, not uncommonly with a certain amount of pretention.

Our material culture, though highly visible and everywhere we look, is often so taken-for-granted that its influence is spectacularly underrated and misunderstood. The natural tendency is to assume that our material culture—from chainsaws to smart phones to all the infrastructure of industry and commerce—is a material manifestation of our beliefs and values, our worldview and ideology. But in fact the reverse is closer to the truth. That is, our ideology is shaped by our infrastructure to a much greater extent than our infrastructure is shaped by our ideology. This is a point made by the anthropologist, Marvin Harris, in his book *Material Culture*, and certainly it seems counter-intuitive at first glance. But it is an important distinction to understand if you want to know where the locus of power actually is within a culture. When it comes to material culture, are humans the leaders or the led? When considering culture, it is always good to inquire into who, or what, is in charge—even if answers to these questions are often not the ones we would prefer.

To truly understand your own situation, within the context of the history of your own people, you must also understand your own culture. But, as it turns out, culture is something almost no one understands. And of course this means that very few people have much of a clue about who they are (in socio-historical context), or any sense of historical cause and effect, and how one thing leads to another leads to another. The first thing to understand about culture is that it's most vital functions are invisible, and, being invisible, must be inferred by their effects. But it is more complicated even than this, because culture is not just one thing (having at least three distinct faces) and cannot be understood apart from the human psychology it interacts with. Many people are not even aware that they are cultural animals, and have no idea that much of the identity that they claim as their own has been imparted to them by culture. This is not ordinarily a problem among peoples with a wholesome culture: they imbibe the directives of their culture, behave as they are expected to, and perhaps live full and interesting lives, never realizing the centrality of culture in everything they have done. For people such as these—and by now there are vanishingly few left in the world—ignorance of culture is no particular deficit. But our situation is different, and ignorance of what culture is and how it works shows every prospect of being fatal, because culture is central to everything we do.

When looked at in terms of the evolutionary history of life on Earth, culture appears as a recent evolutionary innovation that largely supplants instinct as the guidance system of the species. Because instinct is genetically hardwired into the genome of each species, and genetic coding is slow to change, instinctual behaviors may not be readily adaptive to sudden changes in environmental conditions. This, in any case, would seem to be an explaining rationale for why Mother Nature saw fit to make changes in a system that had worked well for several billion years: bestowing this (putative) adaptive edge upon one particular species with a big brain and opposable thumb as their primary guidance system. It is true that a few other species have the capacity to pass on learned behavior to their offspring, but in no instance that I know of does culture take precedence over instinct, as is the case with *Homo sapiens sapiens*—the species who names himself wise, but is not.

As an evolutionary experiment, culture apparently worked without serious flaw for tens and perhaps hundreds of thousands of years—back in the days before agriculture, and the culture that this new lifeway inspired. It is true that not all indigenous people lived a single lifeway. There were immediate return hunter-gatherers and delayed return hunter gatherers, who were mostly nomadic, just as there were a few easy living populations along certain salmon rivers of the Northwest Coast, and proto-agriculturalists along certain large inland rivers. But despite some small differences, born out of different experiences, it remains true that all these people shared a perspective on the world that can fairly be called the Indigenous Worldview, and was at the heart of indigenous culture.

According to the Indigenous Worldview, Mother Earth is sacred, and always to be treated with reverence and respect; She is alive, and possesses the qualities of intelligence, sentience, selfhood, and volition, as well as unknowable mystery. When native peoples speak of 'all our relations' they are acknowledging that all living beings are kin to the human, and that we are all integral to the Community of Life, and live together on this sacred Earth in a condition of mutual interdependence.

Living in the hands of the gods is living in the Gift of Nature's generosity; it is living within the annual solar budget, and off the interest of Nature's bounty. This is in contrast to living in the Theft, which is living off the interest of Nature's bounty while also living off the principal. All mining is Theft, whether that mining is using renewable resources at a pace that exceeds their rate of renewal (drawdown), or mining non-renewable resources for one-time use until all such resources are exhausted (or become uneconomical to extract).

Living in the Theft is how we are living now, and how we have been living since the dawn of agriculture. It began with the theft of other creatures' habitat for the exclusive use of humans, by turning forests into bare-dirt landscapes where topsoil was eroded and eventually poisoned by the salts brought in with stolen irrigation water. Theft also began with the domestication and enslavement of wild animals, stealing their freedom to be themselves and live out their own natural destiny. And though they may not have realized it at the time, when our once-wild ancestors exploited and brutalized other sovereign beings, they also brutalized the human sensibility and transformed themselves into commodities to be exploited by those with the power to control them. When individuals started working for those in power instead of working directly for themselves--and this condition became normalized—we were no longer the wild creatures we evolved to be, but were now, ourselves, domesticated.

These early Neolithic Revolutionaries necessarily came out of a culture which held the traditional Indigenous Worldview; thus, their cognitive dissonance must have been extreme in those early days. Stealing the habitat of fellow Earthlings for agriculture, and stealing the freedom of their fellow beings for slave work and convenient meat, very much went against the belief in the sacredness of all life. Likewise, the newly instituted institution of private property must have been difficult to rationalize when not that long before Mother Earth had been regarded as sacred. How could you "own" your own Mother? The very concept must have caused migraines of consternation.

Thus, something had to be done; and something was done.

It was time to break out the Big Lie. The Big Lie declares that the human being is not an integral part of Nature and the Community of Life, as formerly believed, but separate; an entity unto itself, and not only independent of Nature, but superior to Nature. All of the former sacredness of Earth was torn from her and flung out into the distant heavens. The Earth and all its creatures were ours to take at our pleasure. Nothing on Earth was of any importance except in how it might serve the human being. And thus was born the narcissistic anthropocentrism that has defined the civilized human throughout our history, and continues to characterize us today.

Living in the Theft and living the Big Lie has brought us to where we are today: poised at the edge of ruin. In the face of environmental and social dis-integration, some of us are coming to see that, no, we are not above Nature, nor are we separate from Nature. The Lie of separation has permitted us to live in the Theft, spending down Nature's capital to the point of near exhaustion—a lifeway with a near-term expiration date. And this brings me to the relevance of the Indigenous Worldview.

I am not suggesting that the seven billion of us who are alive in my own time could all become hunter-gatherers on this severely damaged planet. It is doubtful that fifty-million of us could live that way sustainably, even now--and conditions are worsening at an ever-accelerating rate. Evidently, we cannot cease living in the Theft at the present moment. We are locked in to this mal-adaptive behavior, and have little recourse but to continue, until something happens to stop us. But we can, at least, come to the recognition that living in the Gift—within the annual solar budget and off the interest of Nature's bounty-- **is** a viable lifeway, and (it now seems self-evident) the only lifeway with long-term staying power. That would be a start.

But what of the worldview on which this lifeway is based?

Isn't it as passé and outmoded as any philosophy of life could be? Well, actually, no. Many of its salient tenets remain as they ever were. The human being **is** an integral part of the Community of Life. And it is quite accurate to characterize our living, and life-supporting, planet as Mother Earth, just as it is appropriate to treat her with the reverence and respect due to such a being: one who clearly displays intelligence, sentience, interiority, volition-- and mystery aplenty.

Since the Scientific Revolution, in the time of Bacon and Newton, the world has been reduced to inert, "dead" matter, a product of random chance, functioning like a machine, in an indifferent or hostile Universe. No meaning; no purpose; just happenstance. That has been the scientific worldview for four centuries now, and many still hold that view in my own time. But it is looking to me like this is a scientific paradigm that is just about to be overturned and made a laughing stock—very much as we think of the flat Earthers today.

Within the realm of philosophy, there is a small outpost of ontology that calls itself panpsychism, and this panpsychism corresponds in many ways to the animism of our wild ancestors. The fundamental question panpsychism ask is: what is matter, really? And its answer is that all matter, all the way up and all the way down, displays characteristics that we identify as intelligence, sentience, subjectivity, and volition—the very qualities we find in ourselves. And when you think about it, it pretty much has to be this way, because, otherwise, where do these characteristics come from? You can't get something out of nothing, and no scientific materialist has yet given a good explanation of how you can.

When we understand that the world and everything in it is in its own way alive and individuated, with its own sense of self and with its own innate destiny to fulfill, the world becomes personalized—or as our wild ancestors would have

THE INDIGENOUS WORLDVIEW

said, peopled with a multitude of spirits. And in fact many indigenous groups speak of salmon people, bison people, heron people, and all the rest, as other-than-human people—granting them the full dignity of personhood. In my particular time and place, we are in the awkward position of being caught between stories—stories to live in and stories to live by. Our culture's foundational stories (the ones fabricated in the early centuries of agriculture) are beginning to be seen as inadequate and dangerous to all Life, but we have not yet come up with new stories we can agree on, fully believe, and inhabit. And this situation leaves us confused and foundering, with little solid to cling to. Much as I'd like to, I do not expect to see this change in my lifetime, because in one way or other, and to some degree or other, we are all invested in the Big Lie and in all of the systems the Big Lie has spawned. By your time, these may have run their course. In any case, these systems are something you and I are going to have look at in some detail, but first there is a great deal more to know about culture.

CHAPTER 18

THREE FACES OF CULTURE

MOST PEOPLE ASSUME they know what culture is and how it works, but culture is a slippery character and is neither what it appears, nor is it just one thing. I would say that culture falls into three more or less distinct categories: commonplace culture; material culture; and deep culture. Commonplace culture is what most people think of when they think of culture. This would include Beethoven's Ninth Symphony, the Mona Lisa, *War and Peace*, and the plays of Shakespeare—that is, all the works that the "experts" tell us is high art—which then qualifies them as high culture. Beneath this lofty plane reside all the other contributions to art, architecture, philosophy, music, and literature—that second tier of artistic and intellectual endeavor which occupies the great middle ground of our cultural heritage, spanning the range between high culture and popular culture. Commonplace culture may also include the world of ideas, but, for our purposes, only derivative ideas; not the foundational ideas on which our culture is based. These foundational ideas belong to the category of deep culture, which is our chief interest here.

THREE FACES OF CULTURE

To the extent that commonplace culture consists of artifacts, like books, paintings and orchestral instruments, it can overlap a bit with material culture, but should not be taken for the same thing. Material culture includes every one of the thousands of items you might find in your home, from plates and pressure-cookers to sinks and toilets. Material culture also includes the larger infrastructure of our lives, from cities and highways to the electrical grid, and would include all our systems of extraction, manufacture, sales, and transportation implicated in the transformation of the Earth's flesh into consumer goods.

To put material culture into historical context, it might be helpful to think about what anthropologists call a people's "toolkit." For untold human generations, the human toolkit consisted of basics like fire, spears, knives, baskets, bowls, arrows and bows, as well as the tools and technologies for turning animal skins into clothing and shelter. Material culture does not exist in a vacuum, but within the context of a group's larger culture: its myths and memes; its beliefs and values; its lifeway and worldview. The pioneering 20th century thinker, Lewis Mumford, made a useful distinction between what he called democratic technics and authoritarian technics.

It would seem to be common sense to assume that material culture is an obvious reflection of our beliefs, values, and perceptions as a people: our worldview. We think something is a good idea, and then we make it materialize. But a more profound understanding of the actual dynamic may be contained in the insight of anthropologist Marvin Harris, when he insists that is really more the other way around: infrastructure influences ideology to a far greater extent than ideology influences infrastructure.

In the last couple centuries, science and technology have also made substantial contributions not only by way of intellectual achievement but also in a vast array of creature comforts and consumable commodities that have come to define the physical infrastructure of our lived environment—our material culture. Also central to this level of culture are the interlocking systems of extraction, production, and distribution--as well as our technological and economic systems--which deliver, and make possible, our way of life.

If all this (which only hints at its totality) is to be considered "superficial" culture, what in the world might deep culture be? Deep culture is deep in at least three senses: it goes way back in our cultural history, often several millennia back; it works at a subterranean level, and so remains invisible to most; and, it is so deeply embedded within the individual and the group mind that--despite its invisibility, and also partly because of it, it all but determines human behavior, both at the level of the individual and the collective. Deep culture is what gives history its shape, in much the same way that our skeletons give shape and structure to our bodies. Looking back over our ten-thousand-year history, using an X-ray-like lens, it is possible to discern how the patterns and trajectories of our ancestors' lives have been informed and directed by deep culture. Using this culture-penetrating lens, it is also possible to trace how this same deep culture has led us, step by step, to the converging global crises that bear down on my world now, and so must shape the world you have inherited.

Deep culture is far less visible than superficial culture, but far more potent, because it addresses our primal nature as cultural animals. When anthropologists speak of culture, it is generally to this deeper culture they are referring. In this more specialized view, culture is a body of knowledge, a collection of stories, myths, and memes, a repository of values, and--embedded invisibly in language--is passed from one generation to the next. This form of culture provides people with the cognitive structures they use for framing life's vital issues, as well as lenses through which to see and interpret the world. In philosophical terms, a people's culture includes their origin story (cosmology); their notion of what is "real" (ontology); their beliefs about how they know what they know (epistemology), and; their sense of right and wrong (their ethical or moral code). All known cultures ask these questions about life and living, and each comes up with its own particular answers—though, of course, there is much overlap among the beliefs of different cultural groups. Among hunter-gatherers, for instance, while there will be stories and beliefs unique to each particular people, grounded in the place where they live, certain features of their culture will be held in common among nearly all peoples who share their way of life.

Thus, while it is important to acknowledge the particularities and uniqueness of each indigenous group, it is just as important to recognize that beliefs held in common among nearly all such peoples amount to a worldview. Nearly all hunter-gatherers, for instance, speak of Mother Earth and Father Sun as sacred and exalted beings who synergistically provide the conditions for Life to flourish in wondrous abundance. Both Sun and Earth are personified and understood to be spiritual beings, and, because they give the people the means to live and thrive, they are held in high esteem: loved and respected, but not without an edge of apprehension, or even fear. Among these peoples, all the creatures of Earth are considered to be kin, and are understood to be individuals with personhood. Thus they can speak of beaver persons, eagle persons, lizard persons, salmon persons, or cricket persons, granting each individual within each species its own intelligence, sentience, interiority, and volition. And just like human people, each has the spirit nature of its kind, as well as its own unique expression of that spirit. When indigenous people speak of All Our

Relations they are acknowledging the human relationship to the entire Community of Life. While they may rank one species above another in terms of the quality of its spirit—the spirit quality of a panther being quite different from that of a mouse—they do not see the Community of Life as a hierarchy, nor do they put human persons above all the others. This does not mean they are oblivious to the special gifts of humans, but rather that they tend to see these gifts as conferring special responsibilities to the Community of Life rather than inviting special privileges—in accordance with the Law of Reciprocity.

The Law of Reciprocity recognizes that all of the systems that make life possible, from the smallest to the largest, require that those who are served by these systems give back as good, or better, than they get. This is necessary for these Life Systems to operate at their optimum best. Free-riders drag the system down; those who obey the Law—the vast majority of the Community of Life—enhance the Life Systems and help keep the four-billion-year Project of Life alive and well.

Showing reverence for Mother Earth, Father Sun, and the Community of Life, while respecting the Law of Reciprocity, constitutes the essence of the Indigenous Worldview--whose function is to inform and direct the people how to behave in the world. This is deep culture working in accordance with the Laws and Systems of Nature; deep culture that is therefore viable, resilient, and durable. But deep culture also carries the potential to do great harm; harm made more dangerous by deep culture's primal pull on the human psyche, and by its ability to mesmerize, captivate, and colonize those who fall under its spell. Deep culture, with this kind of power over the human mind, can thus be perilous unto ruin—as many of us are now beginning to see.

For hundreds of human generations the Indigenous Worldview orchestrated the way humans lived in the world.

THREE FACES OF CULTURE

Humans were in right relationship with Mother Earth and Father Sun; they were well-integrated into the Community of Life; and they were observant of the Law of Reciprocity. Then, with agriculture, and all the changes that agriculture brought in its wake—private property, social stratification, and the rise of authoritarianism; food surplus and food storage, and the burgeoning populations these made possible; the mining of topsoil, unto exhaustion, with the consequent need to expand into new territory, thereby generating the need for warriors and (endless) war—the old way of living in the world was transformed into something quite different. The old stories, myths, and code of ethics were inconsistent with this new way of living in the world, creating confusion and cognitive dissonance. A new cosmology, ontology, and epistemology were required—along with a moral code to match. Thus, over the early centuries of agriculture a whole new belief system took shape, and in the process our culture of civilization was born—and with it what I call the Big Lie.

The Big Lie is pretty much a reversal of the Indigenous Worldview. In this new version of ourselves and the world the human being is separate from Nature, and Nature, rather than being sacred is seen as subordinate to humans: an antagonist to be overcome, on the one hand, and a storehouse of resources to be raided, on the other. As hunter-gatherers, we had "lived in the hands of the gods," to use Daniel Quinn's elegant phrase; as agriculturalists, we were bent upon taking the food supply into our own hands, at once defying the gods and becoming like gods ourselves. In this process we grew ever more self-absorbed and vain, no longer seeing ourselves as an integral part of the Community of Life, but rather, apart from, and above, all the other beings on Earth. In our anthropocentric narcissism, we came to see ourselves as some kind of wondrous anomaly, unlike any other creature in the world. By the time of the writing of the Book of Genesis, some three-thousand to thirty-five-hundred years ago, all of these cultural memes were well-established, and only remained to be codified in print and sanctified as the Word of God.

Consider the far-reaching implications of these three verses from "the good book:"

"And God said, 'Let us make man in our image, after our likeness: and let him have dominion over the fish of the sea, and over the fowl of the air, and over the cattle, and over all the earth, and over every creeping thing that creepeth upon the earth.'" Genesis 1:26

"So God created man in his own image, in the image of God created he him; male and female created he them" Genesis 1:27

"And God blessed them, and God said unto them: 'Be fruitful and multiply, and replenish the earth, and subdue it: and have dominion over the fish of the sea, and over the fowl of the air, and over every living thing that moveth upon the earth.'" Genesis 1:28

In this story, born of the agricultural way of life, the human being is in charge of the Earth, and every living thing upon it. Dominion implies not only domination but also ownership. Everything on Earth that the human might desire is his for the taking, as his exclusive right. All sense of community and mutuality with the other creatures of the Earth has, by this point, been replaced by a relationship of domination and exploitation. And, as we see in other parts of the Old Testament, this exploitative relationship is not to be tempered with moderation, but pursued to the maximum to build up riches and become a powerful patriarch upon the land. And, of course, have many children.

These (putative) divine injunctions amount to a set of marching orders, and a template for how to live in the world. This is deep culture, and it matters not at all whether we are devout Christians, militant atheists, or something in between in terms of personal beliefs. These injunctions constitute a foundational myth which underlies all, or nearly all, of our stories. Since, as cultural animals, we live by story, we really cannot escape the assumptions about the world that our stories are built upon, subterranean as they may be. Or, as pathological as they may be. Each of us imbibes these stories and memes with our mother's milk and at our father's knee. Deep culture is encoded in language and penetrates all our cultural institutions; and we get a dose of it every time we interact with others of our culture, reinforcing" the story of our people."

Though invisible to most, deep culture (like our skeletons), provides structure to our everyday lives. And it is the foundation on which our superficial culture is built. It is vital to understand this, because whatever might be wrong with our culture cannot be fixed by tinkering with superficial culture. If we don't get down to the root causes in our deep culture, all our fixes will be superficial, and the fundamental changes that are required will elude us.

To illustrate the difference between deep culture and superficial culture, consider, for instance, the Great Chain of Being. With its intellectual roots in the thinking of Plato, Aristotle and Plotinus, the Great Chain of Being is a schematic ranking of all that goes to make up the physical world, as well as what is believed about a (supposed) world beyond. Medieval and Renaissance churchmen painstakingly expanded upon this way of viewing the world, putting God at the top of the hierarchy and Earth at the bottom, with angels ranked above men, men above the beasts, and with all of the animals ranked by type according to perceived superiority, one over another, but well above plants, which are themselves ranked according to their "virtue" and usefulness. Below plants are the metals and minerals, with Earth and its skin of dirt inferior to all else. The Great Chain of Being is a product of more than two thousand years of our cultural history, and this way of thinking about the world so insinuated itself into the culture at large that it would come to influence the way early scientific thinkers viewed the world: that is, as an elaborate, but intelligible, hierarchy. Even today, the scientific discipline of taxonomy, among many others, continues to bear the imprint of these earlier ways of understanding the world. Yet, despite its ancient origins and long cultural life, this elaborate cultural meme still qualifies for what I am calling superficial culture. And that is because its assumptions about the world are based upon the founding assumptions of deep culture, including the Big Lie of Separation.

The Great Chain of Being is the near-antithesis of the Indigenous Worldview, which is not hierarchical, but holistic and holonic: a view that comprehends the interdependent and synergistic nature of living systems; understanding the world in terms of connection and relationship, based upon the Law of Reciprocity. It is a view that locates value and sacredness in Mother Earth herself, and not somewhere outside this living system that both supports Life and **is** Life. The Great Chain of Being degrades the Earth to the lowest possible level in a rigid hierarchy that separates spirit from matter, body from mind. In order to arrive at such a construction it was necessary that the foundational Big Lie of Separation had already been well established and taken its place in deep culture. Deep culture is primary culture, foundational culture, and the secondary culture that builds upon it—what I am calling superficial, or derivative, culture-- could not exist (as is) without its antecedent(s).

Let's say there is a reform movement that sees problems with the Great Chain of Being, and they want to amend all the incongruities they perceive which do not align with present knowledge. Let's say they are atheistic scientific materialists and they want to expunge the entire category of angels: No more seraphim, no more cherubim; goodbye to thrones and principalities, archangels and angels. And of course there can be no God at the top. Then let's say there are some deep ecologists, with a minor in evolutionary biology, who are deeply unhappy about the placement of the human being above all the other animals, because, after all, we are all in this together: plants, animals (including humans), mountains, rivers, oceans, ecosystems--everything that goes to make up the biosphere—including the physical and chemical processes that help make this planet pulse with Life. And let's just say this latter group was influential enough, after writing dozens of peer reviewed articles in all the prestigious journals, to force a re-thinking of this rigidly structured hierarchy of one kingdom or genera or species over another. And let's take it further yet, and suppose that, after much wrangling and debate, a consensus was reached, and the whole Great Chain of Being was discarded as a patent absurdity, with no merit whatsoever, except as an artifact of our benighted history.

What has happened in this hypothetical overturning of a revered (if lately underappreciated) institution is the reform of (or elimination of) one offending secondary cultural institution, without in any way touching the primary culture that is its ultimate source. The idea that hierarchy is the natural order of things, the way the Universe organizes itself, remains. The Big Lie itself—that the human is separate from Mother Nature, the Earth, and the Community of Life-- has never even come into question. Nor has the notion that the Earth is the exclusive province of man, to take for his own whatever he wants. And, naturally, the anthropocentrism that comes along with these self-serving notions stands just as tall and proud as ever. And this is why reform of any of our present systems or institutions will never get us where we need to go: because our dysfunctional deep culture is in no way disabled, nor is its pathological program for planetary ecocide. As if taking sustenance from a fading, failing Earth, this program—written into deep culture-- only grows stronger by the day.

Although deep culture carries the potential for the gravest of dangers, as we now begin to see, deep culture need not be dysfunctional in this way. The deep culture that underlies the Indigenous Worldview, for instance, is evolutionarily adaptive to the ecology of planet Earth, because it is well-matched to the actual (not invented) conditions, and Laws of Life, on Earth. Our artificially concocted deep culture, and the worldview built upon it, is not. But changing several millennia of habit and belief is no easy thing, and is made even more difficult by the artificial culture that has developed over the last hundred years.

In the early part of the twentieth century, Edward Bernays, one of the Founding Fathers of artificial culture, would become a propagandist (working within the Wilson administration) promoting the American role in World War One. Following this success, of "making the world safe for democracy," Bernays founded an enterprise he insisted on calling Public Relations. That is, propaganda with a more acceptable name. Ever since that time, the role of the tribal storyteller has been hijacked by the corporate media and turned into a marketing platform to sell a wide range of consumer goods and a rather narrow range of ideas—mostly those that make the world safe for capitalism and corporations. Thus the human need to live by story and be guided by cultural meme has been subverted to the will of the corporate power elite to impose their story upon us.

This artificial culture, as provided by the corporate media, has insinuated itself into nearly every home in America and Europe and across much of the world, where its distractions, "entertainments," selective disinformation, and celebrity worship all follow a highly orchestrated script. Televisionland is a parallel Universe that bears a striking resemblance to our everyday world, but is as fake as the Fox News slogan: "fair and balanced." What media moguls dub "Public Opinion," is not dispassionate reasoning based upon careful consideration of the "facts," but is instead the product of manufactured memes, first tested on focus groups, then manipulated to produce the desired results.

Artificial culture creatively combines elements of deep and superficial culture in such a way as to seem an authentic cultural voice—and in a certain way, I suppose, artificial culture is a genuine reflection of who we are now: venal, cynical, amoral, self-absorbed. But it is not a reflection of our higher, better selves, and is therefore a rather distorted glass in which to see and evaluate the human enterprise.

Many believe that culture is nothing more than the sum total of the contributions made by all those living today and all those who have gone before us. This view assumes that culture is an exclusively human enterprise: of, by, and for the people-- and that it exists for the sole purpose of serving humans. But it is not nearly that simple. I like to say that the culture of civilization is nothing if not a self-promoting, self-aggrandizing propaganda machine. Invisible, and not exactly benign, it casts a spell over us that few ever break. It colonizes us with its myths, stories, and memes, making us believe that what we believe and value about the world is our own individual perception. In this way our own identity is so entangled with our culture that most of us are unable to untangle the two and still have a sense of personal identity. This bond between the human and his culture can be a wholesome relationship, or it can be a kind of insidious bondage that smothers all instinct—including our very best instincts. As a wise person once said: "Culture is not your friend." Nor is it in any way neutral.

Following the lead of the anthropologist Albert Kroeber, I

reify, or personify, culture, seeing it as an entity with a will and agenda of its own. If culture—and especially deep culture—is consistent with the laws and conditions of planetary health, culture's agenda will then be fundamentally wholesome. But if deep culture is based upon wrong-headed misperceptions or outright lies--as I have been insisting here about our own—that deep culture must be rejected if we are to have any hope at all of halting its program of Planetary Death, and our part in enacting its will. But before you can reject it, you have to SEE it, and see it for what it is.

CHAPTER 19

LIVING IN THE GIFT

ABOUT THIS TIME you may be wondering about all this emphasis on culture, and maybe questioning what it has to do with you. Well, I can't be sure of your situation-- physically, socially, educationally, or in any other way—and can only hope the best for you in all aspects of your life, considering. What I am offering you, as a gift of reparation and regret, may be of no use to you at all—for any number of reasons. But I feel very strongly that my generation owes your generation better than the legacy of ruin we are dumping on you, and though it isn't enough, the best I can do by way of compensation is offer you some conceptual tools with which to navigate the chaos and confusion that must define your world. My motive in this is simple: I want to see the human race continue on terms that are compatible with a living planet—which I take to be small and simple in scale--and I worry that this one last chance for our species will be sabotaged by the cultural program that, in my time, is dismantling the biosphere and turning it into toxic waste.

My great fear is that any survivors of the coming crash

might try to revive civilization and keep alive the culture that makes this way of life possible. As I have noted, I see the culture of civilization as being a self-promoting, self-aggrandizing propaganda machine, and one which has insinuated itself, like a contagion, into the psyche of all who have come under its influence. Among those who, in my own time, are tuned into the converging crises bearing down upon us, and threaten our very survival as a species, the overwhelming majority believe that the first order of business is saving civilization—they are that deeply under its insidious spell. Spellbound, they are unable to see, or even entertain the thought, that it is none other than this very culture of civilization-- based on agriculture, private property, and planetary domination—that is the heart of the problem. Delusions of grandeur and addiction to Power run so deep in this culture that I worry we can never escape their hold over us.

This fear may be a bit irrational on my part, because the kind of material culture we see in my time can never be repeated. By your time, whatever remnants of riches remain in the Earth beneath your feet will be unavailable to you: either because we have exhausted them, or have taken all the easy, accessible stuff, and what is left is not worth the effort of going after. So, I am pretty sure you will not be able to build a super-civilization even more pretentious than our own. But still I worry that some of the poisonous rot of our culture will find its way into yours, and spoil your chances, along with any long-term prospects for our kind.

The question of 'resources' will always be an issue for humans, or for any living being—and markedly so in your case. I don't know what is going to be left for you to work with, but I am reasonably certain that you will be living in a resource-poor world, and I want to give you some idea of how this all came about.

LIVING IN THE GIFT

The first thing to understand is that what is identified as a resource available for human use is dependent upon a peoples' culture. According to the ancient worldview which preceded the culture of civilization-- what I call the Indigenous Worldview-- Mother Earth is sacred, and is to be treated with deepest respect and reverence. Accordingly, the hunting and gathering peoples who held this worldview did not mine the Earth for its buried treasures. Not only would such an act be considered a defilement of the Mother, but a nomadic people on the move have no desire to burden themselves with anything but the most portable of necessities. For people of this lifeway, competence and cooperation are what make for a good life: thus, it is not what you 'own' that is important, it is what you know, and the more you know, the less you need.

The conditions of life on Earth require that the life of one creature must be taken to sustain the life of another, and in this way killing and violence are necessary to Life's continuance. But if this is a Law of Life, it is offset by the countervailing principle that all Life is sacred, and is to be treated as such. This is paradox, and it creates a tension of opposites that must be navigated with great care, with an eye to maintaining balance. Accordingly, among those who hold the Indigenous Worldview, the taking of another creature's life is allowed only under specified conditions, including the asking of permission, and the giving of thanks, through prescribed ritual activity. And, as with all ritual, it is most meaningful when sincerely felt. Respect and reverence for all life forms is appropriate and should arise naturally out of the recognition that all Life is sacred. Accordingly, when a life is taken for human sustenance, nothing should be wasted. Waste shows disrespect. These simple principles have been practiced by humans for tens of thousands of years, and, for the most part, those humans did not degrade or diminish their world—which they recognized was not theirs alone. Living in this way honors the compact between Nature and the human, while also being a conservation ethic which honors the reciprocal relationship between predator and prey. At the same time, living by these guidelines provides a people with their best prospects for continuing to live in their chosen place--unto the seventh generation and beyond.

The hunter-gatherer thrives by preserving his chosen ecosystem in its natural intact condition. In this way the land preserves its wildness, and so does the human preserve his. Resource use by those who call themselves civilized is based upon a different set of principles. Whereas the immediate-return hunter-gatherer lives within the annual solar budget, and makes his living off the interest of Nature's capital, we civilized types go far beyond living off the interest: we have been spending down Nature's capital for centuries now, and at an ever-accelerating rate, in order to support an insupportable number of humans living in an ever-more lavish and improvident lifestyle. How have we done this? And what are its implications for the Community of Life, and therefore also for you?

To begin with, agriculture is an activity that requires the destruction of natural ecosystems—ecosystems that have been billions of years in the making. What began nearly four billion years ago as the appearance of single celled organisms, evolved over eons into ever greater complexity and ever greater diversity, and this complexity and diversity self-organized into guilds, communities, and ecosystems—which, over time, developed ever greater resilience. Resilience is built upon redundancy, which acts as a hedge against the hazards of stochastic events: things like fire, flood, tsunami, asteroid, earthquake, contagion, and so on. If an ecosystem has half a dozen creatures who perform roughly the same ecosystem function, when harsh events visit themselves upon the system and take out two or three key constituents, those that survive continue their usual functions, which helps to maintain the ecosystem's integrity. Without this kind of resilience, ecosystems can be overwhelmed by events and transformed into an entirely different kind of ecosystem. This kind of regime change is captured in the quip by Chateaubriand: 'Forests precede civilizations and deserts follow.' Spending down resilience in this way is a form of mining, and also a form of theft.

Right up until the time of agricultural man, this kind of resilience had been building for millions of years—at least since the last great global stochastic event, perhaps 65 million years ago, that took out the dinosaurs. And it is this accrued resilience that agricultural man has been mining ever since: first by transforming natural ecosystems into unnatural ones, thereby cancelling them out, while extirpating their diverse populations; then by mining the topsoil unto depletion, thereby turning fertile, productive land into waste land of little biological or ecological worth. This same process of ecosystem degradation is, of course, also accomplished by the building of cities, by paving over permeable land with impermeable surfaces, and by creating industrial sacrifice zones. One thing leads to another leads to another, and it all begins with agriculture. And once embarked on this path of transforming natural ecosystems into something entirely different, it seems to have been an easy slide into other forms of transmogrification of the living Earth.

I want now to explore the proposition that certain things that the people of our culture have identified as 'resources,' put here for human use, are no such thing. What we call 'renewable resources' are gifts of Nature, and their use is permitted to humans, as long as they are in fact renewed. When the forests of the British Isles and of Europe are cut down for human use, but not renewed; when we take fossil water from ancient aquifers at a rate that far exceeds its recharge rate; when we deplete the oceans' large fish by eighty percent, and give them no chance to rebound—this is mining a renewable resource, and cannot long endure. Using the Earth's plentitude in this way is, I would say, in violation of an ancient human compact with Nature-- the ultimate source of our lives. It is allowable to live off the interest of Earth's solar budget and to partake of Nature's emergent abundance. It is not permissible to live off the principal, as this is mining, and constitutes theft.

In addition to such 'renewable' resources, the people of our culture have identified another part of the living planet to be used by humans, which they call 'non-renewable resources.' These include fossil fuels such as coal, oil, and natural gas; metals such as iron, copper, nickel, silver, and gold; various other elements, including the rare earths, and any number of gemstones and miscellaneous compounds. All of these are integral to the Earth, are under the Earth's skin, and can be accessed only by ripping into the Earth itself. Inevitably, it is a violent process, whether accomplished directly by humans using sharp prying tools, or giant machines that gouge out the Earth's flesh tons at a time. Few, if any, of these non-renewables come to the surface in pure form. They come with a lot of the rest of the Earth, referred to as 'overburden' or 'spoils,' which is treated as waste. In the case of mountaintop removal, everything that is not coal is bulldozed toward lower ground, including into creeks and rivers. Much of what is brought up to the surface of the Earth, along with the sought-after treasure, is toxic to life. As long as it was buried, its life- and health-threatening properties were no problem. But, once above-ground these poisons are released into the biosphere to work their ongoing harm.

Metals, such as gold, require highly poisonous chemicals, like mercury and cyanide, in the mining and refining process.

Where do these chemicals end up? In the biosphere, of course, and in the bodies of animals and humans, even decades and centuries after mining operations have shut down. To this day, the Rocky Mountains retain the toxic legacy of its mining history, with no relief in sight. The hydraulic fracturing process introduces a dangerous brew of chemicals (including benzene) into underground aquifers, even as this risky process releases methane (a highly potent greenhouse gas) into the atmosphere. The Gulf Oil Spill of 2011 is a reminder of how environmentally devastating deepwater oil extraction can be, while the Alberta tar sands continue to expand the sacrifice zone of that dirty, corrosive project. In the world of mining, a few people get filthy rich, the consumer gets a certain amount 'stuff' of some kind, and everybody else gets the toxic legacy, while the tissue of the Earth itself is ravaged and left for dead.

All of this, by itself, should tell us we are doing something wrong. As a practical matter, simply in terms of costs and benefits, this equation does not add up. The epidemic of cancer and other diseases coincides with a witch's brew of chemicals we are all exposed to through our chemical agriculture, and our deepening reliance on pharmaceuticals just to live 'normally.' Meanwhile, industrial processes release a plethora of dangerous chemicals into our air and water, nasty things like PCBs and dioxins. All but a very few of these compounds come from under the skin of the Earth, and what seems obvious to me is that they should be left there--based simply on cost-benefit calculations which look beyond quarterly profits for the few to the long-term welfare of the whole.

Then, too, it may be that the subterranean zones of Earth constitute their own kinds of ecosystems, whose functions we have not begun to understand. Just for an instance, the iron that is in the Earth may function in important ways in terms of Earth's electro-magnetic field, affecting the stability of Earth's orbit. The point is, we do not understand the implications of everything we are doing. A cost-benefit analysis, even leaving out such mysteries as these, suggests the costs far outweigh the benefits—and this is based strictly on practical, materialistic considerations, leaving out any possible spiritual components to the equation.

But what if the Earth is sacred? What if all Life is sacred? What if the Mayan spiritual perspective, as presented by Martin Prechtel, is a more profound understanding of our Universe, our world, and our place in it, than our own? What if, as he suggests, taking "resources" out of the hide of the Earth creates a "hollowness that's been carved out of the universe" that can only be made right by ritual sacrifice, to reciprocate for what has been taken? What if it's true that: "The universe is in a state of starvation and emotional grief because it has not been given what it needs in the form of ritual food and actual physical gifts. We think we're getting away with something by stealing from the other side, but it all leads to violence." What if he and the Mayans are right and we are wrong? Present day Mayans are not hunter-gatherers, but an agrarian people who once had a 'great' civilization that failed (as all civilization eventually do). So theirs is not a pure Indigenous Worldview, but blends that view with hard lessons learned from failure—demonstrating once again the value of the historical perspective.

So, again, I ask you to consider: What if all that is under the Earth's skin belongs to the Earth and not to us at all—and that taking what we mine from the Earth is indeed theft? That it is culturally sanctioned theft does not make it anything other than theft; it just means we have given ourselves permission to be thieves, and sanction the plunder of the Earth. We have been at this plunder for a few thousand years now, but only in the last few hundred have we gone about the job systematically. And where has that left us? All of the 'easier' resources to get at have already been mined, and what is left is generally of lower quality and harder to get at. All these 'resources' are on the down side of depletion. The availability of oil is likely past its peak. All the non-renewable resources we've come to depend upon are in decline, and it looks as though we are willing to fight with other humans for what remains.

This is violence begetting violence, in a self-amplifying positive feedback loop. "We think we are getting away with something by stealing from the other side, but it all leads to violence. The Greek oracle at Delphi saw this a long time ago and said, 'Woe to humans, the invention of steel.'" As I see it, all the violence and disorder of our own time is the price we are paying for breaking our compact and bond with Nature. If we had stuck to that bargain, and lived only on the interest of Nature's abundance (living in the Gift), and not helped ourselves to the principal (living in the Theft), we and the world would still be thriving in a state of ever-renewing balance.

If we are to ever reach that balance again, it will be by going back to the simplicity and honesty of living in the Gift. And this is my best and highest hope for you: that Mother Earth is in a renewal phase in your time, and that you will have the wisdom to stay small and live a life of gratifying simplicity.

CHAPTER 20

LAW OF HOLONIC RECIPROCITY

THE HUMAN BEING lives by story, and the story we live by will have its origins in culture. By now you must realize that there is something deeply flawed in the stories our culture has us living in. A story, or complex of stories, that has a people systematically destroying their life support system is more than flawed; it is pathological. Even if we recognize this--being the cultural animals that we are, and **requiring** some sort of story to live in—we find ourselves in a trap, because our twisted, Earth-destroying story is the only one we have. What we desperately need is a New Story, but we do not have one—not in my time. But in seeking a New Story I don't believe we need to start from scratch, because there is much in the Indigenous Worldview that has proven itself as viable, and can serve as a basis for our own New Story.

An essential ingredient to the New Story, as I see it, is the concept of holonomy, because it acts as a unifying foundation for so much else within the New Story. Holonomy refers to a fundamental condition or property of the Universe—one of nested interrelatedness. A holon is a self-bounded whole

LAW OF HOLONIC RECIPROCITY

which is part of a larger whole, and which cannot exist independently of that larger whole (or holarchy). Such a holon might be a cell within the human heart. The cell takes its life within the context of the heart, and cannot live separately. The organ of the heart takes its life within the context of organ systems, and these in turn take their life within the context of an entire organism, a living human being. That human takes its life within the context of local, regional, and global ecosystems. The Earth, or Gaia, is itself a self-bounded holon within a larger solar system, and that system is in turn embedded within a galaxy, which is likewise part of something larger still. Everything is connected; everything is interdependent, and there is nothing woo-woo or mystical about this. It is an obvious fact of life. Trouble is, the people of our culture have for thousands of years tried to live in the pretense that humans are separate from everything else-- exceptional, sapient, and autonomous-- and this lie has led to the Earth Crisis we find ourselves in today. The truth is we are not, and could not possibly be, autonomous. What we are instead is holonomous: interconnected with everything in the world in a vast network of mutual interdependencies. We are part of something far grander and much more wondrous than a single isolated narcissistic species. Within this larger, grander identity, we are wholly holonomous.

This new, yet ancient, understanding of the Universe, and our place in it, carries with it some profound implications. All of the interlocking systems, from smallest to largest, depend upon reciprocity. The individual cell depends upon the organ of which it is a part (or holon) for its life, but the organ itself is made up of cells, and requires the contribution of each cell in order to function and have its own being. If a single cell decided it wanted to continue receiving all the benefits of living in the context of the heart, but didn't want to continue making its usual contribution to the whole, that cell would then become a free-rider. The loss of a single cell would not greatly harm the heart, but would be only slightly damaging to its overall performance. If, however, thousands or millions of cells all went on free-rider status, the heart could suffer major, and possibly terminal, damage. This fact of life applies at all scales, from subatomic particle to galaxy: every holon within every holarchy is required to give back to the system which gives it life at least as much at it takes from that system (and preferably a little bit more, to compensate for free-riders). This is what it takes for any system to function optimally, and the requirement, or responsibility, for each holon to give back to its system at least as much as it takes is known by indigenous people as the Law of Reciprocity. I call it the Law of Holonic Reciprocity simply as a reminder of why it is Law: it is Law because all systems are holonomous, and require reciprocity to function at their best.

The Law of Holonic Reciprocity has, in turn, its own inherent implications. One such implication-- and a huge one-- is that the Universe is moral at its heart; that justice inheres in the very nature of the Universe. This is very far from the scientistic doctrine of a random meaningless Universe—very far indeed. But can that doctrine—based not on scientific fact, but on scientific ideology—refute the obvious fact of how systems work? Not in an honest way; not that I can see. But let's leave the ideologues aside for now and consider some of the further implications of a moral Universe.

The Law of Holonic Reciprocity invites us to look at the world in terms of whole systems, and not of single whole systems, but interlocking, interdependent systems within systems—all the way up the scale and all the way down, systems connected to systems connected to systems, from quark to Milky Way. Seeing the world in this way can, and perhaps should, expand our sense of self beyond our isolated individual personalities to include everything that allows us our being: the air we take into our bodies, the trees that respire the oxygen that enriches that air, and which help absorb the carbon dioxide we exhale; the water that keeps us hydrated, including each individual (and individuated) drop, and its immediate source (lake, river, well), but also embracing **its** source within the water cycle, including sky, cloud, ocean, land, precipitation, and evapo-transpiration --all the macro-systems and micro-systems that allow the water cycle to work as it does, and make Life possible. Likewise, every morsel of food we take into our bodies for ongoing sustenance is the product of countless cycles and systems, beginning with the energy of the sun, transformed by photosynthesis into nutrient-rich plants, which may be consumed by us directly, or first passed through the body of another plant eater. Breath passes in and out of us, as does food and water, in ongoing cycles within cycles within cycles. The thing we identify as "me," the individual, is much more illusory and much less definite than we like to believe. We are, after all, eighty percent bacteria, and only 20% human, by genetic code.

Nor are we anything like the solid and constant beings we have long taken ourselves to be. Instead, we--and all organisms--are highly dynamic creatures whose physical being is constantly in transition. Our gallbladders, for instance, completely reconstitute themselves, replacing every "old" cell with a new one every two days. And every part of our body is going through a similar process of dying and regenerating every day of our lives. Given all this dynamic connection with everything around us--and as far away as the sun, and beyond—we may be due for a new definition of self. And with that new definition a much broader sense of the moral order.

Most people regard the Golden Rule as a universal axiom

about how we should live in the world: Do unto others as you would have others do unto you. But this is based on the old cultural notion of self and other, subject and object, in a world of discrete autonomous entities and beings. But, as we now see, this is not the way the world really is. Nothing is truly separate from anything else, except perhaps in superficial appearance. Thus the Golden Rule as it now stands makes only superficial sense—and is pretty much restricted to inter-human relationships. A better maxim to live by, a Holonic Golden Rule, might go something like this: Take great care in all that you do, knowing that what you do to the apparent "other," you are also doing to yourself—both your smaller self and your larger Self, which are inseparable. The Holonic Golden Rule thus applies not only to how we treat our fellow humans but how we treat our fellow Earthlings, and, naturally, how we treat the Earth itself.

As things stand now within the Old Story, Nature is something quite separate from the human being, and is made up of "dead" matter, and of course is without sentience, intelligence, or volition of any kind. Certain animals may seem to have the appearance of such qualities, but, according to Descartes and his followers, animals are really just machines, automatons, and thus can feel or think or want nothing. These culturally sanctioned perceptions provide self-interested rational actors with a license to do whatever they will with dumb brutes on a dead Earth—and especially in pursuit of wealth creation: a preeminent value within civilization. The country of Bolivia has proposed a law that would give Nature legal rights of its own, to help protect it (and the humans that depend upon it) from the most damaging of wealth creation schemes. Of course the people of our culture regard such a notion as ridiculous on its face: how can something that is dead have rights? Only humans have rights. Right?

LAW OF HOLONIC RECIPROCITY

But just suppose that what we call matter, the "stuff" of the Universe, is not dead at all, but is in some sense alive, sentient, and capable of cognition. And in fact there is very good reason to believe that this is actually the case. If these qualities did not inhere in the Universe right from the very beginning, then where did they come from? No one has yet offered a convincing answer to this question. If matter can sense its environment and make choices based on what it senses--and evidence demonstrates that it can, and routinely does-- then our world, and the Universe which contains and sustains it, is not dead at all, but is living, intelligent, and volitional. This is the Universe as seen by our wild ancestors: living, sensing, self-directed--and deeply sacred. Mother Earth and Father Sun, the Givers of Life, were revered with humility and gratitude, and regarded as super beings possessed of intelligence, intention, and a unique personhood, with individuated characteristics of temperament. We now live in a world where almost nothing is personal; our wild ancestors lived in a world where everything was personal, because they recognized the uniqueness of each and all. If every snowflake that has ever fallen has had its own unique identity—and we are justified to believe this is the case—then why shouldn't we believe that everything in the Universe is likewise possessed of individuality and personhood? This is not meaningless speculation, but has far-reaching implications in terms of the Rights of Nature.

If we live in a Universe that has fairness and justice at its very heart, and depends upon the Law of Holonic Reciprocity for its own smooth functioning, then we, the people of civilization, are outlaws .We are free-riders who have declared ourselves exempt from the Law's requirement of giving back as good as we get to that which gives us our life. The Old Story of our culture has given us permission to take and take and never give anything back, and that is what we have done, to the point of nearly exhausting the Earth's amazing abundance and resilience. In a world where all flourishing is mutual, and reciprocity is the Law of Life, we have been blood-sucking parasites, fattening ourselves on the lifeblood of our Sacred Mother and the Community of Life. The New Story of holonomy (which is also quite ancient) requires that we change the way we understand the world, and our place in it. When we who live by story change our story, our behavior must change with it, because that is the kind of being we are.

In a world that thrives on justice, and is meaningfully alive with the subjectivity of personhood and the capacity for knowing and choosing with self-directed agency and intentionality, the role of the human being changes from ruthless exploiter to caring tender of the Gift. What these principles come down to is a philosophical foundation for the New Story we so urgently need. In my time, ideas such as these so go against a long cultural tradition, and the scientific materialism that has been built upon this tradition-- and especially on the Big Lie of Separation. Within this social, economic, and political context, the Rights of Nature threaten not only long-held cultural beliefs, but vast fortunes made on those beliefs, as well as future wealth creation. The concept of the Rights of Nature carries with it the implication that there are limits to what can be appropriated from the Whole. Among the people of our culture, who have lived as if there were no limits for a very long time now, the prospect of recognizing and living within limits threatens not only our deepest beliefs about the world, but our whole way of life.

Even among those of us who see where the Big Lie has led us, and how Living in the Theft must end in depletion, exhaustion, and ruin, we stand helpless to do anything about it. Why helpless? Because right now we have only this Old Story to live by. A few of us may be working on conceptual elements of a New Story, while a few others are trying to live a New Story, based mostly on intuitions felt deep in the gut. But this isn't enough, because the human operates, for good or ill, as a collective—and as a collective, operating out of the group mind, we are stuck in the Old Story. It would be a wondrous thing if we could all embrace a New Story before too many dominoes have fallen, and somehow avert the worst of what is to come. While I don't say that is impossible, I think it highly unlikely. Nor am I sure our systems and infrastructure would permit such an unlikely event in any case. And this is why I am looking to you. If you are part of a small human population that has survived the outcome of the Old Story, you are, I hope, in a position to live a different and better story, and are more than ready to embrace a New Story, if only such a prospect were available to you. And this is where I am hoping to be of some use to you: to offer you some conceptual tools that are not likely to be available to you otherwise. And since we are on the subject of moral behavior within a moral Universe, let's look a little deeper into that issue.

CHAPTER 21

FAILING MORALLY

I KNOW OF only three basic approaches to morality. The one that has been around the longest looks to Nature itself for direction in how the human should live. There have been variations on this view, ranging from the animism of hunter-gatherers, to the shamanism of tribal peoples, to the Taoism of the historical Far East. Then, some four thousand years ago, a monotheistic religion arose in the West, which declared that all morality was decreed by a male god-figure in the sky, and that the Laws of Morality were codified on clay tablets miraculously delivered to the Earth, to be discovered by a special chosen people. This was the doctrine of Judaism, which was later picked up by the Christians and declared to be Universal Law, with the injunction to spread this Law, and this religion, all over the world. Some fifteen or sixteen hundred years later, with the rise of the Scientific Revolution, a wholly different doctrine of morality would begin to take shape. Among scientific materialists, morality would come to be seen as a strictly human invention. Morality might well have social benefits-- they would say--providing some basis for a social contract, perhaps, but had no relevance or validity beyond this limited, and somewhat arbitrary, application.

The better to understand and sort out this muddle, it is instructive to view it in historical perspective: to see how one thing led to another led to another: how the egalitarian spirituality of animism, which located meaning and morality in the spirit-filled Earth, was transformed into a monotheistic religion which put the human at the center of everything, subject to the directives of a distant all-powerful patriarch, while the Earth itself was demoted to lowest possible statues within this rising new hierarchy. With its roots in the Agricultural Revolution, this cosmological and ontological reversal of an ancient understanding of the world took several millennia to fully develop and become codified, but in its effects it has proved to be a cognitive and ideological revolution on a scale never seen before or since. This revolution--which has never been given its proper name—was a usurpation of Power on the most grandiose scale imaginable. At the heart of this revolution was the dual claim that the human was separate from Nature and that the Earth was the sole property of human beings. In place of Sacred Earth we now had Empire Earth—and when enough people came to take this proposition seriously, and commit themselves to its assumptions, the Revolution of Empire Earth was on its way.

This is the historical context in which another, but lesser, revolution was to take place: The Scientific Revolution. And here again it is important to understand the historical situation when Establishment Religion and Establishment Science divided the world between them, in a Power-sharing compact that still informs, and shakes, the world today. In essence, the deal was: The Church would take the 'soft' and less visible side of things: the spirit, the emotions, the soul, along with all the doctrines that attach to their sacred text. Science would deal with the physical and material: those things that could be weighed, measured, and computed. That wholeness does not divide itself so neatly into discrete categories of mind and body, matter and spirit, did not seem immediately troubling to either side of this grand bargain. One reason for this has to do with our Western philosophical tradition, in which (Platonic) Dualism and (materialistic) Atomism had been at loggerheads for two millennia and more. Christianity had long allied itself with the two-different-worlds view of Plato, replacing Plato's world of perfect 'forms' with its (distant) Christian Heaven. The Earth, in both Christianity and Platonic thought, remains as a flawed, and rather despised, lesser realm.

Atomism is monistic and materialistic, and is philosophically irreconcilable with dualism. It is also reductionist, and sees things in terms of their smallest constituent parts—long thought to be the atom. Working within the reductionist-materialist cognitive framework that Science inherited as their part of the bargain, it is not surprising that they came up with the explaining story they did. The world as they saw it through their materialist lens, had no mind, no spirit, no creator, and thus it came to seem that it had no meaning or purpose, either. Instead, at least among the more extreme materialists, the Universe and the Earth would come to be understood as random, meaningless, and indifferent to humans, with the Laws of Life cruelly set up as all against all in pitiless competition for survival. This view, I should point out, has not been derived scientifically, but is instead a bedrock assumption taken for granted and passed on from one generation of scientists to another, as unquestioned, and unquestionable, doctrine. With such a nihilistic worldview it is little wonder that morality is seen by Science as a wholly human construction-- something we pretty much make up as we go along.

When Science parted ways with Religion four or five

hundred years ago, they did not start fresh with a brand-new set of underlying assumptions. Instead, Science embraced the entirety of our long cultural tradition, going back to the beginnings of agriculture. What they did, by way of distinguishing themselves from Religion, was embrace one school of Greek philosophy over another (Atomism over Dualism), making that the basis for their inquiry into Nature, and also the basis of their worldview. That is, Science is nothing more than a schism within the Revolution of Empire Earth. In both the religious and the scientific paradigms, the human being is still at the center of everything; none of the other animals, fungi, or plants has status of any importance, except in how they serve the human being. And the desacralized Earth remains as nothing more than a storehouse of resources, a waste dump, and a Power to be outdone and overcome. The Community of Life is not recognized as an interdependent, holonic community which far exceeds the sum of its parts. Nor is the self-organizing, life-nurturing Earth itself recognized as anything but an indifferent machine. Stuck in a scientific model where organism is simplified to mechanism, and complex, non-linear systems are reduced to a cartoon version of their relational intricacy, it is perhaps not surprising that Science has so little to offer in the area of morality.

It is true that there was once an ecologist who was also a moralist of Nature, and here is an example of his thinking: 'A thing is right,' he said,' when it tends to preserve the integrity, stability, and beauty of the biotic community. It is wrong when it tends otherwise.' Aldo Leopold was an unusual man, and a brave one, because thinking in whole systems like this very much went against the grain of the scientific community of his own day-- and it still does. In fact, this kind of thinking is much more allied with the Indigenous Worldview than with that of the West. His Land Ethic is very similar to that of indigenous people: it 'simply enlarges the boundaries of the community to include soils, waters, plants, and animals, or collectively: the land.' Within our culture, such talk is worse than heresy; it is counter-revolutionary, as it would topple the human from his lofty throne and invite him to transform himself 'from conqueror of the land community to plain member and citizen of it.' An Earth-centered and system-centered Land Ethic 'implies respect for his fellow members, and also respect for the community as such.' Schooled to see the world through the prism of the isolated individual, neither scientists, nor anyone else, is encouraged to notice the kinds of relationships that are implied by the word: 'community.'

The best our most up-to-date science can do is notice, and quantify, whether or not certain moral strictures serve some practical purpose in the real world. They can say that treating cows as sacred in a country like India has particular practical results—which they can demonstrate with graphs and charts. But it is not theirs to comment on this practice as moral doctrine.

Moral doctrine is supposedly the province of Religion—and certainly Establishment Religion claims morality as its own—but their vision of what morality is, is truncated and foreshortened by their myopic and narcissistic anthropocentrism. That is to say, when you look at something like the Ten Commandments you see that it has only to do with how people relate to their jealous god, or how they relate to one another. Nowhere do you find any injunctions about how to relate to the Earth, or to the other creatures of the Earth. Nor is this simply an oversight; instead, it follows quite logically from the Big Lie of Separation and the cultural and philosophical revolution of Empire Earth. If everything is about people, and people only, then it follows that morality can only be about people, too. The thinking is circular, solipsistic, and tautological, but few have seemed to notice just how much has been left out of what passes for morality—namely, the more-than-human world. Having no cultural taboos against destroying other life forms and taking their habitat for our own, and, with no prohibitions against tearing apart the living Earth, paving it over, and choking it on our poisonous wastes, we have systematically committed acts for which our language has no name—and no shame.

We have lately had to invent our own words to describe what are essentially crimes against Nature—words like ecocide or omnicide—but these do not begin to cover the multitude of sins that the Church itself does not acknowledge as wrong. We can speak of the human extirpation of species—which is ongoing at about the rate of 200 species a day—but we have no terminology for this offense. When you kill a king you call it regicide; when you kill off an entire species, you are left speechless, at a loss for words. You can try coining a clumsy word like species-o-cide or planet-o-cide, and someone might have a vague idea what you mean, but the fact is, we have in our culture no prohibitions against depleting the species of the Earth, or against so degrading the Earth that it will no longer support Life. With no such cultural taboos--deeply understood and felt by all--mere neologisms carry little weight.

It is difficult to believe that a dominant culture like ours could live in the world for thousands of years and remain so oblivious to the world that has given us our lives. But this is what we have done: we have built a false world inside the real world, and all we have seen is the one of our own making. The voice of Aldo Leopold is, to my mind, a voice of sanity in a world gone mad, speaking simple, obvious truth: 'A thing is right when it tends to preserve the integrity, stability, and beauty of the biotic community. It is wrong when it tends otherwise.' Integrity and stability are qualities that might be rendered in some measurable form, and may thus seem appropriate to the concerns of the scientifically trained ecologist. But what about this quality of beauty: How does that figure in? I think it is first and foremost a human response to the self-willed and spontaneous beauty of the natural world; not just the sunsets and the grand views, but the aesthetic way in which Nature organizes itself, at all scales: from the microscopic to the telescopic to the everyday. Moreover, beauty does not just exist for its own sake, but is a talisman and marker for something else: and that is system health. In the world of Nature, when something looks good to the eye, it is probably because balance and symmetry manifest themselves from the inside out. Beauty and system-health go together, and whether that system is an organism, an ecosystem, or a planet's biosphere, it is a pretty good guess that when natural beauty has been replaced by its opposite something is amiss.

Western Religion and Western Science fail us morally because they are obsessively human-centered, and made accordingly blind to the larger context of our lives-- blind especially to the health and beauty of the complex systems that make our lives, and all Life, possible. A system of morals that does not recognize biotic systems, and our dependence upon them, is worse than dysfunctional: it is suicidal—along with also being ecocidal, species-o-cidal, and planet-o-cidal. And this is moral failure on the grandest scale imaginable. What is needed in place of our myopic human-centered ethical shortfall is, of course, an Earth-centered moral system that recognizes our dependence upon everything else for our survival. And it is not like we would have to start from scratch to arrive at such a system. Our wild ancestors (and indigenous people alive in the world today) understood (and understand) the relationship between the human and the rest of the living world. They understood (and understand) that all systems, at all levels, are mutually interdependent, and rely upon reciprocity to go on working at their optimum best. These systems require something of us, and we owe them a moral debt, for giving us precious Life. We are born into the world with responsibilities to the Whole, and any morality that fails to recognize this basic truth has failed us and the Life System at one and the same time. This, it turns out, is the price of living the Big Lie. We are not Separate from everything else, and we never could be. All flourishing is mutual, and any morality that does not stand on this truth is a sham.

CHAPTER 22

THE FOUNDATION OF A NEW STORY

I HAVE TRIED to demonstrate to you why the moral system of Western Civilization has failed us, with the clear implication that it would also fail you. Not recognizing the true context of our lives, neither science nor religion, nor any of our other cultural institutions, offers useful guidance about how we should live as beings integrated into the larger whole of the Earth Community. What should be our attitude toward the skies, the seas, the rivers, the Earth beneath our feet? How should we behave toward these, as well as all the living beings we share this planet with-- all of which make up the Whole of which we are merely a part? Our self-absorbed culture has not asked these questions, but other cultures have. And I would suggest that anyone who wants to go on living on a living planet will necessarily have to ask these kinds of questions, and also come up with some serviceable answers.

What I believe you need in place of a list of human-centered prohibitions that tells you what not to do to other humans, is a set of Earth-centered positive guidelines that you can use in your everyday life. At least I know that when I was a young person I felt the need for something like this, and it just wasn't there. It seems to me, looking back, that by the time I was ten or so I had a well-developed conscience and enough of a sense of self to want to be a good and virtuous person. Unconsciously, I had some inkling that the people around me, as carriers of our culture, should be able to help me sort out what was, and was not, permissible in the more-than-human world. But where I expected something there was nothing, so I was forced to make up my own rules as I went along, by trial and error. Only very recently have I come across what I was looking for so long ago, and I hope it is something you can make use of. I'll call them the Ten Precepts:

1. The Earth is our mother; care for her.
2. Honor all your relations.
3. Open your heart and soul to the Great Spirit.
4. Life is sacred; treat all beings with respect.
5. Take from the Earth what is needed and nothing more.
6. Do what needs to be done for the good of all.
7. Give constant thanks to the Great Spirit for each new day.
8. Speak the truth; but only of the good in others.
9. Follow the rhythms of nature; rise and retire with the sun.
10. Enjoy life's journey but leave no tracks.

This is precisely what I was looking for as a youngster, but nothing like this was available to me then. Why? Because of the culture I come from. Certain people of my culture might be able to endorse some of these precepts as making good moral sense. Some might say that, yes, we should live like this, but they would be in the minority. Of course these Ten Precepts did not arise from our culture, and indeed they derive from a worldview mostly foreign to our own: that of the Americans who lived here before we Euro-Americans arrived, and who, though marginalized and partly subsumed by the new America, still retain this much wisdom to live by.

The moral vision behind these Principles is perfectly consistent with the Law of Holonic Reciprocity. If everything is connected to everything else in a far-reaching web of interdependencies, then anything we do will have an effect on the whole. If the Earth is our mother, it makes moral sense to care for her—out of gratitude, yes, but also because anything we do to her we do to ourselves.

What does it mean to honor all out relations? Partly it means just what the fourth precept states: "All life is sacred; treat all beings with respect." Honoring all our relations also means recognizing our kinship and our common destiny. This is even more profoundly true of those relations on whom we rely for sustenance. If we don't take care of them—whether salmon, or deer, or the acorn oak--they won't be able to take care of us. That's another good reason to "Take from the Earth what is needed and nothing more." In that way we won't disrupt or destroy the source of all abundance.

Live lightly on the land, or, "Enjoy life's journey but leave no tracks." The subtext would seem to be that human happiness is to be found in relationship—to the Great Spirit, to fellow humans, and to all our relations—and not in things material. (I personally would take this to include all self-aggrandizing monuments, including cities and their Earth-defacing industries.)

"Give constant thanks to the Great Spirit for each new day." Feeling gratitude and recognizing how sublimely lucky we are to be alive in such a world is a step in the direction of happiness, as is opening one's "heart and soul to the Great Spirit." When you open up in this way, you bring into consciousness an awareness of the larger Self, the Whole, and in so doing you may override the narrow and petty interests of the smaller self, and this is good for your spiritual life, your character, and the larger enterprise of life.

These precepts address not just outward behavior, but the interior state of the individual. Nor, would it seem, is a priestly class required to mediate between the individual and the Great Spirit, or to interpret words in a book. In this tradition, each individual can and should have his or her own relationship to the visible and invisible world. One's peers may be there to offer support, or notice egregious shortfalls, and the tribal individual will likely also have group observances and rituals for purposes of purification and to deepen connections with the spirit world. But in general these Principles toward a Moral Life do not require much explication or elaboration. The important thing is to keep them daily in mind and do one's best to live by them.

Of all these simple but essential Rules, one stands out as having special profundity, and indeed as being an articulate expression of the Law of Holonic Reciprocity. "Do what needs to be done for the good of all." Although very general, and presented in a soft way, this precept asks quite a lot of each of us, including some serious soul searching. For instance, the "all" whose good must be considered can have implications at several holonic levels at once. If you happen at a given time to be part of a group of three, and a moral decision must be made, do what's best for all three, and not just for yourself. That seems pretty straightforward, but what if what's good for the three causes harm or loss to the larger community? This must be factored into any moral decision as well. And one's moral responsibility doesn't end with the human community, but radiates out to the entire Community of Life, and to all the systems that support and make life possible.

Say you've had a very successful day at the river: you and

your two companions have caught more salmon than can easily be carried back to camp in one trip. Those back at camp will welcome every fish you've caught, but you're so tired from the day's fishing that two trips seem out of the question. Should you carry all you can and leave the rest to rot? Should you try to work a deal with your fellow fishermen where they have to come back but you don't? A moral decision is required of you. On what basis will you arrive at an answer?

I can easily picture myself in this situation, because I am a fisherman and have had similar ethical dilemmas. Putting myself in the place of one of these young fisherman, I would know that we should have anticipated our present problem, and quit fishing sooner than we did. But we were having too much fun and none of us wanted to quit. Now, though, we had all these fish to deal with. It's not altogether clear that we have violated the Rule that says not to take more than is needed—not yet, anyway—because, once back in camp, all these fish would be used. Then I recall that all life is sacred, and that we must treat all beings with respect. Leaving fish to rot, or throwing them back in the river, would clearly violate this Law of Life. From what I've heard from the elders, there'd be a very good chance that my people's fishing would soon turn sour if we did such a thing. The salmon spirits would be that angry with us. Maybe there will be someone back in camp who can come for the rest of the fish. If not, then I'm going to have to do it myself, no matter how tired I might be feeling—knowing that I was doing what needed to be done for the good of all.

In this instance, knowing what needed to be done was not that complicated: choices were informed by considering several of the Rules of Life, weighing them against each other, and in combination. In other circumstances, arriving at the best course of action might require considerable deliberation among the group as a whole, and much could depend on the collective knowledge base accumulated over time. The experience of the elders could prove important, as might certain of the old stories. The charge to "Do what needs to be done for the good of all" implies a rather comprehensive understanding of what might be included in that "all"—that is, an understanding of the relationships among several holonic levels, and how an action at one level might affect other levels, including the overall well-being of the Whole.

Among people who have lived in one place for thousands of years, or even for hundreds, a long-term knowledge base accrues about how their particular ecosystem works, and the various cycles their ancestors have observed. This knowledge, and all knowledge specific to place, helps to inform better decision making about how best to live in harmony with one's chosen place, and doing what needs to be done for the good of all.

Take, for example, a group of fish-dependent people who decides to place a limit upon themselves in regards to their fishing. Maybe at some point in the past they failed to show restraint in their fish taking, and so severely depleted a particular run that salmon were in short supply for years afterward. Recognizing that they had taken more than they needed for subsistence, thereby breaking one of the Rules for Life, a group decision was made to limit their take. They would do this by allowing a certain number of days to pass from the sighting of the first spring salmon in their part of the river, and would not begin fishing for them until the appointed time. As is the case with many such moral decisions, by following the imperatives of their moral code, and showing restraint—treat all beings with respect; take no more than you need—they are actually serving their own best long-term interests.

Why should that so consistently be the case? Because everything is connected. What you do to any holon or system upon which you yourself depend, you do to yourself. And the more deeply you look into the matter, the more clearly you see that there is no holonic level or system from which you are absolutely independent. And, again, that's because everything is connected to everything else.

Lacking these simple Principles toward a Good and Moral Life, the dominant culture of our world has managed to deplete fisheries all over the globe, and driven many species to extinction. No one believes this is a good thing, yet we go on doing it. Whatever guidance we've taken from our moral codes has clearly been insufficient to the task. I would suggest that this is because those codes come from a time and place that failed to recognize the holonic nature of our lives and our world. Instead of seeing the Oneness, and all the implications of that Oneness, their worldview seems to have been a muddled conflation of atomism and dualism. From atomism came the idea that everything was made up individual material particles, and that every whole (or holon) could be broken down into individual component parts, and could be understood in terms of those parts. The hyper individualism seen in Western societies, and made into a veritable Cult of the Individual here in America, has its roots in atomism.

Dualism posits that there are actually two worlds instead of one. As handed down to us by way of Plato and his theory of Forms or Ideals, we are asked to believe that the world we live in is a flawed copy of a second world where everything is perfect. This other, perfect world is evidently far away, and its perfections unattainable in this one. Following Plato and his precursors, the Abrahamic religions elaborated upon this dualism and asked of their followers that they concentrate their best hopes on an after-life, in "a better world." Whatever unity there might be between Heaven and Earth was something only understood by God.

Between the two of them, atomism and dualism have been

the underlying foundations of Western thought for three millennia, and have informed both our religions and our science. Our worldview, confused as it is, derives from this amalgam of incompatible notions about who we are and the nature of the world we live in. At a theoretical level, neither atomism nor dualism is totally absurd or without merit. It's just that neither, separately, accurately describes the world we actually inhabit, and, taken together, they've created a moral monster, as our ravaged planet clearly demonstrates. We've known no restraint when it comes to taking from the Earth far more than any of us has needed, and certainly it can't be said that we've left no tracks behind. We've scarred and marred every inch of the Earth that we and our machines could get to, and we're not done yet. And we won't be until we change our view of the world, and our place in it.

Conceptually, the Law of Holonic Reciprocity is easy to grasp—and, I would suggest, it *feels* intuitively right. Once you understand that everything is connected to everything else, one holonic level nested within another within another, all the way up and all the way down, you recognize that a moral order is implicit in the Oneness of All. It's very much as Aldo Leopold has observed: "A thing is right when it tends to preserve the integrity, stability and beauty of the biotic community. It is wrong when it tends otherwise." The charge for the human being is identical to what is required of every other holon within the holarchy: to make a positive contribution to the health and wellbeing of the whole, to keep the entire enterprise going at its optimum best. That's it, it's that simple!

But wait. We're still hung up on atomism and dualism, our unconscious minds committed to the old worldview that isn't working. It isn't working, in part, because we've forgotten that the Earth is our Mother, our sacred mother, and that it is our charge to care for her. Dualism has made this possible by removing all sacredness from the Earth and locating it in some far-away place given the name of Heaven. That's just so wrong! So perverse! Heaven was right here all along, all around us on this beautiful Earth. We've been turning it into a hellacious mess because we've been made blind to where we are, and who we are, by an ideology—an ideology based on dualism. This ideology, whose roots go back to the other side of the Dark Ages, has tempted and corrupted us into believing we could do anything to the Earth that we chose to do, because we were as gods. We had dominion over it all. If we brought loss and harm in our wake, it really didn't matter. Our true home was somewhere else, out there among the stars. We humans-- the anointed, the blessed, the chosen—didn't need to concern ourselves with all the other creatures of this planet, or any of the systems that support life here. This was just our temporary home, anyway, and if we left it a little worse for wear--so what! We're the stars of the show, the ones with souls; the Earth is just a stage-set in our drama, and all the other beings our expendable supporting cast, easily left in the dust when our time comes to rise up in glory to our true home in the sky.

It makes a nice fairytale, especially if you are a prince or princess, and can look forward to living happily ever after in luxury and splendor, the favored among all living beings. It's all about you. You're at the center of it all, just like you were at the age of six months. All things are bestowed upon you, and nothing is required in return. It's like living in extended infancy forever. Take and take and take, with never a thought to giving back. Why should you give back? What Commandment requires that of you?

Well, that's the problem. We really don't live in that kind of world. Reciprocity *is* required of us. That's what the Law of Holonic Reciprocity is all about, and it's why the Ten Precepts are infinitely more relevant to life on this planet than the

THE FOUNDATION OF A NEW STORY

faltering, foundering Ten Commandments. We don't live as atomistic beings, as islands unto ourselves; and we don't live in the lesser of two worlds. We live in the One World, and the One World is an integral part of the One Universe. We live in a holarchy of interconnectedness with everything else that is. We live in a state of interdependence—holonomy-- just as does everything else. We've been given wondrous gifts, and, in the way of gifting, it's time we give back. That's what reciprocity means: take, but also give, for the good of All.

CHAPTER 23

THE TECHNOLOGY TRAP

NOW I THINK it is time we talked about technology. This is a difficult subject, and one few can approach with detachment or anything approximating understanding—and this includes me. All I can do here is tell you what I have learned after several years of inquiry into what technology is, as well as what it does-- while at the same time admitting that my understanding is partial, if not exactly impartial. In any case, technology has played such a huge role in the life of our people--not to mention the destruction of planet Earth-- that we need to take on this issue with whatever conceptual tools we can muster.

Let me start by saying that my best hope for you is that the conditions of your life meet two critical criteria: small and simple. By small I mean that I hope that the global human population in your time is small—certainly less than a million, and maybe just a few thousand. And if you are part of a group, I hope your immediate group size is somewhere between twenty and thirty individuals—a group size that has proven itself optimal over thousands of human generations. I would also hope that you will never join a group that is larger than 150 individuals—the absolute maximum that anyone can relate to as individuated, 'known' persons. When group size exceeds these numbers, much mischief is likely to follow, as the history of our people has so tragically demonstrated.

I am linking technology to group size because, as I see it, the two go inextricably together. Many of the features of life in my own time are scale-dependent. Runaway technology and runaway overpopulation are not only connected to one another, they are also dependent upon our systems of agriculture, private property, and social stratification. These are all interconnected, interdependent complex systems, and they work together synergistically. Agriculture, which depends upon the mining and drawdown of resources—that is, living in the Theft—is a chief contributing factor to human overpopulation. And so is technology. Giant earth-moving machinery, chainsaws, feller-bunchers, tractor-combines, and myriad other human inventions have made the over-exploitation of Earth's resources a matter of simple routine-- all fed by cheap and accessible fossil fuels. Working together synergistically, technology and agriculture have allowed the human species to overrun all the other species in the Community of Life, stealing their habitat and making it our own, thereby disastrously throwing off the balance of Nature, and endangering the entire Gaian Life System.

In the face of such runaway complex systems, small and simple looks very good. But are small and simple even possible as a sustained, sustaining, and sustainable way of life? I believe most people of my own time would say that there is a kind of inevitability in the development of human technology. But I am uncertain just where this 'inevitability' comes from. Is it so organically implanted within the human character and genome that it simply cannot be denied-- or even seriously discouraged? Or might this 'inevitability' possibly be a cultural phenomenon-- or culture in combination with the imperatives of complex systems?

Technology gives rise to things, but is not a thing itself: like culture, it is a process and a system, and it has an agenda of its own, including an imperative for expansive growth. We who have been enraptured by technology like to believe that technology serves our human purposes and is therefore our subordinate, our servant. But near as I can tell, it is closer to the other way around. It controls us to a far greater extent than we have any control over it. You can point to some isolated cases where people have actually said no to a particular technology for a time, but ultimately our answer to technology is always: Yes. Yes, I'll take this, and the next thing to come along, and the next.

We have a story we tell ourselves to rationalize why we always say yes--no matter what--and that is the Story of Progress. According to this story, things just keep getting better. This belief in progress is called meliorism, and it takes many forms, but the underlying faith is that there is a tendency toward improvement built into the Universe itself. In another age, people firmly believed in moral and spiritual progress, for instance. Then the Darwinian Revolution gave us reason to believe in biological progress. What technology seems to offer us is a belief in never-ending material progress, with the corollary assumption that newer is always better. This is a cultural belief that the marketers of new products love to tap into to sell you the very latest iteration of their absolutely must-have product.

Technology is like the serpent swallowing its own tail, in that it is a complex system built upon positive feedback loops, and is self-perpetuating as long as the feedstock lasts. For a long time it looked as though the natural resources of the Earth were as infinite as the human appetite for more and more stuff, but in my time we have begun to realize that we are indeed living on a finite planet, and that our demands will soon outstrip supply. Then what? Utter ruin is what it looks like to me.

Of course there are those who believe that 'human ingenuity' will overcome the material limitations of a finite planet. I call these people either technophiles, technotopians, or, in some cases, technopimps. Certainly they suffer the narcissistic delusions of human exceptionalism that our culture is founded upon, based in the belief that humans are not only very special, and of course 'sapient,' but also not subject to the same Laws of Life that apply to all the other Earthlings. In short: magical thinkers. Or, perhaps, simply true believers in the Story of Progress—and faithful to the bitter end.

So, I believe it is still an open question whether or not the human relationship with technology is written in the stars, in our genes, or only in the cultural stories we tell ourselves about ourselves. If the latter, then there is hope for you—hope for the human potential that comes with simplicity, but is foreclosed by too much complexity.

Now, I know there are those who would say that I needn't worry about your own prospects for living in simplicity: with the legacy we are leaving you, you will have no choice other than simplicity. But I'm not so sure. Of course I recognize that we are depleting all available resources at an ever-accelerating pace, and surely we won't be leaving you any more than circumstances force us to. But unless the collapse of civilization is so complete that our material culture disappears with us, you will have something salvageable to work with. And I want to convince you that this would be a mistake-- not only for you and your generation, but for any possible future generations. I want to make you see for yourself that the human relationship with technology is pathological and fraught with bad ju-ju—certainly for All Our Relations and for Mother Earth, but also for the human soul and spirit, as well as for the human prospect.

The human being is, of all creatures, especially vulnerable to the seductions of Power. And Power is what technology promises: Power to master the world; *and* (it turns out) in so mastering, to throw its intricate ecologies lopsidedly out of balance; *and* in so doing, to endanger the entire Project of Life. Power... the seduction of Power... the habit of Power... the addiction of Power...the corruption of Power...all lead to the failure of Power...to entropy: which is the opposite of Life.

This is why I would wish you small, and simple, and humble: as small, simple, and humble, *Homo sapiens* could never-- and would never-- subject the living world to the carnage that technology and the industrial juggernaut has visited upon the living Earth. In some way, the difference between heaven and hell has something to do with scale.

Near as I can tell, there is a line that should never be crossed, because after it is crossed there seems no going back, short of some cataclysmic event (such as the collapse of global civilization). If there are human survivors of such a collapse—someone like you, for instance—this would mean a second chance to get it right, to turn things around. This line to never cross is one that was first pointed out by the twentieth century thinker, Lewis Mumford, who made the distinction between what he called democratic and authoritarian technics. Any tool, any weapon, garment, implement, or whatever, that a person can make for him or herself remains on the democratic side of the line. This might include bows, arrows, baskets, bowls, eating utensils, digging sticks, spear points, moccasins, bonnets, blankets, and so on---all of those artifacts of material culture that are basic to everyday human life, and can be made, with more or less skill, by an individual.

On the other side of the line are things that cannot be made by a single individual, but require a hierarchical social order with bosses and workers, and, commonly, natural resources not easily obtained close at hand by one person acting alone. Anything motorized or manufactured on an assembly line, for instance, or requiring the mining of either renewable or non-renewable resources, or transportation of stuff across great distances, would likely be authoritarian in nature, and therefore dangerous-- ultimately, to everything that lives.

I pretty much equate democratic technology with systems that remain on the simple side of complex; and, correspondingly, equate authoritarian technology with systems that are highly complex, and often non-linear. When I speak of complex systems, I don't mean systems that stand alone, autonomously—because nothing in the world does. It is in the nature of complex systems to be in interdependent relationship with other complex systems. That is, authoritarian technology depends upon systems of systems, all intertwined, like a ball of snakes. Thus manufacturing depends upon mining, but so too does mining depend upon manufacturing, while both depend upon a transportation and distribution infrastructure, which itself depends upon mining and manufacturing. And all these, in turn, depend upon a highly stratified social order of owners, investors, managers (upper, mid, and low-level), along with an elaborate hierarchy of white- and blue-collar workers, sweatshop slaves, and various other humans laboring in forced servitude.

Is the human being capable of staying on the simple side of complex? I don't know the answer to this. I hope that is a real possibility, because if it is not, there is no way we can continue here. Of this I am pretty certain, and I am not alone in this assessment. One thinker has said: 'we shape our tools and then our tools shape us.' Another, in the form of a poem, has noted that 'things are of the snake,' and, 'there are two laws discrete, unreconciled: one for things and one for man,' the upshot of which is that 'things are in the saddle, and ride mankind.' More recent thinkers have spoken of Progress Traps and the Vicious Circle Principle, in which scarcity leads to technological innovation, which leads to increased resource availability, leading to increased consumption, which in turn results in population growth, resource depletion, and scarcity once again.

What is for us a boom and bust Progress Trap, is for Mother Earth and her Community of Life a single errant species so out of control, so spendthrift with the lives and ecosystems of others, so improvident with the accrued riches of Earth's subterranean realms, that the entire project looks likely to crash in successive waves of ecological failure. And, of course, if it crashes humans crash with it. We have pretended that we don't need a viable Earth as a life support system, but that is a Lie.

So, again, I admonish you to keep your life as simple as you possibly can. Don't give these complex systems a chance to take it over as they have taken over ours. Give the natural world a chance to rebuild itself, to again accrue the kind of resilience it had before my culture of civilization took it upon itself to spend it all down. You will be the winner for this, and so will our species, if only you can restrain yourself and somehow beat the addiction to Power that our kind is prone to.

And one last piece of advice, based upon what I have seen of the extreme force of material culture on human life: Start over; start fresh; ideally, invent a whole different language to speak and think in. And don't get near anything left over from our ruined civilization. Treat it all like the toxic waste that it is, and isolate yourself from it—and far, far from it, if you can. And do not ever believe the lie that technology is 'neutral.'

The lie goes: technology itself is neutral; whether technology is positive or negative depends upon how people use it. Not so. Every artifact of technology comes with a program or agenda of its own. Thus, splitting the atom can be used to make bombs to kill people (not to mention all sorts of other living beings), or it can be used 'peacefully' to generate power. This assumes that generating power is an unambiguously good thing, and of course neglects to mention that there is no safe place to put spent fuel rods, and no way to cool them down without lots of water and a way to pump it. Nor does this presumptive 'good' use of nuclear power factor in all the terrible accidents that have already happened---Chernobyl, Three Mile Island, Fukashima—or all the others that will inevitably occur should industrial civilization somehow break down.

Nuclear fission is a violent process, and one over which humans have minimal--and temporary-- control. Our involvement with it has been a perilous usurpation of Power, and many of us now wish that we could somehow put the genie back in the bottle. But we cannot. It is out and about in our world now, and having its way with us. We couldn't say no to it while it was still at a safe distance from the living world (still in its bottle), and we cannot say no to it now. The Progress Trap has sprung on us again. The Vicious Circle Principle continues to hold us under its suffocating spell.

But let us look at a piece of technology that is much simpler: the ax. Or, let's look at two different axes: the stone ax and the steel ax. I am going to assume that the stone ax is a piece of democratic technics that an individual could make for himself, and will further assume that the stone ax is a rather inefficient tool for serious deforestation. I am not saying it is benign, but limited in its mischief.

Now let us look at the steel ax, which is an artifact of authoritarian technology. To make this piece of technology, iron must be mined from under the skin of the Earth and smelted under great heat and forged into the shape of an ax head. For both the stone and the steel ax a tree must be selected and felled to make a serviceable handle, unless just the right branch of a downed tree can be found. In the case of the stone ax, a person who knows his way around the woods may well have spotted just such a branch, and found it more convenient than (unnecessarily) chopping down a tree with his stone ax, whose head does not want to stay in place under heavy use.

With the much more efficient tool, the wielder of the steel ax has fewer physical constraints, and, lacking cultural constraints, is likely to fall more trees than the stone ax-man, because it is easier to do. Of course the chainsaw makes deforestation a systematic global reality in my time, but I want to stick with the ax because it demonstrates, at a very basic level, how material culture dictates human thoughts, values, and behaviors.

I recall a twentieth century anthropological study where three steel axes were introduced to a tribe of newly contacted natives. These had been an egalitarian people, but the social dynamics of this group quickly changed with this new technology. The three men who took charge of the axes suddenly became Power figures within the group, each attracting his own followers. One ax-holder seemed to feel that the ax in his charge should be put away and not used until an obvious use for it came along. But the other two developed a kind of rivalry in which there was competition to attract followers away from the other. Of course, both had to fall some trees to demonstrate their new power. But then there was the question of what to do with all these fallen trees. One of the ax-holders came up with the idea of building a structure in one of their seasonal camps, and there were some who agreed this was a good idea. As the ax-holder, and self-styled architect of this new project, this individual seized this new Power to direct others in the construction of this new building. As it turned out, many more trees needed to be felled to complete this project—too many trees, according to some in the group, who were afraid that the animals they hunted would leave the area in protest at losing their forest. This battle over the trees led to much internal conflict, and finally to the social disintegration of this particular group.

What I want you to especially notice is how very 'un-neutral' this technology was within this group. The material culture—what one anthropologist refers to as 'infrastructure'—is much less the *result* of the group's values and behaviors than it is a *driver* of how the people live their lives. Given time, group behavior leads to the stories and values that rationalize and make sense of what it does. However counterintuitive it may seem, technology doesn't follow; it leads. In fact, it can be argued that it downright determines the way people behave and believe.

I am hoping it is possible that you can beat the Technology Trap, though this is far from a certainty. I want to believe that seeing the trap for what it is will give you an edge that my people never knew. We were seduced by the Power it offered and failed to notice how it took over our lives, and made us a party to its agenda—an ever-expanding agenda with an unhappy ending for Life. My hope for you and your own people is that you will have evolved a culture, based on the human near-death experience, that is determined to live within the means that the Earth freely offers to you, and will know better than to take more than the Earth can afford to give. You must know this as a foundational principle of your own, and the races', survival—and act accordingly.

I know that culture can be, and is, a powerful force in human life. I just hope it can take on, and overcome, the temptations of Power that the complex systems of agriculture, private property, hierarchy, and technology—in synergistic combination-- seem to offer. Each and all of these have been fully enshrined in my own people's culture, and turned into revered cultural institutions. So, in a sense, it is culture against culture: one (mine) consuming its life support system to feed its runaway gigantism, but looking at the moment like an unbeatable Goliath; the other but a simple stripling youth, but-- one would hope-- with the backing of a rebounding Community of Life and a smiling Mother Earth.

Can simplicity ever win out over complexity, and continue to hold the advantage? I hope that you and your people are able to answer this in the affirmative. Pretty much everything that values, affirms, and nurtures Life, depends upon it.

CHAPTER 24

EDUCATION IN CULTURE

GETTING AN EDUCATION was once a straightforward proposition: you spent time in the company of skilled and knowledgeable people—an uncle, a grandmother, or some other member of your small band—and, by paying attention and applying yourself, you developed these knowledge-based skills as your own. This is education at the human scale, dependent upon close personal relationships with others and also upon a deepening relationship with place. Knowing where to find the best basketry, arrow shaft, or cordage materials was as much a part of life and learning as how to fashion these into useful implements and tools. Likewise, learning the lore of the hunt and the hunting ground, or where and when to find the preferred edible and medicinal plants, was ultimately a matter of individual and group survival. So, too, in its way, was learning the stories and traditions of one's people, engaging in ritual activities, and never forgetting the wisdom of the ancestors. This has been the way of teaching and learning for as long as we have had language and walked on two legs--or was for as long as we made our living directly from the natural bounty of the land, as mobile hunter-foragers.

This may again be the way of education in the human future, and I very much hope that it is. But I don't expect the journey to that place to be a painless or easy one, because of our present trajectory and where it is likely to lead. I worry that when our present civilization fails, whoever of us is left will fall into barbarism. All civilizations eventually fail, and when they do they tend to fall into a Dark Age of intractable ignorance and violence. Within the context of failed institutions, the highly educated are likely to be scorned as individuals and denigrated as a type. In any case, the complex economic and social institutions that once supported higher levels of education will no longer be functional. It may even be that books themselves will fall upon hard times, and feed the bonfires of a devolved social order.

It is impossible to know exactly how things will play out, or at what stage in civilization's fall you will appear on the scene— if at all. There are so many sound reasons for me to doubt that this 'message in a bottle' will ever wash up on just the right shore and be found by the one person it is intended for. And sometimes I feel foolish for even attempting to communicate across time in this way, with so much potential chaos intervening between my life and yours. Yet, I am convinced that I have experienced a unique phase in our history, when a generation or two of ordinary middle-class young people were given an unprecedented educational opportunity, never seen before, and never to be seen again. So, I don't know how you will be able to use this offering on the subject of education (if at all) but I'm hoping this at least provides some insight into why I keep emphasizing the importance of the historical perspective, and how I came by this insistent conviction.

Among all the empires of the world, going back to ancient

Egypt, Greece, and Rome, education was reserved for the power-elite in society, though specialized training was permitted to the technocratic class who did their bidding. Ordinary citizens--who might be serfs, craftspeople, soldiers, or slaves—were offered no formal opportunities to improve their minds, and were in any case too busy in service to the overlords for any such pursuit.

A rigid class system has always gone hand-in-hand with civilization, but as a young person I had been sheltered from the harsher aspects of patriarchy, and was encouraged to believe that I lived in a democracy that was also a meritocracy. Having survived a world war, and now coming into our own as a global economic power, we Americans were on top of the world. Throughout our relatively short history, first as a colony then as a nation, we had suffered from a cultural inferiority complex. Europe and Britain had in the last centuries produced an impressive array of artists, philosophers, scientists, musicians, and statesmen, while we upstarts were busy pushing our frontiers ever westward, serving as a resource colony to our cultural betters. Now that we had won their war for them, as we liked to believe, we would show our snooty European cousins a thing or two about cultural and educational attainments. And central to this grand project was a course of study designed to instill cultural literacy into the masses, though the name it went by was unassuming enough. It was called a liberal arts education, and for a time it was available in colleges and universities all across the land.

When I arrived at my small hometown college in Ashland, Oregon, after three years in the army, I thought I wanted to be an architect, and had no idea what lay behind the phrase 'liberal arts,' or if this differed in any way from what they called general studies. By design, the first couple years of college amounts to general studies, in any case, and by doing what was expected of me I managed to sample a broad range of academic disciplines. After two years of this, I liked it so well that I resisted narrowing my focus to one particular specialty, and spent an extra two years refusing to declare my major. This is why it took me six years, and a bunch of extra credit hours, to finally get my Bachelor's Degree in English. Here I was--after eleven years of ennui and the worst sort of boredom, slogging through the public school system--now rapturously in love with learning, and never wanting it to end.

Always a generalist by disposition, a generalist's education tuned out to be an excellent fit. And that is essentially what a liberal arts education is: an exposure to as many lines of inquiry as you can fit into your years of university experience. What you discover by sampling a broad range of classes is that each academic discipline comes not only with its own standardized body of knowledge, but with a set of beliefs about that knowledge—the consensus ideology of the day. For instance, at the time when I was taking several psychology courses, with an eye to majoring in that field, it was the consensus view that the human came into the world as a blank slate to be written upon by experience. When asking the question: "is the human personality formed mostly by Nature, or by nurture," the conventional wisdom of that day was to favor nurture and dismiss inborn influences as negligible. My instinct told me that this was an unbalanced view, but my professors told me otherwise. I chose to follow my own gut intuitions and try to work out my own conclusions. I would weigh what they said--in this and in all my classes—but I would not uncritically accept academic orthodoxy just because it was the agreed upon doctrine of the day. This resolve came in the context of inner conflicts about what to believe, at a time when I was new to the academic scene and had little reason to believe that I could possibly be seeing things more clearly than these experts in the field. And yet I felt compelled to follow my gut instincts and intuitions, even in the face of the social pressures that come with dissent from the consensus view. Looking back now, with the hindsight of fifty years, I can see that my then-tentative resolve set a pattern that I would continue to follow throughout my life. I might not always be the independent critical thinker that I held up to myself as a model, as I could get caught up in fashionable thinking just like anyone else, but I had an ideal of what intellectual integrity meant, and this was the goal I would strive for.

Every department within academia carves out a particular territory which it demarcates and claims as its own. This behavior amounts to a fragmentation of knowledge, and is a function of specialization, as well as the hierarchical structure of academia itself. This entrenched authoritarian stratification in turn plays upon the psyches and egos of the academically ambitious--who patrol the boundaries of their specializations, guarding against and attacking interlopers who might intrude upon their hallowed territory. Within this context of jealously guarded departmental boundaries, what a good liberal arts education does is give you the confidence to crash these artificial borders, and, in your own mind, tear them down. Ultimately, what the liberal arts education is good for is helping you to see things whole and in context, prompting you to connect a broad range of dots over a large field, in pursuit of an ever broader and deeper understanding of the Big Picture of life in the real world.

Throughout the evolutionary history of our species we humans have always been omnivorous generalists, excelling in many areas of endeavor: our large and active brains (along with the intelligence of our hearts) reveling in our broad range of competencies. When we lived, hunted, and foraged in small egalitarian mobile bands, some might be better than others at flint-knapping, basket-making, or bringing fresh meat back to camp, but specialization was necessarily limited: by group size and lifeway, but also by a fiercely-held ethos of egalitarianism. This changed with the rise of settled agriculture, which concentrated more people into a smaller geographical area, while the revolutionary institution of private property concentrated wealth and power into the hands of the propertied few. Under these changed conditions, division of labor and social stratification was becoming the new normal. But not until the Industrial Revolution, the rise of the corporation, and assembly-line manufacturing, were masses of human beings required by the new conditions of life to foreswear their genetic heritage as generalists and become narrowly focused specialists—often performing the same mind-numbing task again and again and again, *ad nauseam*. When linear machine-logic is forced upon living organisms in this way, compelling complex, variety-loving human beings to behave as if they themselves were machines, something unhealthy happens to the human personality, manifesting in a variety of pathologies and addictions.

Blue-collar assembly-line workers who perform the same specialized task hour-by-hour, day-after-day, are prone not only to repetitive motion syndrome but to a psychological syndrome which is characterized by a generalized sense of alienation from life and other people. Known in some circles as 'alienation of the worker,' this syndrome is a condition not limited to the drudgery of mining or manufacturing jobs, but affects the white-collar worker as well. Bureaucrats, technocrats, and corporate management personnel all have roles to play within the machine-like system of their organization, roles that rarely engage the whole person, but only some narrow, specialized part of the human potential, according to the "needs" and imperatives of the system itself. Being overworked while also being under-utilized and unappreciated as a whole, multi-faceted person, leaves the typical worker feeling not only dehumanized but in some way lost to him- or her-self. This is a pathology created by the top-heavy systems that seem to be required for a mass-society like ours to function. Apologists for such soul-crushing systems—namely, those at the top who benefit financially—say there is no other way. Some aspects of the system may be regrettable, in terms of wasted human potential, but there is no better alternative. Now get back to work.

What I am hinting at here is that the billionaires, the bankers, and the corporate CEOs have a vested interest in suppressing the kind of education that encourages the asking the larger questions about how the world is now constituted, including the present distribution of wealth and power. It does not serve their purposes that anyone outside their small circle might have the ability to see things whole and in context, or dare to question the social, political, and economic order as it stands. It does serve their purposes that knowledge be fragmented, narrowly focused, and jealously guarded, as it now is in the world of academia—an institution infiltrated and deeply influenced by this same power-elite.

I mentioned above an unprecedented time in history when a high-quality liberal arts education became available to ordinary middle-class people like me. Of course I didn't realize it at the time, but it turned out that I and my generation was the beneficiary of a little blip in history when a wave of democratic idealism swept over America and made higher education for the masses seem not only highly desirable but historically inevitable. This new vision of what was possible for ordinary Americans came on the heels of World War Two, and was partly enabled by the GI Bill, which helped defray the costs of a higher education. This post-war period of the 'fifties and late 'forties was boom-times in America. While the GIs had been off fighting the war, American manufacturing concerns had gone into overdrive in support of the war effort. This heightened industrial capacity, combined with a returning workforce, fueled economic growth across all sectors of the economy, and not least of all among institutions of higher learning. Low-interest educational loans, along with the financial incentives of the GI Bill, created a surge of demand for higher education, and now academia went into overdrive, too, building capacity to meet pent-up demand.

When I entered college in the early 'sixties it was still boom-times in America and institutions of higher education all over the land were continuing to grow in both size and ambition. This was a time in our history as a people when a spirit of idealism swept over us: a time when it seemed that anything was possible and we could have it all. We had a brave and charismatic young president with a beautiful young wife, and in just the right light it did indeed look like we might be living in Camelot. Within the context of the cold war, the war in Vietnam, and ongoing skirmishes in the fight for racial equality taking place in the south, life on campus was electrically charged with a positive belief in the human possibility. We wanted peace, love, and understanding, and were convinced we could have it. Meanwhile, we were making do with sex, drugs, and rock and roll.

We thought we could change the world, and in small ways we did, but mostly the world changed us. Our starry-eyed idealism took a blow from which it never fully recovered on a November day in Dallas, 1963, when our president was shot and killed. Something went out of us then: something to do with the kind of people we were, the kind of system we lived under, and the kind of world we could make for ourselves. The idealism didn't necessarily wink out in everyone on that day, but the new world we hoped to create lost its sense of inevitability and nearness-at-hand. Maybe we could make the world a better place in our individual lives, but as a world-changing social movement, something vital (perhaps our innocence) was ripped from us on that horrific day.

As a war-baby, I was not quite of the post-war baby-boom generation myself. Being slightly older, never one to identify with large groups, anyway, and temperamentally averse to group-think in any of its manifestations, I was deeply sympathetic to this counter-cultural movement, but also skeptical that it could achieve its larger aims. That is to say, I reveled in its energy but never fully shared its faith. It was, in any case, an exciting time to be on a university campus, and my own idealism was doubtless aroused by all the good energy around me, making a positive contribution to my own education.

Setting the scene in this way, I am trying to provide you with historical context—including a sense of the *zeitgeist,* or spirit of the age--of a time when education in America was on the rise. In a small way, I am attempting to replicate one of the most valuable attributes of a generalist's liberal arts education: the historical perspective. Most academic disciplines offer the student some sort of historical overview of that discipline's development over time. I found this to be true in just about every course I took in the biological sciences, the social sciences, as well as the humanities. Even history classes offered a glimpse of the history of the writing of history. In my study of English and American literature, the provenance of any particular work, and the likely cultural and historical influences upon the author, was always considered highly relevant to understanding the work of art. Along with the particulars of history I was picking up in these various classes, I was also learning the value of the historical perspective as a way to make meaningful sense of the world.

From an early age I was taught that a vibrant democracy

depends upon an informed electorate. This belief was advanced by Thomas Jefferson and other Founding Fathers of our unprecedented American experiment in self-government. These men had fled the tyranny of European monarchy, and it was fresh in their minds as they attempted to found a new political order. As the educated elite themselves, they well knew that autocratic rule and repression of the masses had characterized the entire history of our civilization. It is true that they formed a representative republic, not a true democracy, set up to serve the interests of propertied white men of commerce. Nevertheless, this notion of a well-informed electorate has always made sense to me in the abstract, even if I have come to doubt that a democratic republic is actually the form of government we live under. (A corrupt plutocracy comes closer to our lived reality.) Nevertheless, I remain enthusiastic about the idea of democracy as an enlightened form of self-rule, and believe it to be an ideal worth working toward. Theoretical though it may be, if we ever **did** have a democracy, the best possible training for good citizenship within this power arrangement would be a broad liberal arts education. And central to this generalist's way of apprehending the world would be the historical perspective.

To understand anything beyond the immediate moment requires that we ask one central question: How did things get to be this way? We can be asking about the fourteen-billion-year history of the Universe, the four and a half billion year history of our own planet, the 3.8 billion year history of life on Earth, the five million year history of hominids, the ten thousand year history of agricultural civilization, or something with origins closer to our own time. If you don't know at least the outline of such histories, you are missing something vital to comprehending your own situation. Any area of interest, and certainly any academic discipline, inevitably comes with its own origin story and history. Knowing little or nothing about these stories is a huge deficit--and a bar to a comprehensive understanding of very much at all. The more of these stories you have some familiarity with, the larger your view. Also, the more comprehensive your sampling of origin stories and the histories of the different disciplines, the better prepared you are to cross-check and confirm consistencies across various fields, while also picking up on disparities and contradictions. You have to recognize that everyone tells their own story, and that of their chosen field, with a certain spin and from a limited point of view. They may fully intend to be honest, and what they call 'objective,' but biases, ideologies, and mistakes inevitably insinuate themselves into any telling of what is, and how it got to be this way. If you are on a quest for truth, and not satisfied with the easy answers of orthodoxy, you will make it your job to engage the living world in its wholeness, and also search out a corresponding wholeness in our human understanding of that world.

This would be the job of a certain kind of individual within a particular sort of society: one in which both the individual and the society maintained some sort of essential integrity. I have no rational reason to expect that a survivor of the fall of civilization will be anything but a broken person in a broken world, and yet I want to believe otherwise. I want this for your sake, and also for mine. I am convinced that I have something of value to pass on to the human future, and I want there to be someone there to receive and use it.

Much of what I have learned about the world I have learned from books, from decades of formal and self-directed scholarship across a broad spectrum of disciplines. Because of the biases built in to this background, I may be making some wrong assumptions about you and your situation. It is difficult to believe that a survivor of the ecological cataclysms that must come between your time and mine would have access to the kinds of books that have been so central to my own quest for truth. But maybe your quest will follow a different path, as has the truth quest of many a preliterate people, including not a few illiterate but far-seeing shamans. I am hoping that, however you achieve it, you will be seeking the large, long view.

With an eye for historical patterns, I am worried about the future descending into a dark age of barbarism: an age when the historical perspective is both unknown and unknowable. At the time I quit my doctoral program in the mid-'seventies, the liberal arts education had already lost its luster. The nation now had a glut of us, and didn't know what to do with the broad-spectrum critical thinking we brought with us to a highly specialized labor force. We were trained to be democratic philosopher-kings in an age of corporate hegemony, when employees were expected to bow to the hierarchy above them and not question whatever they were told. By the time of Reagan, in the 'eighties, the ethos of a broad, general education had fallen into disfavor among the corporate elite, and universities were charged with providing students with a much narrower, more specialized, curriculum. And this has been the direction of higher education ever since: to abandon their short-lived mission of turning out a well-educated, thoughtful citizenry, prepared to take their place within a democratic political economy, and to instead provide the market economy with well-trained (if narrow) specialists. This shift in emphasis has meant (among many things) that a wide-ranging historical perspective is now hard to come by in academia, because it is not highly valued. Nor is such a perspective easily attained on one's own, and never without an effort of long duration, impelled by a belief in its importance.

If I have managed to give you an inkling of the importance of a general education and the historical perspective, I hope it is not to leave you in vain frustration, with no way to build such a perspective of your own. Instead, I wish you all of the benefits of this wide-angle depth-of-field lens upon the world, and the chance to use it to full advantage.

CHAPTER 25

LAND MANAGEMENT FATALITY

SUPPOSE THAT SOMEONE you respected and cared about was in denial of a major chunk of reality--simply refused to see it-- and had constructed an elaborate rationale in support of their myopic half-vision. Imagine further that this individual was an influential member of the community, a teacher who was actively passing on to others this partial, and therefore inaccurate, vision of the world--and denial of anything beyond this truncated version of the world was becoming general within your community. The situation has become daily more problematic because this worldview is materially affecting everything in the larger world as well, and not in a good way. Now, if from where you stand you could see a large part of the damage being done, and could trace a cause-and-effect relationship between this particular worldview and the ever-worsening damage, wouldn't you feel compelled to say something about it?

This is quite similar to my own situation, except that it is not a lone individual within a single community that is the problem: it is the entire world that is under threat, and the worldview that is facilitating its ruin is that of scientific materialism. The criticism I bring to this view of the world is meant to be the constructive criticism of a friend: a friend to science, yes, but as more than a friend to the natural, living world, which, being much larger than a certain perspective on the world, inspires a larger loyalty.

The scientific worldview that informs much thinking today began to be formulated in the time of Newton, Bacon, and Descartes, with further details later added by Darwin, Spencer, and others. Newtonian physics inspired the metaphor of the Universe as a great machine—a metaphor that has an element of truth as well as an element of utility—but ultimately gives a false impression of the nature of the world. A machine can be simple or complex, but the machine is by its nature linear. Anything mechanical operates according to machine logic and is understandable by anyone who comprehends this logic, making the machine potentially fixable, predictable, and manipulable. All of this is excellent as long as we don't get into category confusion and start seeing organisms as machines, or confuse non-linear complex systems with the much simpler linear kind. But unfortunately we do this all the time, and the results are often disastrous. This oversimplification began with the first clearing of land for agriculture, in which a complex adaptive non-linear system (an ecosystem) was transformed into a manipulable linear system, a farmer's bare-ground field.

This act established a precedent that the agricultural people of civilization have followed ever since, and expanded into the mining of all possible resources, below-ground and above, renewable and non-renewable, to where global macro-systems are now under threat of collapse. One such non-linear macro-system is the global weather system, which is made up of myriad regional weather systems, many of which depend upon what has been called the biotic pump to keep air and water circulating. Many regional biotic pumps depend upon standing forests to keep cycling water and air currents from land to sea and back to land again. When wholesale logging leads to deforestation these regional pumps shut down, creating air stagnation and drought. When enough of these regional systems are so compromised, the Earth's entire circulatory system is in danger of collapse. Simplistic linear thinking may work in the world of manmade machines, but it does not work well in the natural world, which consists of many complex adaptive systems interacting in non-linear, externally uncontrollable, ways. For too long we have been working on a mechanistic model that vastly oversimplifies the living word—and it shows.

Machines and organisms may operate on a few of the same principles, but to believe that mechanism and organism are identical is not only wrong, but is dead-wrong. Same goes for mistaking non-linear systems, which are inherently unpredictable (except probabilistically), for their much simpler third cousin, the human-controllable linear system. This is a deadly serious cognitive error, and it is taking the world apart piece by piece, species by species, and we ourselves are not immune to its cascading consequences.

It is interesting how one cognitive error can create corollary cognitive errors. For instance, the law of cause and effect is presented under this model as a simple one to one relationship, which, in linear systems, can actually be the case. With this understanding of the way things work in the world, many a scientist and layperson has assumed, for instance, that a single genetic trait can be traced to a single gene. The early genetic work of Gregor Mendel with peas, where he selected for obvious traits like purple flower or white, wrinkled pod or smooth, made it look just this simple: one gene equals one phenotypic characteristic. But this is seldom how Nature accomplishes her wonders of complexity. More typically, one trait can be influenced by several, or dozens, of genes, just as several disparate traits can be influenced by a single gene. And influence is the right word here: the final phenotypic outcome is far from the strict determinism posited by the mechanistic model, but is instead the result of complex, non-linear interactions among different genes, and even different kinds of genes, including those that regulate gene expression. Regulatory genes customize the degrees to which various interacting phenotypic traits are expressed in the individual organism, in a highly fine-tuned way, which looks very little like the simplistic machine model of the world, or even the apparent linear simplicity of Mendel's peas. Indeed, very little is as simple or as linear as it seems, even our constant companion, the weather.

Our daily local and regional weather offer examples of complex non-linear systems that defy prediction based upon a simple one-to-one cause-and-effect relationship. This is because multiple factors are involved, and because effect is not always that easy to sort out from cause, when you have both positive and negative feedback loops interacting, chasing their own and each other's tails. Many, and perhaps most, natural systems work in just this prediction-defying way, which helps explain why so many of our attempts at 'scientific management' have produced such a range of spectacular failures.

The wolves of Yellowstone National Park offer a well-known example of 'scientific management' gone terribly wrong. Thinking in linear and mechanistic terms, park managers decided, for a variety of reasons, that it would be a good idea to rid the park of its wolves. In this they ignored one of the first principles of ecology: you can never do just one thing. And sure enough, that is how it turned out. With their top predator absent, large herds of elk lounged along the Yellowstone River, contentedly chomping down the young aspen and willows that had formerly shaded the river and kept its temperature cool and constant. With the willows gone, the beavers had no tender bark to chew on or suitable material with which to build their dams. Without beaver dams to slow the upper river's flow and create habitat for hatchling trout, and without riparian willows and aspen to protect the river from overheating, the trout population took a nosedive, as did that of the river's aquatic vertebrate and invertebrate population, in what can be seen as a cascade of ecosystem failures. Both the wolf and the beaver are keystone species, and with them gone a once-famous blue-ribbon trout stream was reduced to a bare-banked down-cutting ditch with little life left in it. With the return of the wolves, the elk could no longer comfortably hang out by the river, doing their daily damage. Allowed to grow, the riparian willows and aspen returned to serve their ecosystem function, to include providing forage and dam-building material to the beavers, who returned to fulfill their own ecosystem function. In this way, the entire Yellowstone River ecosystem mended and renewed itself—to the delight of many a fly fisherman, and even to the Park Service itself.

For twenty-two years, I was a seasonal employee of another land management agency, the U.S. Forest Service, and I got to see first-hand the results of mechanistic, linear thinking as it manifested on the ground within forest ecosystems. Or maybe I should say, what had once been natural forest ecosystems, but now were something else. A natural forest ecosystem tends to have a number of characteristics that identify it as a product of Nature, such as a variety of tree species (not just one), trees of different ages, girths, and heights, along with a diverse understory of shrubs, flowering plants, and ground cover such as feather moss. Natural stands of trees with these characteristics of biodiversity are uncommon to rare in my part of the world, which is the West side of the Cascades in central Oregon. That is because 'scientific management' has reduced the complexities of the primeval forest ecosystem to vast swaths of industrial clear-cuts, which are then replanted to a single species (Douglas fir in my region), in straight-line rows, which then grow into an even-aged, even-sized trees within a plantation that is far more vulnerable to blights, infestations, and wildfire, than is a naturally diverse forest.

Land managers and industrial logging interests like speak of the trees they 'manage' with chainsaws and feller-bunchers as a renewable resource. And it is true, up to a point, that fallen or burned forests do renew themselves, but one crucial detail is left out of this self-serving meme. Former forests can normally be counted upon to renew themselves when they have the wherewithal to do so. But when most of the remains of a forest are removed, as in clear-cutting, or salvage logging after fire, renewal becomes ever more problematic, because renewal requires something to work with. Thus, after three successive rounds of clear-cutting and tree removal--even if spaced over a century or more--there is not much left to contribute to the renewal process. In the ideal growing condition of the Pacific Northwest, and barring misfortune and stochastic events, trees may be counted upon as a 'renewable resource' for as many as three successive generations of 'harvest' and tree removal. Beyond that, there is not enough fertility left in the soil to grow a healthy forest—not least of all because the topsoil left naked after clear-cutting is blown and washed away by the winds and rain that visit this mountainous country all through fall, winter, and spring. In equatorial rainforests, soil fertility is so tenuous that land laid waste by chainsaw will likely never see forest again. Europe itself was once heavily forested, as were many other parts of the world that will never be forest again. So, to speak of forests as a 'renewable resource' is really just a cover story to disguise a practice that is best understood as mining a deplete-able resource unto exhaustion.

The long-term unsustainablity of this land management

agency's forest clearance policies is mirrored by its anti-ecological wildfire policy. Following a particularly destructive wildfire season in 1912, the Forest Service adopted a rule that said all fires must be put out by ten o'clock the following morning after a fire. This was the guideline to be followed whenever possible, but failing this ideal outcome the standard policy was that all fires are to be put out as quickly as is safely possible. This would appear to be a reasonable policy, but it makes certain assumptions that are very far from the facts on the ground. It is, first of all, a standardized policy that is meant to apply uniformly to all forest ecosystems no matter what. The rub here is that no two forest ecosystems are identical, and to pretend that they are often leads to very poor outcomes. The forest ecosystem I live in, for example, is on the west slope of the Cascade Mountains and experiences a pronounced maritime influence, which moderates both summer heat and winter cold. All forests are fire-adapted ecosystems, but each forest has its own particular fire regime. Here, with our relatively cool summers, we do have both human-caused and lightning-ignited wildfires, but these seldom grow very large. It may be that every hundred or two hundred years conditions will have been such that a fire of great severity has swept over the landscape, taking out vast swaths of forest, burning them to the ground. A stand replacement fire such as this is a nightmare scenario to anyone who lives in this mountainous forested region I call home, and the Forest Service presence here, with its large fire crews, and its put-'em-out fire policy, offers some relief from late summer jitters, when fire danger is extreme. What is difficult for any of us to comprehend—not least of all the Forest Service--is that even the most severe of stand-replacement fires serves an ecological purpose. When we put out all wildfires, no matter what, and when we do this systematically for more than a hundred years, we are imposing a human-devised system that we claim to be 'scientific' upon a complex, highly evolved system of Nature, and these two systems are often badly mismatched—somewhat like forcing a square peg into a round hole.

Another forest ecosystem with which I have some familiarity is on the Lower Klamath River in northern California. The Six Rivers National Forest is mostly steep mountainous country with a major river and a number of tributary streams running through it. For thousands of years this rugged landscape has been inhabited by three distinct tribal peoples: the Yurok, Hupa, and Karuk. Each of these peoples tended to inhabit whatever flat places they could find within the narrow strip of bottom land along their chosen river—the Trinity in the case of the Hupa, the Klamath for the Karuks and Yuroks. Having lived in this fire-adapted landscape for dozens or hundreds of human generations, these Native peoples came to a profound understanding of their home landscape—and they dealt with fire in their landscape accordingly.

The Six Rivers national Forest is not a single forest ecosystem, but more an aggregation of distinct forest ecosystems which share some commonalities, including, typically, very hot and dry conditions in late summer and early fall. These people who lived on, and from, the land were intimately familiar with every ridgeline, creek, meadow, and hollow, in their territory, and they knew it in all stages and seasons. Accordingly, they knew precisely where and when to use fire proactively, to achieve their own 'land management' goals. This included burning older patches of willow to prompt new growth for premium basketry material; post-harvest burning beneath preferred tanoak groves, to minimize parasites, and; opening up favored hunting meadows encroached upon by young saplings, by putting fire to them. And then there were the more general precautionary burns conducted ritually in mid to late fall. These were low-intensity burns, usually achieved by lighting from the top of a grade and letting it back slowly downhill. Creeping around on the forest floor, taking out no more than the lower rungs of the ladder fuels, these carefully monitored burned-over areas were not likely to attract wildfire for several years to come. In this way, the highly volatile fire regime endemic to this area was managed by a people who had every incentive to do the job right, and with serious consequences for getting it wrong.

When the Forest Service took over in this area following World War One, the one-size-fits-all wildfire policy of the parent organization was imposed, with no little force, upon this fire-prone landscape. Indians caught burning forest land in the old traditional way were rewarded with long prison sentences. And of course whatever fires could be put out, were put out, post haste. Predictably, fuel loads were allowed to build, and when wildfires did visit the area they burned fierce and hot, feeding on the accumulated fuels.

When one of these extra-hot fires got going in this steep canyon country Forest Service fire crews would be called in, very often from states with widely different topography, vegetation type, and natural fire regimes. Whatever local knowledge the fire bosses might have was knowledge of a different locality. On a really big fire, a crew and its overhead might cycle in for as long as three weeks at a stretch, which often proved to be just enough time to make some serious mistakes, but not enough time to gain useful local knowledge. And of course an Incident Commander did not have to live with the consequences of mistakes in judgment. Consequences were left for the locals to deal with.

A practice that the locals never learned to love is one called backfiring. The rationale behind backfiring makes sense on paper: if a fire is burning hot and fast and is likely to jump fire lines, what you do is light from that line, hoping that your drip-torch-lit fire will back slowly away from you and toward the oncoming conflagration, creating what is called a black line. In terms of firefighter safety, this option is generally seen as among the better choices, and it is one that a locally inexperienced fire boss is likely to go to by default. And here is where ignorance of the local topography and wind patterns, and no experience with how fire has behaved here in the past, can influence strategic decisions with long-term implications for the land itself. I know of an instance where backfires were lit from a gravel road that was two and a half to three miles from the oncoming fire. Certainly there was a convenience factor in this decision, and it would definitely have been some trouble getting firefighters closer in to the blaze to start their backfiring, but a lot of good forest land was sacrificed in the process—and the timing could hardly have been worse. In the heat of mid-afternoon, and with red flag warnings of strong east winds coming over the radio, the fire crew was ordered to light their drip-torches and create a black-line all along this mountain road. Driven by hot east winds, the back lighting soon developed a head of its own and rushed across tens of thousands of forested acres toward its counterpart. As the land between the two onrushing fires shrunk before the oncoming clash, the superheated living trees exuded their volatile aerosols then burst into explosive flame. When the two towering infernos met, they blew up into a firestorm so hot and intense its all-consuming energy filled the sky with destruction absolute.

After this fire burned itself out, and the fire crews had found their way home, it was evident to the locals--especially the Native locals--that much of what had long been forest might never be forest again. The intensity of the heat had sterilized the soil to such a depth that it would probably be centuries before anything beyond a few brave pioneer species might again inhabit this land, with a living forest a very distant prospect, indeed.

These kinds of land management failures cannot be blamed solely on 'scientific management,' but more deeply upon the assumptions which underlie such policies and practices—which ultimately takes us back to the Big Lie. The foundational assumption of the Big Lie is that everything here on Earth is for the exclusive use of humans—which, naturally, includes trees and forests. This is the reverse of an ecological understanding of how things work in the world. With the assumption that the world is all about us comes a self-referential myopia, accompanied by an attitude of indifference toward other creatures and the natural ecosystems that support them. With no loyalty to the Whole, but only to ourselves, saving trees from wildfire makes perfect (linear) sense. So, for that matter, does industrial-style clear-cut logging. What these policies and practices don't add up to is any kind of ecological sense.

Under the spell of the Big Lie, anthropocentrism, and the metaphor of the machine, so-called scientific management of land and natural resources is doomed to fail—fail, that is, if the goal of management is to conserve, or preserve, these same 'resources.' If the goal is to mine and deplete resources unto exhaustion, then scientific management is a glorious success, one which is global in scope.

The metaphor of the machine is closely allied with another doctrine within the scientific materialist paradigm, and that is reductionism—which is what I want to talk about next.

Long after had science established itself on the principles established by Newton and Descartes, certain scientific developments would bring some of these underlying assumptions into question, the emerging disciplines of ecology, chaos theory, and systems thinking.

LAND MANAGEMENT FATALITY

In principle, the primary purpose of science is to understand the natural world. For a few, understanding, for its own sake, is enough, and more than can ever be attained in a lifetime of seeking answers. A burning curiosity, and its occasional satisfaction, is what mostly drives inquiry this level of scientific practice. This approach has sometimes gone by the name of pure science, but science has rarely been pure and is vanishingly rare today. The motive force behind most science, today or ever, has been to know Nature in order to control it, to have power and mastery over the living world, including other humans, and to convert Nature into prosperity for some (humans) and wealth for an elite few.

CHAPTER 26

THE SCIENCE-NATURE SEPARATION

REDUCTIONISM IS BASED on the notion that the whole equals the sum of its parts, and that the whole can be understood if each part is carefully scrutinized. But there is a problem with this approach and the premise it is based on, because the whole is always larger than the sum of its parts. What is left out of this atomistic supposition is the way the parts are organized—and this is no small matter—as well as the various relationships among the parts, which are also vital to understanding the whole. Reductionism has had some utilitarian success in the world, or it would have been abandoned long before now. Sometimes it is exactly the right tool to use, but its uses are specific and limited. Unfortunately, reductionism has escaped the hallowed halls of science and entered society at large, becoming the all-purpose saw-wrench-hammer wonder-tool in the minds of the general populace, and is used indiscriminately as **the** way to frame and understand the world. Reductionism also has the psychological appeal of making the complex seem simple, the unfathomable fully comprehensible.

The essential problem with reductionism is that it focuses

THE SCIENCE-NATURE SEPARATION

full attention on one particular aspect of something while ignoring the larger context of the whole. I think my first awareness of this problem came when I was an undergraduate and my genetics professor told the class that, in terms of biology, we humans (or any other animal) became redundant once we had mated and passed on our genome to the next generation. An individual human might live for five or more decades afterwards, but as far as biology was concerned all that followed the act of reproduction was irrelevant. At the time, such a notion seemed absurd to me, but only because I reckoned that human life in general, and my life in particular, had many other meanings besides the single one I was hearing about now. And of course an immediate objection was: what about this new genetic event that has been brought to life? Who but its parents are going to nurture this unique genome in the form of a child for the next twenty years or so? Surely that care and nurturing is part of biology too.

I recognized immediately that science, in this instance, was suffering from some kind of a vision problem, and wasn't seeing things whole, but I didn't then comprehend that this distorting myopia was rooted in ideology—that is, in a belief system that was itself not scientifically derived. I don't recall my professor talking much about the selfish gene, a notion advanced by Richard Dawkins in a book by that title, but this is the source of the biological orthodoxy that, in the long evolutionary view, human significance begins and ends with its role as carrier of genetic material that gets passed on. For me, this is the tail wagging the dog, but then I am not a true believer in the ideological orthodoxies that underlie, and would seem to support, this waggishly disconcerting hypothesis.

These orthodoxies of scientific materialism include the following beliefs: that the Universe and Life on Earth are the result of random chance functioning over long time; that the

Universe is indifferent or hostile to Life on Earth, including human life; that life on Earth is best characterized as a struggle for survival in a bloody competition of all against all; that the province of science is matter, and that matter is essentially inert, and is without any of the qualities that we ourselves possess, such as sentience, intelligence, selfhood, and volition; that if something cannot be weighed, measured, or computed, it falls outside the province of science; that spirit or spirituality have no measurable dimension and therefore are assumed not to exist; that the Universe is in no way goal-directed—it has no intention, aim, or purpose, and thus human life itself has no meaning or significance, except what we might invent for ourselves.

Add up all these doctrines and what you get is the philosophy of existential nihilism, and its corollary, the anomie of meaninglessness. All that exists is assumed to be full of sound and fury, but signifying nothing. Trouble is, this is nothing like the world I see around me. Nor has this view of the world been confirmed by the scientific method, but is instead an a priori assumption with roots in the accidents of history: indeed, in the messy and bitter divorce that took place between Religion and Science back in the so-called Age of Reason. In passionate reaction against Establishment Religion, with its proprietary claim to the spiritual and moral realm, Science has not only foresworn those realms but has come to deny their very existence—based on little more than a defiant will to disbelief.

I want to be clear here. I am not siding with the 'revealed truths' of religion. Not at all. Instead, I am suggesting that there is more than just these two possible ways to see and make sense of the world, ways that do not necessarily share the common assumptions of Religion and Science, which both spring from the same cultural tradition, and are based on the same deep myths about the nature of reality and the

THE SCIENCE-NATURE SEPARATION

human's place within it. Central among these myths (myth in the anthropological sense) is a near-fanatical anthropocentrism, which places the human being at the narcissistic center of everything, while maintaining a dismissive indifference to all other living creatures, except in how they can serve the pleasure of us all-important humans.

I see Religion and Science as like branches on a tree, branches pointing in distinctly different directions, but sharing a common trunk, and beneath that trunk a shared subterranean root system.

Really, how could it be otherwise when Western Science and Western Religion arise from the same civilization, the same troubled history, and the same deep culture? Science and Religion are certainly at odds with one another, seeing some things in diametrically opposed ways. They are in a power struggle over the hearts and minds of the people, and it looks as though the newer narrative may be winning more converts than the archaic one, but this fight is still going on. Amazingly, some people accept both of the competing narratives as true, and somehow live with the irreconcilable contradictions--which can invite quite the muddle. Others can be hotly militant in their partisanship for their chosen worldview and fiercely hostile in their rejection of its counterpart. I am not in the least denying the antipathy that can exist between these two schools of thought—both intellectual and emotional. All I am saying is that both traditions are rooted in a common set of beliefs about the world—a common cultural mythology—and to the extent that these foundational beliefs are pathological or dysfunctional, both science and religion suffer the same unwell condition.

The extreme anthropocentrism that characterizes the mindset, perceptions, and values of the civilized peoples of the world does not stand alone, but is part of a larger complex of cultural myths and memes that, taken together, form a complex belief system. For instance, the conviction that the human being is the smartest, most capable, and most deserving of all Earth's creatures—that we are in all ways exceptional--is very much tied up with the bedrock belief that the human is separate from the Earth's Community of Life and from the Earth itself. This deeply influential foundational belief--that the Earth and all its life forms are subordinate to the human, and have no value in themselves, but only in how they can serve the human drive for comfort, riches, power, and domination--is a core principle that feeds, and is fed by, anthropocentrism.

Religion sees the human as the special creation and darling of deity, while science sees *Homo sapiens* as the pinnacle of evolution. In either case, it is all about us very special humans. According to one narrative, we have been chosen to take dominion over all the beasts of the Earth, the birds of the air, and the fish of the sea, and use them as we see fit, in this temporary dwelling place that is not our true home. According to the Christian-inspired Great Chain of Being, the human ranks just below god and the angles, but towers far above all the other creatures of Earth, who are seen as Other, and with whom we share no kinship. The human, in this view, is an isolate, an anomaly: a cosmic orphan far from Home. Within this rigid hierarchy, the Earth is the lowest of the low, contemptible in all ways except as a stockpile of resources. Within this narrative, anthropocentrism, human exceptionalism, and man's separation from Nature combine to produce a set of beliefs about the human's place in the world as well as about the Earth and its Community of Life: we are the misfit Master, and its sole purpose is to serve our ends. When science came on the scene just a few hundred years ago this belief system had been deeply entrenched in Western culture for millennia, and was taken for granted to be the self-evident way of the

THE SCIENCE-NATURE SEPARATION

world. Not surprisingly, science went about building its own edifice upon this highly questionable, self-important, foundation-- and to the extent that this faulty tradition informs and infiltrates the thinking of the larger culture, and specifically the sub-culture of science, to that extent the presumptions of science, including many of its treasured doctrines, are, at the very least, suspect.

One such treasured doctrine is the belief that everything in Nature is knowable by humans, and that science is the single viable path to this knowledge. But knowledge for its own sake is not enough: being the master-species that we are, and above Nature, it is our destiny to use this knowledge to 'manage' and manipulate the natural world and to subject it to our will and absolute control. The necessary corollary to this doctrine is a passionate embrace of technology, for technology is science materially manifested in the world, and the means by which we dominate the living world.

This is science in its essence, what civilized science is all about: knowledge for the purpose of control. In the capitalist and market-oriented countries of the world (which by now is just about all of them) science and technology are also about making money, and lots of it.

Science, being a youngish sub-culture within a much larger and older over-culture, naturally inherits its own salient characteristics from its parent culture. The beginnings of the culture of civilization go back roughly ten thousand years to the early days of agriculture and the domestication of plants and animals. What became the cultural institutions of Western civilization--including the ideas, perceptions, and values they were built upon—would take centuries and millennia to develop into a mature, and apparently coherent worldview. By five thousand years ago, and certainly by three thousand, we see a people very much like ourselves living their lives according to stories and memes we recognize. When we read Homer's *Odyssey,* for instance—written some twenty-nine hundred years ago--we are immersed in a world with a distinct family resemblance to our own. By this time in our history, and in the development of our culture, the cultural institutions that shape and inform our way of life were already well-established; they were, and still are, taken for granted by almost everyone, and remain all but invisible to the unschooled eye—including the eye of Science, which can find nothing in culture to weigh, measure, or compute, and therefore believes it can safely ignore.

What I am talking about are cultural memes, beliefs, and institutions that penetrate all strata of a society, such as: authoritarianism, hierarchy, patriarchy, colonialism, classism, speciesism, sexism, and racism. There is a pattern here among all these isms: a pattern based on a perceived superiority of one class of beings over another. The idea of hierarchy, whether inter-species or confined to humans, presumes inequality among individuals or classes of individuals. Patriarchy and male chauvinism assumes a male superiority over females; racism and colonialism assumes that one skin color, culture, or social order is superior to others; classism elevates one sub-group above their presumed 'inferiors;' speciesism, a close relative of anthropocentrism, assumes that one species outranks another, with humans (of course) at the very top of the hierarchy; authoritarianism describes the power relationship between those at the top of the social order and those (believed to be) beneath them. None of these self-serving isms are innocent matters of opinion; none are practiced by individuals or groups upon others without doing great, grievous, or fatal harm. All are deeply entrenched in Western culture and have been passed on from generation to generation, including generations of scientists. Science—which does not exist in a vacuum—has thus been influenced by these and many other isms deeply embedded in our culture, and all have skewed the questions that Science has thought fit to ask, which have in turn skewed its findings.

These biases—far from the 'objectivity' science claims for itself—are particularly noticeable in the so-called social sciences, such as anthropology. It is the rare anthropologist indeed who does not assume that his own culture of civilization is superior to and more 'advanced' than the tribal people that he (or she) studies. If after spending many years with a particular people the anthropologist comes to regard his 'subjects' as more grounded and well-adapted to their environment than his own civilized people, he is seen by his peers, and those who support his work, as having 'gone native,' and is thereafter held in disrepute. In this or similar ways all the isms that underlie the culture of civilization are enforced, reinforced, and perpetuated.

The sociology of science is a fascinating and little-studied subject, even though peer review and other social pressures upon individual scientists (not to mention economic pressures) are central to the way science is actually conducted. Of course it is possible that some of these cultural biases have some basis in fact--at the social level if not at the biological level—but my point is that these are taken-for-granted, untested assumptions which form the basis for much of what passes for science.

What laboratory scientist, for instance, questions the speciesism entailed in the routine testing, torture, or killing of lab animals--including dogs and our close primate relatives? My own first introduction to speciesism in a scientific context occurred in the laboratory section of my freshman zoology class. There must have been about thirty of us seated at benches, awaiting delivery of our very own live frog. When mine arrived the first thing it did was pee in my hand. We were instructed to hold on tight to our frogs until everyone in the lab had one—which I did. Standing up front, the teacher showed us how to use the sharp ice-pick-like tool we'd all been provided to 'pith' the frog. Pith is scientific jargon for scrambling the frog's brain, which doesn't kill the frog outright but renders it cooperative. There was a girl in the class who spoke up and said she wasn't going to do this, which prompted the instructor to ask if anyone else was too 'squeamish' to pith their frog. One hand went up, and those two were allowed to observe as others performed this operation. Doing what was expected of me, I stuck the sharp point into the back part of the frog's skull and moved the probe around in circle, as we'd been shown. It felt a bit like scrambling eggs in a pan. With my frog disabled and compliant, I poked him in places with my probe, learning I'm not sure what—maybe something to do with nerves and muscles. Whatever it was, I wasn't getting into it. In fact, I was feeling really lousy—regretful and vaguely nauseous--because I had destroyed a living creature for reasons that made no sense to me. The lesson that day (I now believe) had very little to do with understanding the nervous system of a frog, and everything to do with normalizing this kind of treatment of fellow sentient beings to the next generation of potential scientists.

If doubts and questions like mine should arise in the breast of a practicing scientist, in the course of witnessing extreme pain and suffering among captive fellow creatures, these must either be suppressed or the 'squeamish' scientist must find another line of work. Given the reductionist indoctrination of most scientists, how many would dare to contemplate the notion that all the Earth's creatures are sovereign beings, with their own selfhood, will, intelligence, and sentience, and that the proper attitude, informing human behavior toward each such individual, is one of respect for its inherent dignity and right to self-actualization? Within the scientific materialist paradigm, such notions as these would be considered heresy, and summarily dismissed as extreme New Age woo. The continued 'work' with laboratory animals depends upon speciesism—with jobs, projects, and funding all on the line. The rationale for most of such 'work' is that it may prove beneficial to humans; and being beneficial to humans serves as justification for just about anything a human might want to do, according to anthropocentric doctrine.

Another couple isms that greatly influence the scientific materialist worldview are atomism and individualism. The philosophy of atomism, coming out of ancient Greece, posits the notion that everything in the Universe is made up of tiny indivisible and indestructible particles called atoms, which are the material building blocks of all that exists. Since, in this view, the atom was (once) believed to be the elementary particle out of which everything is made, the atom was singled out as the primary unit of interest. We now know that the atom is not indivisible or the most elementary of particles, but this is immaterial to the principle of atomism, which is: that all that is real is matter (or matter in the void), and that the whole can be understood by studying the parts that go to make it up. Atomism valorizes the part over the whole, seeing it as the prime (and perhaps primal) unit of interest, in much the same way that the hyper-individualism endemic to our culture glorifies the lone, isolated individual as the primary unit of interest, ignoring social relationships and how these provide the support and context for the individual's very existence. To ignore context, organization, and relationships is to see only part of the picture, while myopically insisting that the part--the atom, the individual--is the only unit of interest.

This kind of reductionism and mechanistic thinking has derived scientific credibility from Newtonian physics, but its roots can be traced back to ancient Greek atomistic philosophers such as Leucippus and Democritus, as well as to the either/or logic advanced by Aristotle. Looking even deeper into our cultural past--to our foundational beliefs as an agricultural people-- we find the Myth of Separation (the Big Lie) and its close relation, anthropocentrism—both of which act as conceptual enablers to the reductionist and mechanistic worldview.

What all of these isms and myths share in common—including the Myth of Separation, anthropocentrism, atomism, reductionism, and equating the world to a clocklike machine--is an anti-ecological view of the world: a refusal to look at the connections and interdependencies that unite the one with the All. Indeed, the Big Lie was (and is) a willful repudiation of the Indigenous Worldview, which goes back hundreds of human (and perhaps thousands of hominid) generations, and was supremely ecological and holistic, and came with an imperative to give back to the Great Sacred Mother as good as was given, borrowed, or taken in support of human life—thus honoring the Law of Reciprocity. This willful repudiation of the Indigenous Worldview, including the Law of Reciprocity, became necessary in the face of the cognitive dissonance engendered by the revolutionary, highly exploitative, and anti-ecological agricultural way of life. Thus an old and enduring culture was overridden and over-written by a brave new culture, with effects that would only gain momentum and multiply over time.

All of the institutions of civilization have been affected by a worldview based upon the domestication of the wild, and its necessary partner, private property. Science likes to portray itself as above the fray, as if it were built upon a foundation of its own objective and dispassionate making. I hope I have persuaded you that such a feat is not possible; that science does,

THE SCIENCE-NATURE SEPARATION

and must, partake of the larger culture, and that the taken-for-granted assumptions of this culture—and especially the deep, foundational ones—are naturally incorporated into the foundations of science.

To again invoke the metaphor of the tree: Science is a branch on the tree of culture, and pretty far up the tree at that (because in our history Science is a relative Johnny-come-lately). Further down the tree, and pointing in a different direction, is the religious or supernatural view of the world. Both of these branches take their own particular stories about the world from the stories of the larger culture—the legends, myths, and memes (including their embedded ontology, epistemology, and cosmology) held within the tree's substantial trunk, and fed by a root system that few to none can see, but which in the case of our culture take their essential nourishment from the Big Lie.

I am trying to make you understand that science, as presently constituted, is neither what it seems nor how it presents itself. As I said at the outset, I am a friend to science as a mode of inquiry. At its best, science asks many important questions, and often arrives at provocative--if partial and provisional--answers. What I object to in science, and hope you will object to also, are scientific materialism's many orthodoxies, which are themselves products not of science, but are instead culturally derived, unquestioned assumptions. What these assumptions all add up to is a collection of unscientific doctrines that pose as science, but are actually scientism. That is to say: these are nothing more than articles of faith in what amounts to a secular religion. Believers in scientism tend to adamantly deny the religiosity of their faith, and I am sure they are sincere in their inability to see that they have swallowed the doctrines of scientism along with their science education. But I am hoping that you will be able to see through this ongoing program of indoctrination, because these unscientific doctrines posing as science have done a lot of damage in our world, and it would be a grievous mistake to let them do damage in yours.

CHAPTER 27

CORPORATE RACE TO EXTINCTION

YOU MAY BE wondering how it is that the human population went so deeply into overshoot in my time, and why we seemed so helpless to do anything about it. The quick and dirty answer is that it couldn't have happened without agriculture and cheap oil, but so much more is involved in our race toward extinction—details and relationships that I think you will benefit from understanding. But first let's take a quick look at the population dynamics of our wild, pre-agricultural ancestors, just to put things in perspective.

During the period of human dispersal across the globe—between sixty and ten thousand years ago—the natural world offered a rich array of ecosystems fairly overflowing with life forms, and thus with opportunities for humans to make a good living. As long as this condition prevailed, and there was new territory to expand into, there was no particular incentive to limit group size, except as it became unwieldy for group encampments and migrations, or as social tensions prompted a group to split up and go separate ways. But once all--or nearly all-- available niches were filled with other humans a new urgency impressed itself upon our kind: we had to match population size to the available resources on a finite Earth. Failure to find this balance could lead to nothing but grief.

In the hunter-gatherer lifeway, the individual and group incentive is to take good care of their resource base. Human lives depended upon fully functional ecosystems as well as on maintaining a balance between prey species and the human appetite for them. Harm the resilience of the ecosystem, upset the balance of the predator-prey relationship (by over-exploitation, say), and you can be sure human lives will suffer the consequences. Living within the Earth's annual solar budget in this way is living in the Gift. It is living off the interest of Earth's natural capital, off the abundance of a fecund and generous Mother Earth. And there is a built-in disincentive to spending down the principal.

Agricultural man lives by a different life-strategy, which can fairly be described as living in the Theft. This lifeway is based upon the principle of spending down the principal; it has no staying power because it depends upon the mining of resources—both 'renewable' and non-renewable-- unto exhaustion. But as long as the party lasts, great fortunes are made by a few individuals, while many others enjoy living in improvident luxury (including myself)—all at the expense of a living planet.

It is not possible for the Earth to support the more than seven billion of us without agriculture, without oil, or without living in the Theft. We couldn't all be here if the world was still a commons and hadn't been privatized. All of these cultural institutions make it possible to overpopulate the planet with humans—and this is beginning to be acknowledged by some of my contemporaries. But few ever contemplate the question: what makes it impossible (or all but) to stop growing our population-- or, better yet, reverse our trajectory, and thereby lessen the pressure of our gigantic boot-print on the face of our Mother? Even among those who recognize that we are deep into overshoot, there is little understanding of why we cannot force a change in this self-destructive trajectory. But this is something **you** need to know.

Let's begin with the enabling cultural injunction, found in the Book of Genesis, but already part of our culture before it ever became codified in print: 'Go forth and multiply!' It matters not a whit whether one is a practicing Jew or Christian for this directive to have resonance, because it is enshrined in our deep culture, and has been for thousands of years. Populating the Earth without limit has been planted deep in our collective psyche, as part of our operating program, and it shows.

Even if, by some miracle, the entire human population were to undergo an instantaneous global mind change at this very moment, and could shed this deep programming; even if we all felt compelled to severely limit the human population, I seriously doubt that we could act upon it, because of all the snares we've managed to entangle ourselves in. Some of these reside in our deep culture, and give us marching orders we are barely are of. For instance, within the same document that enjoins us to be fruitful and multiply we find sanctified approval for wealth creation and the storing up of great riches by favored individuals. This of course runs exactly counter to the egalitarianism of the hunter-gatherer, where all is to be shared equitably among everyone in the group; where no more is to be taken from Mother Earth than can be used immediately—thus insuring fairness and justice within the group itself, while also conserving the Earth's Gifts for later, including for future generations.

As with the injunction to expand the human population, this encouragement to seek power and wealth had to have been well-established within the culture long before it was ever enshrined in print and made official doctrine. That is to say, it runs deeper than any one religion, and has, by my time, been taken for granted by almost everyone within civilized society. And also taken for granted is the (unacknowledged) fact that wealth creation is not possible by living in the Gift, but only by living in the Theft--that is, by spending down the Earth's principal: its complexity, diversity, and resilience, accrued over 3.8 billion years of Earthly evolution. Living in the Theft is a life strategy that can work for a few, for a while, but inevitably must fail completely.

With overpopulation and wealth creation as foundational principles, other cultural institutions would inevitably appear to facilitate these cultural marching orders. And this is where we began our problematic relationship with complex systems: systems that promised Power—and delivered—but not without exacting a soul-withering price for our elevated status as Masters of the Planet. Indeed, it may not be overly fanciful to see what has happened to the civilized human in the light of a Faustian Bargain or Deal with the Devil.

Complex systems are not well understood, and have only been the subject of close study for three or so decades—and looked into mostly by those trained in the traditions of materialist science. Thus, complex systems are assumed to be without personality or personhood of their own, and are thought to be more like mechanisms than organisms. And this may actually be the case--no one really knows-- but I think it dangerous to underestimate what they are and what they can do. Accordingly, I find it useful to personify them to some degree and to see them as having agendas of their own: *as if* they were volitional beings with a will of their own. I wouldn't call them the Devil, or Mephistopheles, or the incarnation of evil, and yet, their effects can run so counter to the purposes of all Life as to seem purposefully intent upon the destruction of a living Earth. If they are just mechanical entities operating out of a handful of principles, rules, or laws, and otherwise have no intentions of their own, you have to wonder why these rules are as they are, and why they couldn't have been formulated in a way that was friendlier to Life.

Usury is the lending of money that must be repaid by a certain time-- with interest: often, very steep interest. Usurers were long regarded as blood-sucking parasites that preyed upon the weak and poor, and were all but banned from civil life. Then came the Industrial Revolution, and with it the need for finance capital, and thus bankers became respectable and important members of civilized society. The problem with usury, beyond its predatory proclivities, is its built-in imperative for growth. Interest on debt is by its nature a pyramid- or Ponzi-scheme: it requires that new money enter the game, and not just new money but new players—new people born into the world, to service the debt of their elders. Usury only works in a world of perpetual growth.

Manufacturing depends upon the mining of resources; the mining of resources, in turn, depends upon machines and other manufactured goods to go about its business. Both mining and manufacturing depend upon a transportation network to move stuff in and out of their locations, and to transport goods to distribution centers. All of these interlocking systems are mutually interdependent, and they consist of both organizational and physical infrastructure. These are systems of systems as well as systems within systems. Some of these systems are linear, and therefore predictable. Others are non-linear and pregnant with surprise. What they share in common is a growth imperative: they all want to get bigger and bigger, and bigger still.

Our economic system—capitalism—also depends upon perpetual growth. Politicians like to talk about 'growing the economy'—and preferably at a rate well above 3% per year. The prosperity of the (American) people depends upon it. Anything below this threshold creates anxiety among our Captains of Industry and causes them to hold their cash reserves close: no expansion; no hiring; no new ventures.

It is the nature of corporations to want to grow, to consolidate, to become a vast empire of interrelated businesses. Financial, organizational, and Power incentives drive corporate systems toward vertical integration and economies of scale. The byword is: Get big or get out. And the bigger you get, the more political clout you have, which translates into ever more favorable governmental policies, regulations, and tax loopholes. All the incentives built-in to the organization of our corporate systems favor, and select for, more Power, more business, more money—and the way to accomplish these goals is to grow larger and larger, and larger still. The pressure is on: Get big or get out.

Everything central to our way of life is in the growth mode: the banks, the corporations, all our extractive and service industries, and, not least of all, our population. More people means: more willing buyers of homes, cars, electronic gadgets, and all the trappings of modern life. More jobs, more prosperity, more everything. More, more, more. It is in the interest of banks and corporations, as well as businesses large and small, that the market for products continues to grow. More, more, more. Grow, grow, grow.

On a finite planet with degraded natural systems and diminishing natural resources this growth imperative, built-in to our systems and into our lives, is an irresistible force coming up against an immovable object. It is us hitting a wall, and doing so at speed. More and more people in my time now see this crash coming. Of course there is also plenty of willful and studied stupidity on this subject. But here again, consider the incentives. As we spend down the last of what is left, there are still fortunes to be made. But it is not only the power elite who gain by the liquidation of natural systems as we turn the Earth inside-out and upside-down in our frenzy to mine everything that can be mined. We are all implicated, all more-or-less willing accomplices, in this final dismantling—because we are dependent on all these systems not only for our improvident lifestyle, but perhaps even for our very lives.

It would seem to make perfect sense, given our trajectory toward doom, that we should reverse our course as quickly and completely as we can. One way to do this would be to de-grow our population. Another would be to make far fewer demands upon this ailing and injured planet. Doing both at the same time would be better yet. But there are a few problems with this obvious fix, not the least of which is our agricultural system which --(get this now)-- takes ten calories of energy (by way of cheap oil) to produce one calorie of food energy to power people. The industrial agricultural system has been in place for less than three quarters of a century, but it is responsible for more than tripling our population in that short time. Without the high-grade energy of cheap oil there could never have been more than seven billion of us. But the fact is: there are more than seven billion living human beings. And what individual, or group, is going to take the responsibility for whittling this untenable number down to size? Even if all seven billion of us could agree that our numbers must be reduced—which we emphatically do not—how would we go about implementing this concerted will that we do not have?

Or let's say that we could all agree that we wanted to live under a no-growth steady-state economic system (for which, again, there is, emphatically, no agreement). What would happen to all these interlocking systems-- in which we are invested and enmeshed-- that only work under conditions of growth, and falter under contraction? We really don't know exactly what would happen, because non-linear complexity is involved, but it is a good guess that it would look quite a bit like dominoes falling—and they'd be falling on us.

I want you to understand why it is, when there were at least a few of us who could see what was coming, that we did nothing, or next to nothing, to slow this juggernaut down. I can see where you might be harboring bitter resentments against those who left you a world so broken in so many ways. I don't know if you yourself hold the value of intergenerational justice, but if you do, you will likely feel that you have been thoroughly betrayed. And you have, but not out of maliciousness; not even out of indifference—at least not complete indifference. I personally know individuals who feel strongly that we are doing you a terrible injustice—and we are. But I want you to realize that we really didn't have a choice in the matter. Whatever little any of us might have been able to do on your behalf wasn't going to be nearly enough, because this growth catastrophe is systemic.

We are all invested in these systems, one way or another, and have grown utterly dependent upon them for whatever there is left to value in human life. The thing is, almost none of us can see how we could possibly live without them—and truly almost none of us could. The bind we are in is this: it is suicidal to go on as we are, and it would be suicidal to stop, and collapse all these systems that support our lives. Most of us live day to day, putting one foot in front of the other, more or less on automatic pilot, taking whatever satisfaction we can from our life in bondage to these systems. Even if we realize that something vital to our being has been taken from us, and that our lives are hollow, this is still all we have: a life of sorts. Your life, on the other hand, is mere conjecture—a phantom in the mists of a future that may never arrive. And so we go with what we know, in the here and now.

Would you, in our place, behave any differently?

CHAPTER 28

LOVE YOUR PIECE OF LAND

NOW THAT YOU have seen the population mess we got ourselves into, and what was behind it, I want you to consider your own prospects in that department. And here much depends upon whether I am more or less correct in my assumptions about population dynamics, or if many of the so-called experts are closer to the truth. As it happens, I am acquainted with a group of population activists, who see very clearly that we are now in overshoot. What they do not see clearly, in my opinion, is what actually drives humans to overpopulate. Nor do they see population dynamics as scale-dependent, and so would perceive your situation, or the situation of our hunter-gatherer ancestors, and the situation today as identical in principle. They are the experts, but I believe they are wrong in this. I leave it to you to decide which view best accords with your own sense of how thing work in the world.

One of these population activists has stated the problem thus: "We are genetically engineered to reproduce, and so we do; we are genetically engineered to consume, and so we do; we are genetically engineered to use our intelligence to maximize the above, and so we do." This is fairly standard thinking among those trained in the traditions of scientific materialism, and tends therefore to be mechanistic and deterministic in outlook. My own educational bias would have me replace the words 'genetically engineered' with 'culturally conditioned,' thus making the population problem less about biological imperatives that drive and rule us, and considerably more about our proclivities as a social, cultural, and psychological animal who functions as a member of a group.

While it is undeniable that the human being comes with a strong sex drive, this is not identical to being genetically engineered to maximize reproduction. This construction seems to assume that the human being possesses little free agency, if any at all. We just behave as we have been genetically programmed to, with no choice in the matter of making babies. I believe it is much more nuanced than this: that the human tends to have a lot of children when it is perceived that the resource base will support many new humans. So, perception is a key factor, and is relevant at both the individual and group level. And because the human is a grouping, as well as a cultural, animal, group sentiment about population size will weigh heavily with couples considering parenthood possibilities. There is very little incentive to produce more children than the land base can support, because only grief can come from exceeding the carrying capacity of the land.

The concept of incentives—and disincentives—is in fact central to my understanding of population dynamics, and human behavior generally. I would think this should be self-evident to all, but somehow it is not, so I will try to spell out just how incentives can work to limit population.

Let me tell you a story about some people I know—a story with implications for your own situation. These are tribal people, three different tribes, who live on the Lower Klamath

River, in the extreme north of what is now the state of California. The aboriginal territory of the Karuk Tribe encompassed about a million acres, extending from just above the confluence of the Trinity River with the Klamath in the west, to some seventy miles upriver beyond what is now the hamlet of Happy Camp. According to tribal tradition, they have occupied this land from time immemorial. According to the carbon dating of Western science, there is evidence of tenancy along this stretch of river going back nine thousand years.

The Karuk's neighbor to the west is the Yurok Tribe, and their territory begins where the Karuks' leaves off: from the where the Trinity and the Klamath Rivers join, downriver some forty miles to the Pacific Ocean.

The territory of the Hupa Tribe begins near the mouth of the Trinity and straddles that river for roughly thirty miles upstream. Historically, the Klamath and the Trinity Rivers have had abundant runs of migratory steelhead, eels, sturgeon, and salmon, with roughly a million fish entering the estuary in an average year.

Because of their location at the Klamath's mouth and the lower forty miles of river, the Yuroks had first access to the fish that entered the estuary, giving them a possible chokehold on the finny resources they shared with their neighbors.

According to a worldview proclaimed by many scientists, and accepted by many non-scientists: humans are naturally selfish, competitive, and warlike. We are genetically engineered to be this way, as are all the other creatures in this dog-eat-dog world. This view is a form of Neo-Darwinism, but far removed from Darwin's own careful observations of the natural world. It is a doctrine, an ideology, held by a certain faction within the scientific community-- one which is not based in science, and, in fact, is clearly contradicted by many of the behavioral sciences, including much paleo-anthropology.

THE CULTURE TRAP

I bring all this up because these three tribes of the Lower Klamath River did not (and do not) behave according to the dictates of their presumed 'genetic engineering.' They did not overrun their resource base and they did not overrun each other. Why? Because they had strong incentives to live at peace with one another, and within their means.

You might think that because these three peoples spoke widely different languages that their cultural practices would also be widely different. In fact they are amazingly similar, and a prime reason for this is that intermarriage among these three peoples has been commonplace going back hundreds and even thousands of years. This intermingling of families and languages and traditions over long time has led to natural alliances as well as a blending of lifeways, spiritual practices, and cultural beliefs.

All three share a deep connection to their fish-rich rivers, and to the fish themselves-- which is the mainstay of their collective lives. Then, too, the geographical area they share is one of the most biologically diverse in the world, giving rise to an incredible number of tree species, including five separate species of acorn-bearing oak trees-- including the tanoak, their agreed favorite, for its superior texture and flavor.

Deer and elk are also plentiful, as are mushrooms, grouse, huckleberries, and scores of other plants and animals indigenous to this mountain and stream country of the Lower Klamath. Rich in diversity of landscapes as well as life-forms, this country is as much a delight to the eye as to the palette. This is, in short, highly desirable territory: a place where these people's ancestors lived for untold generations, and where future generations might have gone on living indefinitely, had invaders not intervened.

I could tell you the brutal story of an idyllic life interrupted by gold-crazed white savages with murder in their eyes and hearts: of genocide, land theft, betrayal, and the spending down these peoples' resources until little was left of this once-cherished world. But the ecocide and genocide perpetrated by European invaders is not the focus here. Instead, I want to look at some of the reasons why these people did not overpopulate their land base or make war upon one another when that is presumed by some as an all-but-inevitable outcome of our 'genetically engineered' human nature.

These three tribes of the Lower Klamath were particularly fortunate in their choice of where to call home, including the fact that they were so geographically isolated from the rest of the world that for millennia they were able to live their lives undisturbed by outsiders. This is fortunate for us, too, because it gives us an exceptionally long-lived undisturbed social experiment with scientifically verifiable results—results that in many instances turn conventional expectations on their head.

Those of us who have spent a good portion of our lives on a family homestead may claim some knowledge of what it means to feel attached to a particular place. Farming and ranching families very often claim to feel a 'love of the land.' City folk, who have never become intimate with a large piece of natural landscape, really have nothing significant in their experience to relate to the kind of attachment to place that I am going to talk about next. And if you yourself have spent your whole life in a bunker or a cave because it is too dangerous to go out into the light of the sun, I do not expect immediate and empathic comprehension of these people's motives and mindsets. I would only ask that you use your imagination; that you put yourself in the moccasins of these fortunately situated people, and consider what you would do, if you had their lives to live.

Historically, we transplanted Europeans have been a footloose people, and though our ancestors may have yearned for a place they could call their own, very few families have been allowed land tenancy for more than a handful of generations. In such a case we are talking about a particular piece of land belonging to—that is, being 'owned' by—a particular family, for let's say a hundred years or more. Along with the title for the land comes the presumption that this piece of ground can be used in any way that the 'owner' chooses, with virtually no prohibitions or taboos. Land is private property, real estate, and is valued as a more or less fungible economic commodity. Can a white man love the land he lives on? Of course. It happens all the time. But owning land—even if tenderly nurtured and cared for—is quite a different proposition than belonging to the land.

What does it mean for a people to belong to the land?

What does it mean for the people themselves, and what does it mean for the land?

When your ancestors' bones, going back dozens or hundreds of generations, are buried in the ground beneath your feet, this gives you a special claim to the land you stand on. When the stories of your people tell about these ancestors, and put them in particular places on the landscape that you frequent yourself, this makes you feel rooted in this land your people claim as their spiritual home. When you've grown up learning from your uncles and elders where to find the best acorns, dig the best balsamroot, or find deer grazing at dawn ; when you have spent untold days on the river fishing with cousins and brothers, harvested medicinal plants with your grandmother, and picked huckleberries with a lover in the mountains; when you've learned where to gather the wild mushrooms, and when; where to find the best basketry materials, and the prime time to pick wild iris for the making of cordage; when you have gone to the sacred Elk Mountains to seek a vision, gone swimming in the deepest creek holes of summer, and hiked with friends to the high lakes for the refreshment of their clear waters—then you have begun to know what it is to belong to a place.

This is belonging that comes from knowing the lay of the land in all its physical variety, and in all seasons. This way of belonging is shared with others on a daily basis, and includes lore passed down from the ancestors--and with it a deepened sense of continuity in place. But knowledge of belonging to this place runs even deeper than this, because of the cultural lens through which all this is experienced. Unlike the reductionist lens through which materialist science would have us see the world-- with matter itself as inert, lifeless stuff lacking in any of the qualities with which we humans are imbued, which of course begs the question of where our own intelligence, sentience, personhood, and volition comes from, as if something can come from nothing-- these native peoples, and most indigenous people everywhere, recognize that the Earth is inhabited by what they would describe as spirits. In their world, which is known to them to be sacred, everything is individuated and possesses the dignity of personhood. Of course everything has its own particular kind of sentience and intelligence, its own reason for being, and the will to become what it is meant to become.

This view of a world that is fully alive and sacred has far-reaching implications for how a people will live their lives, including how many children they will see fit to bring into the world. I have said that perception is a vital component to reproductive choices, as are perceived incentives. If you and your people have belonged to a particular place for a very long time, and it is a good place for your people to go on living, you have a strong incentive to avoid careless or reckless behaviors, and to live circumspectly in place, informed by attitudes of reverence and gratitude.

THE CULTURE TRAP

As for the mechanics of population control, there have long been several options open to humans. In the case of these particular peoples, the men and the women have traditionally slept in separate quarters: the women and children in the long house and the men and older boys in the sweat house. This segregation by gender has been accompanied by a culturally cultivated prudishness toward sex, and taboos against secret trysts. Most sexual activity, and most pregnancies, occurred in the high country during the berry season of high summer. Other birth control strategies, among these people who had a thoroughgoing understanding of their local pharmacopeia, included herbal equivalents of morning-after pills and plants that would induce miscarriage. They also practiced the nursing of infants until their fourth or fifth year, physiologically discouraging unwanted pregnancies thereby. And if all else failed, there was always infanticide.

The motivation of these people to control population was strong. Recognizing that they lived in a territory that provided high-value nutrition, but could support only a limited number of humans, the people were forced to make a choice. If they allowed their population to exceed their resource base, children, elders, and others they loved would die. The single other option would be to expand their resource base by killing off their neighbors—many of whom were also family. One group having no particular technological or numerical advantage over the other, the outcome of such an enterprise was likely to be highly unsatisfactory all around. All-out war made no sense, but this is not to suggest that there were never tensions or clashes among neighbors.

All three tribes built temporary weirs out into the river to trap and retrieve migrating salmon. Usually these were built in pairs: one from one side of the river, the other from the opposite bank and just upriver. When constructed according to tradition, these weirs allowed considerable escapement of fish to proceed on their upriver journey. But what if some enterprising young Yuroks decided to build a third weir above the other two and thereby take fish that would normally be harvested by their neighbors upstream? Two things would happen. The womenfolk would know of this right away, and many of these would have kinship ties to the Karuks, the Hupas, or both. Not wanting to see her relatives suffer privations, they would talk to her own menfolk about taking out that third weir. If they didn't respond favorably, she would get word to her relatives upriver. And soon a contingent of hotheaded young men would be down in Yurok territory taking things into their own hands. Blood would likely be shed, but whoever's blood it was, that third weir would come out—as would, in time, the other two.

Everyone would know that it wasn't right for one people to take more than their fair portion of a shared resource—including all but a few of the Yuroks. 'Take no more than you need' is a fundamental principle of the hunter-gatherer lifeway, and it is not just some abstract ideal. It is a guideline that conserves the resource base over long time even as it respects the sacredness of all life forms.

Empathy is a key factor here, in both the human and the other-than-human realm. In addition to the intermarriage which brings these peoples into each other's orbits, their ritual lives also intersect. All three tribes are fix-the-world peoples whose World Renewal Ceremonies are nearly identical, because they have been invited guests to one another's multi-day ceremonies and have shared in their spiritual practices. This close interaction among groups has had the effect of investing their neighbors with their full humanity, thereby countering any tendency to demonize them as an alien Other, who might then be treated with disrespect. Empathy and mutual respect make for better relations among humans than their opposite, and both can be cultivated at the personal as well as the group and cultural level.

When it comes to enforcing cultural norms, scale is critical. Like their more mobile forager cousins, these people of the salmon tended to live in groups of twenty to thirty people, with one or two strategically located villages reaching as many as fifty individuals. There were no 'chiefs' among these tribes, though there was slightly more stratification than among immediate return hunter-gatherers. That is, some families and village sites had more prestige than others, and healers and ceremonial leaders were held in higher esteem than others. In general, leadership tended to arise out of the particulars of the moment and then recede as the situation was resolved. For instance, each of these peoples had worked out its own schedule of fines to levy against wrongdoers, ranging in severity to match the wrongful deed. Everyone knew the cost of each infraction, but a particular individual would have to emerge to extract the fine from the perpetrator and pass it on to the victim(s). With no police and no judicial system, these people regulated behavior with simple peer pressure—as humans always have—and when group pressure wasn't sufficient to control all behaviors, this system of fines was used to enforce group norms.

In a group where everyone knows everyone else, what is perceived to be the common good is socially enforceable on a day-to-day basis. This would include the number of people that any village's land base could support in an average year, and thus the number of children that any such living unit could safely allow into its fold.

In a mass society, like the one I live in: where we have lost this intimate connection with the people around us, and are ruled by anonymous authoritarian systems of externally imposed enforcers and laws that may or not be just; where the growth demands of our systems take precedence over, and short-circuit, our own deepest interests and human needs; where land may 'belong' to people, but almost no one belongs to the land, and no one is thinking about the seventh generation; where we are so out of touch with Nature and Mother Earth that we behave as if our resource base has no limits; where everything has grown far beyond the natural human scale, and the inborn capacities that our evolutionary history has provided us with—it is easy to see how some get lost in the abstractions of biological determinism, and believe that we are run by locked-in automatic programs that we have no capacity to override; that we are feckless victims of our own biology.

If those who say that we are genetically engineered to reproduce and consume, and to use our intelligence to maximize our reproduction and consumption, then I would say that you (and our species) are doomed—doomed to consume and over-reproduce yourself into oblivion, like the snake that eats its own tail, and keeps on eating until there is nothing left but teeth and gaping appetite.

I cannot believe that the Project of Life is built on such a model, that it could have endured for four billion years based on a balls-out 'genetically engineered' zero-sum winner-take-all program of maximization. This model is, I believe, a reflection of our human-devised predatory/parasitic economic system, and has been made into an ideology to rationalize our living so out of balance with Mother Earth and all our relations. It is a rationalization to justify our living by Theft.

I believe that Nature works on the principle not of maximization--for one particular (favored) species-- but of optimization for all. This has been called the Balance of Nature, and it operates on the principle of reciprocity, in a world where all flourishing is mutual. I believe you are being asked to choose between two worlds; one made by Nature and one made by man. And what you believe about your world will go a long way toward making that world what it is.

PART II

The Sophia Myth and Other Essays

CHAPTER 29

THE SOPHIA MYTH

Introduction to Four Essays on the Sophia Myth

THE STORIES WE are living in are destroying the living world, and are therefore also destroying any chance for a viable human future. However deadly our Old Stories might be, we cannot help but cling to them, because they are all we have, and we are incapable of living without story. This is the trap we are in—the culture trap. But what if a New Story were to appear on the scene, and this New Story had none of the toxic qualities of our Old Story, and in fact offered a viable way to live in the world—one that nurtured Life rather than shutting it down? I believe there is such a story; it is called the Sophia Myth and it explains the origin of the Earth and the human species in a way that is different from the cosmologies we are accustomed to. It also opens up a new/old way for the human to live in the world as a friend—rather than an enemy-- to all Life. It is a multifaceted story, rich in nuance, and not easily summarized. That is why it has taken me four separate essays—none of them short—in an attempt to penetrate the depths of its implications. And I haven't gotten to the bottom of this story yet. I am posting these essays here, in serial fashion, for the very few who might find it worthwhile to invest the time in what I consider to be one of the last best hopes we have to avoid our own extinction—a New Story to live in.

The first essay—"A New Story to Live in"-- frames the Sophia Myth within the context of the stories (the two Master Narratives) we are living in now: those of Monotheistic Religion and Scientific Materialism. If you find either of these two (mostly incompatible) Master Narratives blameless, and personally convincing, you are probably not going to like what I have to say about them here.

The second essay—"The Sophia Myth: from Fragments to a Nearly Integrated Whole"—draws heavily upon the work of John Lamb Lash and his excellent book, *Not in His Image: Gnostic Vision, Sacred Ecology, and the Future of* Belief. This is a summary, using strategically selected passages in Lash's own words, in order to give the reader a fulsome sense of the story without having to read the 400 page book. Also included are Gnostic insights into, and criticisms of, certain doctrines of Judaism and Christianity that the Gnostics found fault with. For their trouble, the Gnostics and their writings were all but eliminated from the world, beginning with the murder of Hypatia in 415 A.D.

The third essay—"A Fallible Goddess versus the Almighty Yehweh"—takes a critical look at the god of the Old Testament and compares this deity with the goddess who became the Earth. This chapter is sure to offend true believers in either of the two Master Narratives, and might easily disconcert others who take for granted certain first principles, such as the belief that matter, rather than consciousness, is primary. All I can say is, at this point, where much is at stake and time is short, I think we need to take a hard look at the foundational principles of our culture.

The fourth essay—"Myth, Truth, and Meaning"—begins by looking at some of the deficiencies of the Gnostic material, as it has come down to us, and suggests a way to remedy what is missing. It goes on to explore where a change in our perception of first principles might take us, were we to think differently about the nature of reality, and accept the cosmology inherent in the Sophia Myth. (A necessary 5th essay is contingent upon events in the world, and remains to be written.)

I don't regret all the research, thinking, and writing that went into these essays, which I expect will become chapters in my book, *The Culture Trap*. When I sit down to write, something special happens: I get to discover, in an articulate and organized fashion, what has been going on in the depths of my unconscious. That is, I get to find out what I actually think and believe about whatever has been inarticulately mulling in my mind. The work involved in this process is a labor of love, and it comes with its own rewards.

Part 1: A New Story to Live By

> (What follows is a brief introduction to the Sophia Myth of the ancient Gnostics, along with the claim that this story is far superior to the two master-narratives we are trying to live in today, and in whose name we are systematically dismantling the living world.)

WE HUMAN BEINGS have the odd distinction among our fellow sentient Earthlings of living not out of instinct but out of story. We live by story and within story, whether we recognize this fact or not. For instance, the American Dream is a prominent cultural narrative in our society and is taken for granted by most as a valid story to live in. But even if a person rejects the Dream as a sham, this story will inevitably shape the trajectory of their life simply because this story is believed and acted upon by others within their group. Same with the Myth of Progress: no matter what we personally believe on this subject, the idea that more and better is inevitably on the way has been a driving force in our society for decades, centuries, even millennia, and there is no escaping it. These are just two of the many interlocking narratives which inform us about who we are and how we should live. There are many others, and, taken together, they provide us with the scripts we act out in our everyday lives. But there is a problem here.

Looking back over evolutionary history, it is evident that for the 3.8 billion years since the first appearance of life on this planet, something we call instinct has lent itself to the survival and well-being of every species on Earth. Instinct, as a guidance system, has proved itself to be remarkably successful over long time. Culture, as a guidance system, is a Johnny-come-lately innovation, and is proving to be daily more problematic—and likely ruinous. Unfortunately, living by cultural narrative—by story—is all that remains available to us. While instinct may still live somewhere within our collective racial memory, it has in most of us become inauspiciously shrunken and deformed, made unreliable by thousands of years of our culture's overwriting and overriding instinct's sure directives. So, for better or for worse, what we are stuck with is story.

Unfortunately, the stories that come out of the culture of Western civilization, and continue to inform our lives, are just about as wrong as could be, imperiling everything that lives. Our stories are perversely twisted and dangerous to Life because they are based upon lies. At the very foundation of Western culture is the Big Lie, which insists that the human being is separate from, and superior to, Nature. Because this view is anti-ecological at its heart it is also, therefore, anti-Life: that is because the world is by nature ecological, and to live in denial of this fact courts psychopathy and omnicide. Absurd (and dangerous) as the Myth of Human Supremacy may be, it nevertheless penetrates and contaminates all of our social institutions, while simultaneously tainting what we believe about ourselves and the nature of the world. But what are we to do even if we clearly recognize how ill-suited our stories are to life on Earth? If story is all we've got, and there is nothing for it but to live by story, what do we do then? The obvious answer is that we abandon all our broken stories and find a new story to live in. Easier said than done, no doubt, but maybe not downright impossible. And I just happen to have a candidate for a New Story that might actually serve.

This is the story of Sophia, the Wisdom Goddess, who indwells the Earth, and is the Earth. The Sophia Myth bears some resemblance to the Gaian Myth, but is far richer in meaning and implication. The Gaian Myth--as borrowed from the ancient Greeks by contemporary scientists to tell the story of a planet behaving as if it were a self-organizing super-organism--is a way of understanding the material processes whereby Earth, and the creatures of Earth, produce and maintain conditions friendly to Life. The Gaia Theory is a huge advance over the anti-ecological precepts of reductionist mainstream science—which sees the Earth and the Universe as a cold and unfriendly place governed by hard-edged chance and devoid of purpose or meaning. Necessarily, Gaia theory is itself largely limited by these same precepts and dogmas which hold sway over society—including, even, scientific pioneers. Gaia theory is an advance in understanding how systems (and systems of systems) work on a planetary scale, but few in the scientific community would acknowledge the Earth's sentience, intelligence, or volition, let alone her personhood--because scientific ideology declares otherwise, and groupthink prevails in science just as it does elsewhere.

By contrast, the Sophia Myth is a cosmological narrative (origin story) of our particular solar system, as it was born within the third arm our own Milky Way galaxy. It tells the story of the Aeon (Goddess) Sophia and how she, our benefactress, became the Earth; how she and the Aeon, Thelete, designed the human genome (the Anthropos) at the core of the galaxy—which is what gods and goddesses do to entertain themselves in the safety of the Pleroma (the galaxy's core). Sophia, it seems, was a passionate and headstrong young goddess, prone, perhaps, to the obsessive and compulsive behaviors of youth. At least this is offered in partial explanation for the strange anomaly that follows. In her uncontained enthusiasm for her co-creation, the Anthropos, and yearning, as she does, to see it develop to its full potential, she breaks with precedent and wanders alone to the very edge of the galaxy's core. Then, somehow, she finds herself beyond all known boundaries, falling through space and time. Sophia's fall takes her from the safety of the galaxy's core out into the further reaches of its spiral arm, where matter and energy take on unfamiliar qualities of density. It is here that an unprecedented transformation takes place. The divine luminosity of the goddess Sophia combines with matter to form a living planet—the very one that would become our home and the home of all that lives (as far as we know): our own planet Earth.

This story of Sophia comes to us by way of the Gnostics, a group of visionaries, scholars, teachers, and mystics who practiced their specialties throughout the Mediterranean and the Near East in the centuries leading up to the birth of Christ. The Gnostics also lived alongside the early Christians in places like Alexandria, Egypt, right up until 415 c.e., when a group of Christians openly murdered the distinguished Gnostic scholar, Hypatia, right out in the street. Following this declaration of war upon the Gnostics—who publicly found fault with Christian religious doctrines--these early Christian zealots went on a programatic spree of persecution, torture, and extermination, whereby the Gnostics were driven out of society and into near oblivion. Meanwhile, the writings of these advanced scholars were consigned to the flames of righteousness, and in this way the Sophia story was suppressed for the greater part of two millennia, until 1945, when a cache of Gnostic writings—called the Nag Hamadi Codexes--was found in a cave alongside the Nile River, in Egypt.

In the years following, scholars have worked at deciphering the meanings inherent in these texts, including an independent comparative mythologist named John Lamb Lash, whose excellent book, *Not in His Image: Gnostic Vision, Sacred Ecology, and the Future of Belief,* is probably the single best source for understanding the Sophia Myth and its far-reaching implications.

This many-layered story tells a nuanced tale of how things got to be this way in our particular galaxy. But where does such an origin story come from in the first place? How does it originate?

The origin stories of many indigenous groups appear to to derive from shamanic trance. The job of the shaman is to penetrate the depths of other worlds and come back with useful information. This same principle would seem to apply to those visionary Gnostics who started telling a story about a galactic Goddess who not only co-created the human genome but went on to become the life support system of every living being.

The Sophia Myth is a complex story with several subplots and many a relevant implications. All this is worth examining in detail, but for now I want to focus on this one part of the story: Sophia's plunge from the Pleroma into the far reaches of the galactic arm (the Kenoma), finding, as she fell, that her own Organic Light was merging with an alien form of matter--and losing in the process all sense of who she was, or might become. Disoriented, homesick, and alone, she is for a time traumatized and in a sorry state of bewilderment--as well she might be, since nothing like this had ever happened before in this galaxy. For a goddess from the Pleroma to become a planet in the Kenoma was a galactic anomaly with no precedent.

In a mission of compassion for her plight, her fellow Aeons in the Pleroma send the Aeon Christos to comfort and guide her through this dark period. Eventually she would adjust to her new reality and became the creative nurturing Mother Earth who succors life in all its varied forms, but who, (so the narrative goes), favors the Anthropos (us special humans) above all other creatures.

Sophia is a supernatural being, with super-intelligence and an immense array of powers, but these powers are not absolute. She is not omnipotent, omniscient, or omnipresent. She is finite, bounded, and ever in the process of becoming. She is sentient in the extreme, feeling everything there is to feel. She can be impetuous and is given to sudden mood swings. She is like us, only very much more so, she being supernatural, a goddess of the galaxy's core.

The Sophia Myth, as told by the Gnostics, resembles the origin stories of many indigenous groups, especially as Sun, Moon, and Earth are considered to have intelligence, sentience, and volition—not to mention a highly individuated personhood. Our wild hunter-gatherer ancestors were animists who knew themselves to live in a world filled with spirits—each an individual in its own right—just as every living being in the world is a distinct individual, and worthy of respect as such. Theirs was a world filled with individuated personalities, whether animal, vegetable, mineral, or spirit. Collectively, these individuals make up a Community of Life, all of whom interact with one another in vast networks of interdependent relationship, creating a unity, a Whole. The Indigenous Worldview, being ecological in outlook, grants the non-human creatures of the world a status little beneath that of the human. The surviving Gnostic material, fragmentary as it is, has little to say about the larger Community of Life and its relationship to the Whole. Although this is a deficiency—due, I am guessing, to the self-obsessed narcissism that has defined our cultural ethos for the past six thousand years--it need not be a fatal one. Simply substitute the ecological insights of the Indigenous Worldview for the vainglory of human exceptionalism, in this way giving our fellow Earthlings their due in the scheme of things.

No narrative, however fully articulated, can cover everything we need to know about how to live within a particular story. Inevitably, we must extrapolate from, and elaborate upon, a story's founding principles, and do what makes sense in terms of the larger outlines. It is precisely here, in terms of these larger outlines and principles, that the Sophia Myth proves itself superior to the leading stories of our culture. This includes the two master-narratives of our peoples: the Story of Monotheistic Religion and the Story of Materialist Science.

The first thing to understand is that both these master-narratives derive from the same foundational premises about the nature of reality—the Big Lie of separation-- and who we, as a people, are. It is easy to lose sight of the roots and the common trunk that science and religion share, especially when you compare their contrasting cosmologies. According to the more ancient of these stories, a male deity, possessed of the extraordinary powers of all-knowing omniscience, almighty omnipotence, and who is everywhere at once (omnipresent) while at the same time residing somewhere far, far away. This is the god who created the human being as his masterwork (and favorite), but with flaws. According to Christian doctrine, all humans are born sinners, and are therefore in need of salvation. When you consider that this all-knowing, all-powerful godhead had the power to make the human to exacting specifications—and presumably did so—you have to wonder what motivated this divine artificer to so botch his master creation. This jealous and vengeful god of the Old Testament does seem to enjoy reducing his children to frightened, groveling toadies, their spirits weighed down with shame and guilt—shame and guilt for being the very creatures he made them. Something in this dynamic does not smell right, as the Gnostics themselves sharply observed—calling Yahweh an imposter god of ill-intent. (More on this later.)

According to the Old Testament, this all-powerful god created the heavens and the Earth in just six days. "In the beginning was the Word, and the Word was with God, and the Word was God." (Gospel of John, 1:1) These words about the Word speak poetically of the Unknown: of Mystery. However, this document insists, the creation of the Universe was absolutely no accident, but came about through divine intent-- and that intent gave meaning, purpose, and direction to the lives of those who believed in this story. In the predominantly Christian countries of the world, believers in the outline of this story (however nominal) constitute the majority of the population. Yet, in the minds of many others, key tenets of this worldview are not only called into question, but have been programmatically supplanted by a starkly different cosmology: the view of scientific materialism.

According to key tenets of this worldview, the Universe is one big accident, precipitated by nothing more than time and random chance and some sort of disposition toward doing things in a certain way. The fundamental property of the cosmos is matter, and in such a material world if a thing cannot be weighed, measured, or calculated it may be safely ignored as irrelevant to science. Telos, or intention, cannot be shown to have weight, dimension, or calculability within this self-limiting system of dogmas. Neither can Spirit, purpose, or meaning, so all these qualities are assumed not to exist, except perhaps as a comforting fiction among the scientifically illiterate. The story that mainstream reductionist science tells is a grim one indeed: the Universe is indifferent or hostile to all life, including human life. It is a dog-eat-dog world of deadly competition for survival, red in tooth and claw. Competition is considered as fundamental to life, with cooperation playing a very minor role in the "struggle for survival." Consciousness, in this view, is a product of matter and is produced (somehow) by the brain, and is regarded as a fluke, an illusion, or both. Yes, they are talking about the same consciousness that is the ground of our being and without which the person that you and I identify as distinctly ourselves would not exist. Their argument is weak, defying the common experience of us all, but at least this view is logically consistent with certain other doctrines of scientific materialism, such as their reductionism, which falsely reduces the whole to the sum of its parts, or the false equation that organism equals mechanism—thus treating the living world as nothing more than machinery.

As a body of doctrines, the paradigm of scientific materialism is more or less self-consistent, but as a philosophy it is darkly nihilistic, and it makes a terrible, blood-soaked story to live in. And, just as the doctrines of the Old Testament offer a dark and distorted view of human nature, so too do the dogmas of scientific materialism. We humans, who are group-oriented animals, are made to see ourselves as isolated individuals in a competition of all against all. We, who display a highly developed moral sensibility and understand the importance of morality to human interactions, are told there is no basis on which to sort right from wrong. We, who are by nature meaning-seeking and meaning-making beings, are told that there is no such thing as meaning in this hard, cold, random-chance Universe.

The deficiencies of the scientific materialist paradigm run much deeper than simply being a bad match for the human organism and its inborn hierarchy of needs. The assumptions built-in to this worldview are ultimately lethal to the Community of Life on a living planet—because nothing, in this view, is, or ever could be, sacred. When nothing is sacrosanct, nothing taboo, the only rule is: might makes right. If Power prevails, and there is no other moral imperative, then the race is on to gain ever more Power, and to do so without restraint. In these days of ecosystem breakdown and full-throttle exploitation of planet and people, we can clearly see the results of a story that denies the moral order of the cosmos.

And it is not as if the Ten Commandments have much more to offer by way of moral guidance—thanks largely to the Big Lie of separation. The Ten Commandments summarize the rules of engagement between an insecure vengeful god and his vulnerable worshippers. There are also a few obvious precepts about how people should treat other people: Don't kill them, don't steal from them, don't tell lies about them. There is nothing at all about how to treat the larger Community of Life or the Earth that nurtures us, except to take dominion over them, with the clear implication that they exist solely for the purpose of human exploitation, wealth creation, and the aggrandizement of God's chosen.

The beauty of the Sophia Myth is not that it spells out a list of moralistic do's and don'ts, because it doesn't. Neither does it suggest that there are no rules, and no basis on which to sort right from wrong. Instead, the story of how a goddess from the galaxy's Pleroma falls through the ever more alien environment of the Kenoma to become the living Earth itself, invites identification with, and compassion for, a being with qualities like our own, only very much more so. Like us, she is intelligent (extremely so), with an enormous capacity for feeling. She has a will of her own, and makes choices with consequences. And she has a personality all her own, just like we do. This is not the kind of story we have become accustomed to. In fact, it is so different that it takes a while to realize how far-reaching its implications are, not only in themselves, but as a story to live in. This is what I want to look at next.

Part 2: From Fragments to a Nearly Integrated Whole

> "A myth is a traditional story consisting of events that are ostensibly historical, though often supernatural, explaining the origins of a cultural practice or natural phenomenon....Myth can mean 'sacred story,' 'traditional narrative,' or tale of the gods." (Wikipedia)

THE SOPHIA MYTH differs from most other creation myths in that it does not begin at the beginning, with the creation of the Universe itself. This narrative confines itself to our own Milky Way galaxy and to a time when galactic evolution is well advanced. This is a story about how the Earth and the solar system were formed and how the human (the Anthropos) came into being. Although the ancient Gnostics were contemporaneous with the ancient Greeks, living in the same part of the world and sharing a similar culture based in the agricultural way of life, the story told by the Gnostics is much more narrowly focused and lacks the moral confusion found in the multiple story lines of Greek mythology, where murder, incest, treachery, and betrayal are common practices among the various gods of Mt Olympus. The gods in the Greek pantheon are fully differentiated named characters who act and interact in a drama of strife and cross purposes. The story of Sophia makes reference to the gods and goddesses who inhabit the galactic core but names only three: Christos, Thelete, and Sophia herself. The Sophia Myth is rich in moral implication, and yet is not at all prescriptive. Once you know the story of who and what the Earth actually is, it is up to you to decide the proper relationship between yourself and the Mother who gives you life.

What follows leans heavily upon the work of John Lamb Lash and his book, Not in His Image: Gnostic Vision, Sacred Ecology, and the Future of Belief, from which I quote extensively. He makes many subtle and nuanced points that might easily be lost through paraphrase. I hope to make an original contribution to the discussion not in telling the Sophia story but in exploring its implications to the lives of people living today, and to a possible human future.

Here I quote the following paragraph in its entirely, not only for its mythic content but for its perspective on how that content might be viewed. "What next occurs in the Pleroma is a collective act, the collaboration of all the Aeons, not just Sophia and Thelete acting as a distinct pair. In episode 3, the entire company of Pleromic gods unites in a choral dance to project the encoded singularity into manifestation. They seed it in the outer cosmos, the galactic limbs turning like a vast carousel around the Pleromic hub. The singularity nests in a nebular cloud. Although the language here is mythic, or mythopoetic, the description can be read as applying to the inner dynamics of the Galaxy. The myth clearly suggests astrophysical processes yet unknown to science, but perhaps beginning to be glimpsed in plasma physics, complexity theory, and the new vision of emergence." (p.174) At this point, the human genome has been projected (seeded) into the outer arm of the galaxy, where it awaits the proper conditions (a home) where it might flourish. How that home appears is central to the Sophianic myth and to the story of our kind.

"Fascinated by what might happen to the Anthropos as it unfolds its potential in a planetary setting, the Aeon Sophia absorbs herself in dreaming, the cosmic process of emanation. But she does so on her own, unilaterally, without a counterpart, at variance with the cosmic law of polarity by which harmony and balance are maintained in the myriad worlds. Enthralled by the possibilities of the human singularity, the Anthropos, she drifts away from the Pleroma, departs from the cosmic center, and plunges into the realm of the external, swirling chaos outside the galactic core." (p. 159) This "fall" from the galactic center is a highly unusual phenomenon, and it produces its own fateful anomalies.

"Sophia's plunge from the Godhead produces an unforeseen impact in the realm of chaos, spawning a species of inorganic beings, the Archons. In Sophia's fascination with the Anthropos (human species), and in her previsioning of how it might evolve, the Goddess did not anticipate the arising of these weird entities. They represent an anomalous or deviant factor that may impinge on the evolution of humanity. The Archons gather around a central deity, the Demiurge, who falsely believes he is the creator of all he beholds. The demented god proceeds to construct a celestial habitat for himself from atomic matter: this is the planetary system exclusive of the Earth, Sun, and Moon." (p. 159) What we call our solar system is at this point still very much in process.

"As the scaffolding of the planetary system arises, a newborn star emerges from the nebula where the Anthropos is embedded. Owing to its superior mass, the star causes the emergent planetary system to cohere around it. It becomes the central sun of the Archontic heaven, a realm of celestial mechanics dominated by blind, inorganic forces. Sophia shames the Demiurge by declaring to him that the Anthropos, though yet unborn, surpasses the Archons in intelligence, for humanity is an emanation of the Pleroma, whereas the Archons arise outside the cosmic core, without an act of emanation. Witnessing this reprimand, and shocked by the arrogance of the Demiurge, the newborn star undergoes a conversion: it chooses to align with Sophia against the realm of Archontic forces, i.e., the inorganic planetary field. The fallen goddess recognizes this choice and produces from herself a daughter in her own likeness, the life force Zoe, who unites with the sun, the mother star of the planetary system." (pp.159-60) Thus, our solar system consists of five (or more) inorganic planets inhabited by inorganic being (the Archons) and a single organic planet inhabited by organic life. More than this, our planet, the Earth, is not only alive but is the Aeon Sophia herself. How did such a thing come to be?

Sophia's original home at the center of the galaxy (the Pleroma) is a vastly different environment than what she finds in the galaxy's arm (the Kenoma). "The Kenoma, the carousel armature of a galaxy, is the realm of chaos where finite, bounded potential develops. It is composed of dark elementary matter arrays (dema), atomic and sub-atomic fields, including proto-organic elements, residue of past worlds. Suns are born in the galactic arms and planetary systems emerge there." (p. 174) Although the Aeon Sophia is a supernatural creature endowed with an immense complement of powers, she is, nevertheless, an emotional being capable of experiencing many different moods, and her fall into this alien environment leaves her stunned and depressed.

"After the conversion of the Mother Star, Sophia finds herself getting rapidly denser. As the solar system captures the emergent earth, the planet becomes increasingly subject to gravity, electromagnetism, and other laws that are totally new to the Goddess. The velocity of her high-porosity currents is winding down, her body of Organic Light dimming to a substance like soft leaded pearl, the germ of the nickel core of the terrestrial globe. In grief and confusion, Sophia gradually morphs into the planet Earth." (p. 310) This morphing of an Aeon into a planet is, evidently, an unprecedented event (at least within this particular galaxy) and so there is no knowing what might happen next.

"When Sophia reaches the stage where the planetary body begins to sprout with life—that is, the point when the biosphere is formed—the emergent life-forms are so rampant and prodigious that she is unable to manage them (episode 8). The gods in the Pleroma observe that their sister is being overwhelmed by the immense diversity of life she is producing. She cannot manage the behavior of her progeny, and fails to keep them within their proper boundaries. In short, her autopoiesis is at risk of disintegrating. Her plight elicits a response from the Pleroma, a rescue mission, an intercession." (p.310) The Aeon Christos arrives on Earth and "brings order to the biological diversity of Sophia's world. Upon making this intercession, the Christos leaves a kind of radiant afterimage in the biosphere, then recedes from Earth and returns to the Pleroma." (p. 160)

The Aeon Sophia becomes reconciled to her new condition, but not without residual feelings of homesickness for all she has formerly known. "Now totally identified with the life-processes of the planet she has become, Sophia finds herself bizarrely stranded, and isolated, in the experiment she has previsioned in the Pleroma. This is a world where one particular strain of the Anthropos (current humanity) now proceeds to live out the potential endowed in it by Sophia and Thelete, thus to demonstrate human novelty on earth." (160)

The human being is Sophia's darling, and her fascination

with what we might become has, from the beginning, been a driving passion of hers. The Gnostics say that there have been other experiments with the Anthropos in other parts of the galaxy, nine before our own, and that all the others have, in some way or other, failed. Nor is Sophia's experiment with Anthropos Ten going particularly well right now. Something in our makeup, something of which there is too much, is pushing us to untenable extremes. The Archons are our enemies, and they mean to do us harm, but it is important to understand that the human race has flaws of its own, and that all our misdeeds cannot be blamed on the Archons. Keeping this fact firmly in mind, it is equally important to understand who and what the Archons are, and why they wish us ill.

The Archons are an unintended result of Sophia's fall from the order of the galaxy's core into the relative chaos of the galaxy's arm. "This anomalous species comes into existence prior to the time when the earth emerges by direct transformation of Sophia's own divine substance. Archons are Sophia's offspring, in a sense, but in an entirely different way than humanity and other organic species are. They do not emerge from her divine substance, Organic Light, but from its impact upon particulate matter in the dema. They are a freak species of inorganic composition, but they are alive and conscious in their own way.

"At first the Archons have no habitat. They swarm around like an insect colony blown savagely across interstellar space, sucked toward Sophia's currents and repulsed again. Since they were not initially projected from the Pleroma, they lack autopoetic encoding. They have no innate intentionality, ennoia. Archons present an extra-Pleromic phenomenon, a cosmic aberration, anomia. Their emergence from the field of primal matter is premature, so they are compared to an aborted fetus. This is perhaps the most bizarre, arresting image in the Gnostic materials. The Archon legion of embryonic insectoid forms attaches itself to Sophia like an infestation of swarming lice. The cosmic miscarriage of the Goddess will have extenuating circumstances for humanity." (p. 181) Indeed, the Archons mean to reduce us to a creature beneath themselves.

Precisely because the Archons are the sworn enemy of humanity, it is important to understand their nature and how they go about the business of bringing us down. "From the Archon legion emerges a second form, a mutation called the drakontoc type in the NHC [Nag Hammadi Codices]. The Apocryphon of John says that Sophia herself caused a leader or master entity to emerge among the Archons: And Sophia desired to cause the thing that had no innate spirit of its own to be formed into a likeness and rule over primal matter and over all the forces she had precipitated. So there appeared for the first time a ruler out of chaos, lion-like in appearance, androgynous, having an exaggerated sense of power within him, and ignorant of whence he came to be. (NHC II, 5: 100. 1-10) This entity, called the Demiurge, is a weird, frightening mutation, 'having a lion-like body with the head of a drakona, a reptile.' (Berlin Codex 37.2-25). Two types of Archons, a neonate or embryonic type, and the drakontic type, are not elaborately described in the surviving materials. They are indicated with the utmost brevity, but clearly enough to give the idea that something very bizarre is happening. The leonine-reptilian Archon, who is also called Yaldabaoth, is dominant and aggressive compared to the more passive Archons whose form resembles a prematurely born fetus. Although the 'chief Archon' is androgynous, it rapidly assumes a markedly male, macho posture. He now takes charge of the extraordinary situation produced by Sophia's plunge, or at least he tries. At the conclusion of episode 5, the Demiurge proceeds to create a habitat for himself in the vastness of the galactic arms." (pp. 181-2)

According the Gnostic teachings, the Earth, Moon, and Sun constitute a three-body system (trimorphic protennoia) that was previsioned by Sophia and her consort within the Pleroma; furthermore, "Earth does not belong to the planetary system but is merely captured in it....The steroma of the Demiurge is the planetary system exclusive of the Sun, Moon, and Earth. These three bodies make up an independent cosmos. Earth, Sun, and Moon form a symbiotic system enclosed on itself and dynamically distinct from the clockwork mechanism of the other planets. Outrageous as this notion may appear, it is not inconsistent with scientific thought." (pp. 183-4) The Archons, who are themselves non-organic cyborg-like creatures, inhabit the non-organic planets within the solar system, and cannot survive the oxygen-rich atmosphere of Earth. But they do have ways of influencing life on Earth.

"Gnostics taught that the Demiurge cannot really create anything because he lacks the power of intention proceeding from the Pleroma and ultimately based in the Originator. Archons cannot originate anything, but they can imitate, copy, duplicate. Their memetic capacity is called phantasia to distinguish it from the real-life animating power of the Aeons, called ennoia. Yaldabaoth is called the antimimon pneuma, the 'counterfeit spirit' in the Apocryphon of John and other cosmological texts. The celestial mansions he contrives are called steroma, a stereometric projection like the holograph of a living thing. The holographic image is not alive but can represent or copy something that is. Using the Coptic word HAL, 'simulation,' Gnostic cosmological texts explain that the many-mansioned heaven of the Demiurge is a virtual cosmos, a virtual reality (VR) world." (p. 182) Mention is made here of an Originator, but very little is said in the texts about the larger Universe, or its originator. The focus of the Sophianic

THE SOPHIA MYTH

Myth is our particular solar system and the galaxy in which it came into being.

Meanwhile, back in our own solar system, the Lord Archon is busy with his own self-importance: "Arrogant by nature, the Demiurge deems himself to be at the center of creation, lord of all he beholds. Gnostic texts state plainly that Yaldabaoth is insane, a demented god, or imposter deity. The Demiurge is indeed a sort of god, a cosmic entity in his own right, but he is not a Pleromic Aeon. He is a self-deified inorganic phantom deluded about his own identity. This is not meant as a figure of speech or a mythological trope. Not by a long shot, for the Gnostic material clearly shows that the adepts of the Mysteries perceived Yaldabaoth and the Archons as real, physically existent inhabitants of our planetary system, who wrongly attempt to penetrate the biosphere....God exists, but he is insane. And he works against humanity. Such is the startling message carried in the Sophianic vision of the Mysteries." (p.185) Even more shocking to the Christian and Judaic sensibility is this revelation: "Yaldabaoth is the Demiurge, a.k.a. Yaweh-Jehova, a demented god who works against humanity." (pp.283-4) Given the Gnostic take on the Judaic/Christian god, as well as other doctrines of the faith, it is perhaps no mystery why the Mystery Schools were hounded out of existence, their heretical writings set ablaze.

The Gnostics strongly, and publicly, objected to a triad of dangerous doctrines that were propounded by the Jews and adopted, in modified form, by the early Christians. They found particularly objectionable the doctrine of "the chosen people," as advanced by an extremist sect of the Jews called the Zaddikim, and embraced in a slightly altered form by the early Church Fathers. They also found fault with the apocalyptic vision of this same sect and the "superhuman and inhumane standard of perfection that informs the religion and ethics of Jewish apocalypticism [which was] inherited, but modified, by Christianity and Islam." (p. 406) The Gnostics were also deeply unhappy with the doctrine of Salvationism: "Gnostics explicitly warned that the Archons work through Salvationist religion, not to destroy us, however, but to deviate us from our proper course of evolution, our share in Sophia's 'correction.' They do this, Gnostics claim, because they envy us. Archons lack both ennoia (singular intentionality) and epinoia (moral-creative imagination), and they want to have this specific endowment of ours, to assimilate or steal it." (p.289)

The doctrine of the chosen people promotes division, pitting "the chosen" against "the unchosen" of the world. In a similar vein, the end-times vision of apocalypticism invites the destruction of all that is real for the sake of a fanatical delusion. Both of these destructive dogmas pose a threat to peace, and even to life itself. It is easy to see why the Gnostics found them so odious. Less obvious are their reasons for rejecting the Christian doctrine of Salvationism: "The directive script of Judeo-Christian-Islamic monotheism impels our self-betrayal, because the script replicates indigenous narrative, the story of coevolution that we really could be developing and enacting, but deceptively insinuates antihuman and antinatural values in its place. Hebrew monotheism is often associated with ethical idealism, as if the model morality dictated by the father god guarantees the best possible behavior on Earth. But if humans possess an innate capacity for moral discernment, such a capacity cannot be commanded from without, nor imposed through rules and formulas from on high." (pp.235-6) The presumption (or insight) of the Gnostics is that the human being possesses its own internal guidance system, including an acute moral sensibility. By surrendering this inner moral authority to external forces, and allowing those forces to dictate by rule, formula, and commandment what is right and what is wrong, the human colludes in self-betrayal. "Salvation by superhuman powers, rather than through the divine potential innate to humanity and aligned with Sophia, is the hallmark of extra-terrestrial religion." (p. 284) Religion, in this view, is a toxic social and cultural contagion disguised as a story by which to live; a myth of redemption, based on an origin story concocted by a mad divinity, to lure humanity off its true path and into self-betrayal.

The Demiurge and the Archons might appear to some as the embodiment of pure evil, but this is not the Gnostic view. Indeed, the question of good and evil is answered by the Gnostics in a rather novel and interesting way. "In the Sophia mythos the Archons emerge because of Sophia's plunge into elemental matter, before the Goddess morphs into the earth and continues her Dreaming as Gaia (episode 5). This unforeseen event is called 'the generation of error' because the anomaly triggered by Sophia's plunge produces a subliminal effect in the human mind, exaggerating our natural tendency to err and shifting it beyond the scale of correction. The presence of the Archons in the solar system dangerously widens the margin of human error, thus impacting the way we learn and evolve. At the very least, the Archons can be taken for a brilliant parapsychological metaphor that explains how humans can think and act out of scale, inhumanely. The self-betrayal of humanity through the redeemer complex happens, in part, because we can think ourselves right out of our own minds and into an alien mind-set.

"No matter what one makes of the Archons in a literal sense, the Gnostic theory of error is certainly one of the supreme achievements of human reasoning. The Gnostic seers insisted that Archons cannot control or manipulate us unless we give them power to do so. This happens when we do not optimize nous, our endowment of divine intelligence. Our omission is their salvation. Gnostic error theory states three simple, interlocking truths: (1) humans are creatures who learn by making mistakes; (2) to learn from our mistakes we must detect and correct them (hence our collaborative role in Gaian evolution and Sophia's 'correction'); and (3) when we fail to detect and correct our mistakes they can extrapolate wildly and spin us beyond human limits. The Archons intrude at just that point where we let our errors go uncorrected, and lend their deviant force to what is already going off course, taking us with them in a wayward spiral. Without our cosmic cousins in the picture we would still commit errors, but would always be able to stand back and correct our course before we got too far out of alignment with Gaia and our own potential." (pp. 290-91) Here is what we have so far learned about the nature of our enemies, the Archons: they are a galactic aberration, an anomaly; they have no intentionality of their own; they are inorganic beings that live on the inorganic planets of our solar system; lacking creative originality, they are nevertheless masterful mimics who deal in deception and simulations of the real; they are motivated by envy, and their intention is to deviate the human from our divine potential, to reduce us to a stature beneath themselves. But how do these off-planet creatures work their black arts upon the human psyche?

Somehow, perhaps because we both share in the nature of our Aeonic Mother, the Archons are (according to the Gnostics) highly attuned to the strengths and weaknesses of human psychology, and highly adept at insinuating themselves into the human mind. These mind parasites work their mischief by means of telepathic remote influence, from their realm among the inorganic planets of our solar system. They achieve their intrapsychic intrusion not only at the level of the ordinary person, but also by targeting key individuals who have, or will come to have, an inordinate influence upon the larger culture. One such individual has come to be known as the father of the three Abrahamic religions: Judaism, Islam, and Christianity. "The ideological virus released on a pandemic scale by Saint Paul was incubated among the ancient Hebrews by the Archons—so says Gnostic counter-mythology. 'Yaldabaoth himself chose a certain man named Abraham...and made a covenant with him.' From the outset, the delusional beliefs of an alien mindset infected the Judeo-Christian religion, but Gnostics saw the infection as it set in. They taught that finding humanity's true path depends on refuting and rejecting these beliefs, all the way back to their origin." (p.117)

In the glossary of Not in His Image we find this definition of the Abrahamic religions: "Judaism, Christianity, and Islam considered as variations of a common belief system characterized by monotheism, patriarchal values, a linear time scheme for history, a divinely prescribed moral code, redeemer ideology, sexual apartheid, and the dominator agenda, including domination of nature and the assumption of human superiority over all other species." (p. 387)

When an isolated individual is deviated from his or her true course and nature, it is a shame, and may even have tragic consequences—at the level of person, family, and possibly community. Self-actualization of one's full potential is what Life is all about, not only for humans but for all living creatures. The inner urge is to become the most fully realized version of who and what we are, given the circumstances of our lives. The poet, Gerard Manley Hopkins has captured this truth in just four lines: "Each mortal thing does one thing and the same: Deals out that being indoors each one dwells; Selves—goes itself: myself it speaks and spells, Crying What I do is me: for that I came." This is Life's own purpose, direction, and meaning: for each individual creature to attain its optimum potential, in alignment with the Whole. When the will to self-actualization is diverted, subverted, and subsumed by an outside force, something of great value is lost—not only for the individual but also to the larger systems of which the individual is a part, including one's society and culture as well as the ecosystems that serve (and are potentially served by) the deviated individual.

But what is the result when an entire culture has been deviated in this way? When John Lamb Lash speaks of the Abrahamic belief system as an "ideological virus on a pandemic scale," this is no exaggeration. For consider what has been subtracted from human life and what has been put in its place. Before the rise of agriculture and religion, our wild ancestors were lovers of the Earth, and not only because their lives depended upon this Being who could bless the people with plenty or grudgingly withhold her bounty. They thought of her as having her own distinct personhood, including all the qualities we associate with a living, intelligent, feeling, willful being—one capable of significant mood swings. A creature like us, only very much more so. They knew Mother Earth as a Being of immense creativity, imagination, and resourcefulness; a lover of beauty as well as of utility; a friend to the human, as long as you stayed on her good side. Powerful and mysterious, Mother Earth was a daily presence in the lives of the people; she was revered, respected, and loved—not only for what she could give or take away, but for all her excellent qualities as a Being, as appreciated through long acquaintance and close relationship.

Echoes of that relationship remain as part of our racial memory, our collective unconscious. As young children, we are predisposed to be in close relationship to Mother Earth. This nascent relationship never comes to fruition for most of us because we live in a man-made world apart from Nature, and because we have been infected by an ideological virus that devalues Mother Earth while elevating the human to a position of supremacy over all.

In place of the genuine article that is the world of Nature, we are lured into a counterfeit world of simulations. Think of Disney World and all the more obvious forms of virtual reality--including television, motion pictures, video games, computers, and Smart phones (to which most of us are addicted)—and how these divert us from engaging with the natural world, or even with each other. "In Gnostic terms the replication of nature in lifeless form exemplifies HAL, Archontic simulation. In the shift from organic form to abstraction an entire range of values is lost and other values contrary to organic life are adopted as if they were equal, or even superior to, the lost values." (p. 230) This shift from the real to the simulated is a hallmark of the age we live in, and now seems on the verge of completely devouring whatever remains authentic and organic in human life, propelling us into a transhumanist future where artificial intelligence rules. If this diversion of our humanity into cyborgs and smart machines carries the day, whatever our best human potential might have led to will be more than "diverted." Humanity simply will be no more.

The Sophia Myth, as reconstructed by John Lamb Lash from the fragmentary materials known as the Nag Hammadi Codices, offers a coherent narrative about the formation of our solar system, with a special focus upon our own home planet and the origin of the human species (the Anthropos)—along with the bombshell story of the Archons and the Demiurge. We owe a debt of gratitude to this independent scholar for his inspired piecing together of fragments of scrambled and damaged manuscripts, uniquely fashioning them into a shape with (potentially) profound meaning. In addition to these major story lines we also get in-depth critiques of certain

Judeo-Christian doctrines, including the assumptions and implications that underlie them. What the Gnostics offer us is a take on the world that is outside the traditions of mainstream Western thought, and yet, paradoxically, comes out of the very same cultural traditions that we recognize as our own. After sixteen centuries of being lost to the world (that is, deliberately and violently suppressed) we are left to make of it what we will.

Should we consider the Sophia Myth as more or less literal truth? Should we instead see it as true, but only in a metaphorical sense? This is the way most of us approach those mythologies we identify with culturally, such as Greek mythology. We seem to recognize that some kind of truth resides in these stories—truth we may identify as archetypal, or see as having some other form of psychological validity. Or we might just be skeptics to the end and see nothing of value in a story that runs so counter to the master-narratives that rule our lives: i.e. scientific materialism and monotheistic religion. My own inclination is to ask a different question entirely: what in this (or any) story is useful? And by useful I mean having a practical application. Recalling that the master-narratives which dominate our lives are driving us and the planet to utter ruin, I am open to considering what it might mean if some of us, or many of us, took the Sophia Myth as a story to believe in, and to live in. (This is where I want to go in the next installment, and I hope you will join me.)

THE SOPHIA MYTH

Part 3: A Fallible Goddess versus the Almighty Yahweh

IN RECENT YEARS a fair number of books have been written about the intelligence of the Earth.* Most of these speak in terms of systems, or systems of systems, steering away from any sort of personification of the Earth's intelligence. Given the rigid doctrines of materialistic science, this is not surprising, especially considering the discomfort most people feel when defying orthodoxy. It is generally easier, and safer, to stick with the crowd—which is why consensual reality tends to hold sway and control what is acceptable to think and believe.

The Sophia Myth invites us to believe that the Earth is no mere mechanistic system of systems operating automatically out of some kind of algorithm, but is instead a living being endowed with sentience, volition, an individuated personhood, as well as a highly developed creative intelligence. In this way she is like us, only very much more so—she being supernatural and we being the product of her and Thelete's divine experiment. Sophia's role as our co-creator would seem to imply a rather steep hierarchy, putting us humans in the subordinate

---

* Since the Gaia Hypothesis of James Lovelock and Lynn Margulis first appeared in the 1970s, inquiring minds have looked into different aspects of this theory and come away with differing views on the subject of a self-organizing Earth. Typical of the scientific materialist mindset is Gaia's Body: Toward a Physiology of Earth, (2003) by Tyler Volk. Rigorously academic in approach, and leaning heavily upon physics, chemistry, and mathematics, the book is nevertheless fascinating in describing various Earth processes and how they interact. Volk will go so far as to say that the Earth behaves as if it were a superorganism, but not that it is one. In this way his credentials as an upstanding scientific materialist remain intact, as does the materialist agenda itself. As long as the Earth can be considered as nothing more than a system of physical and chemical processes--with no sentience, intelligence, or intent, and certainly nothing like personhood—business as usual may continue unabated, until nothing is left to take.

role of supplicants in the face of an almighty power. Yet there is nothing in the Gnostic materials, as presented by John Lamb Lash, to suggest any such relationship.

We know that the jealous, narcissistic, and authoritarian father-god of the Old Testament requires that his vassals bow down to him in fear and trembling—or else! "Thou shalt not make unto thee any graven image, or any likeness of anything that is in heaven above, or that is in the earth beneath, or that is in the water under the earth: Thou shalt not bow down thyself, nor serve them: for I the Lord thy God am a jealous God, visiting the iniquity of the fathers upon the children unto the third and fourth generation of them that hate me." (Exodus 20: 4-5) This is a capricious god who seems to suffer great insecurity within himself, who likes to throw his weight around, squishing people at will and leaving the rest to squirm and grovel in fear of his wrath.

More than a century's worth of anthropological work tells us that most indigenous groups revered and respected the Great Spirit and invested considerable group energy into rituals and ceremonies designed to cultivate good relationship with Mother Earth and the Invisible Powers. They seem to have been motivated not so much by fear as by a sense of identification with all of life, and in the recognition that Mother Earth and Father Sun were the source of all that lived and breathed, of all that was good and beautiful in the world. Gratitude was a central motivation, but so, too, was the courting and practice of humility. Our indigenous brothers and sisters knew very well that the human is prone to pathological levels of hubris, arrogance, and self-glorifying pride—and that trouble cannot be far behind. It is not that the gods demand homage of the human; it's that the human requires a check on his overweening self-regard with a regular dose of ritual humility. Or so the evidence would seem to suggest.

But what of the Goddess Sophia: what, if anything, does she require of us? And what sort of relationship is it possible to have with her?

To get at answers to these questions, it may be helpful to explore some of the ways that Gnostic cosmology and ontology differ from those of the Abrahamic religions. According to the sacred texts of Judaism, Christianity, and Islam, the heavens and the Earth were created by an all-knowing, all-powerful, immortal male deity who makes exacting demands upon all the beings of his creation, but especially upon the one he has fashioned after himself: us special, but deeply flawed, humans. The Bible speaks of eternity but seems to assume a world and universe that is essentially static, with everything now just as god made it. And god himself is depicted as the quintessence of perfection, but perfection is hard put to maintain its purity and consistency, except in a world that is static--a world that does not evolve or grow but stays forever the same.

It should be noted that perfection, as envisioned by early sacred texts, as well as by Plato, does not occur in the real world we inhabit, but in a sort of heaven of ideal perfection that is one hundred percent theoretical. In such a world the Earth would be a perfect sphere maintaining an orbit in the form of a perfect circle. The shape of the actual Earth only approximates a sphere and its elliptical orbit makes a very lopsided circle, indeed. Yet this arrangement has persisted for some 4.5 billion years, and this demonstrable fact should tell us something about the nature of reality, and also about human fantasies of perfection.

By way of contrast, the Gnostic writings portray Sophia as a supernatural but mortal being who, at the time of her fall was young and impetuous, and who as the newly-formed Earth was overwhelmed by feelings of homesickness and depression. When she had been safely ensconced within the galactic core, co-creating the human genome with her partner, the Aeon Thelete, her feeling space was animated by hyper-curiosity and the urge to create something of significance. The Gnostics may not have elaborated a theory of evolution, but they did seem to understand that the world and everything in it is in dynamic process. As the pre-Socratic philosopher, Heraclitus (c 535-475 B.C.) has noted, and as our best science now affirms: "You could not step twice into the same river" because "all that endures is change." When Sophia strays from the Pleroma and falls through the Kenoma, to eventually become the Earth, this is a break with precedent, an anomaly that generates consequences, but it is not the breaking of an absolute Law. And herein lies an important distinction between the Gnostic worldview and that of the Judeo-Christian tradition.

Within the Gnostic worldview, perfection is necessarily relative. The concept of relative perfection may be a misnomer, when what is really meant is that something--some part, some holon--functions well enough to survive more or less in harmony with the Whole. Implied in this view is a network of connectedness, a web of interdependent relationships, such as is suggested by this pithy insight of Heraclitus: "All things come from the One and the One from all things." If all is in dynamic motion-- as in an expanding, evolving Universe— being in synch or in tune with the Whole is the place to be. In such a world, nothing could possibly attain, let alone maintain, absolute perfection. What is possible, and what constitutes the world as it is, is a flexible adaptability among constituent parts to harmonize with the evolving Whole.

The notion of absolute perfection, as found in scripture and as carried forward by culture to the present moment, is based on the false concept of a Universe in stasis. When expectations of absolute perfection are applied to human beings, these impossibly high standards become a trap for the unwary, leading to torments of guilt and shame, along with feelings of inferiority, because no human, no organism of any kind, including Goddesses, could ever measure up. Weakened by self-doubt, the conscientious and the devout become vulnerable to those who would seek power over them, and especially to an authoritarian, fear- and guilt-stoking priesthood. Consider the fire-and brimstone sermon by Jonathan Edwards, "Sinners in the Hands of an Angry God," and multiply this soul-withering message by however many clerics, over however many centuries and all around the world, have seen fit to expound upon this harsh theme of judgment and damnation.

The Judeo-Christian tradition and the Gnostics offer two very different views on the nature of reality, as well as on the nature of the divine, and these differences have far-reaching implications. One can scarcely overstate the proposition that ideas matter, and that what you think about the world and yourself manifest as very real consequences, in your own life and in the world at large. The sorry state the planet is in right now is a direct result of our people living out lies over centuries and millennia. I have already mentioned the Big Lie of Separation, in which Western man imagines himself as separate from, and above, everything else in the world, including Mother Earth herself, who is regarded as nothing more than a collection of resources to be used, without restraint, by humans. Much of the planetary exhaustion that we are experiencing today, including "resource" depletion, poisoning of the biosphere, the sixth great extinction, and ecological failure at all scales, can be traced back to this single anti-ecological, catastrophically mistaken, idea. But the Big Lie has spawned other lies that have also proved themselves toxic to the human enterprise, as well as to the Project of Life, and prominent among these is the institution of patriarchy.

When the books of Genesis and Exodus were written some

2500-plus years ago, the way of life they chronicle and codify was already well-established. These were pastoral people and growers of wheat, and there was considerable division among themselves and enmity toward neighboring groups. The ownership of land and livestock separated the prosperous from those with less, and was the basis for the rigid hierarchy that defined their social order. At the apex of this society was the patriarch, and he wielded great power over those below him, including his wife (or wives), his children, his servants, his livestock, and whoever else fell below him in the social hierarchy and came in his way.

The god who created, or was created by, this privileged individual not only mirrors the high-status patriarch but sanctifies and glorifies this way of life, lending his own patriarchal authority to this highly stratified lifeway. In the voice of Abraham's servant we are told: "And the Lord hath blessed my master greatly; and he has become great: and he hath given him flocks, and herds, and silver, and gold, and menservants and maidservants, and camels and asses." (Genesis 24:35) To be favored by this god was much to be desired, especially for the material prosperity that might come of it. But you definitely didn't want to get on this god's bad side. Bad things happen to those who displease the almighty, or who disobey him. Sometimes there seems no reason at all for the torments he visits upon his children, except for the joy of watching them squirm, as with Job.

This is a highly partisan god, who aligns himself with his chosen people (as long as they stay on his good side), and who promises to do harm to their enemies on their behalf. "But if thou shalt indeed obey his voice, and do all that I speak, I will be an enemy unto thine enemies, and an adversary unto thine adversaries." (Exodus 23:22) "For mine angel shall go before, and bring thee unto the Amorites, and the Hitites, and the

THE SOPHIA MYTH

Perizzites, and the Canaanites, the Hivites, and the Jebusites: and I will cut them off." (Exodus 23: 23) "And I will set thy bounds from the Red Sea even unto the sea of the Philistines, and from the desert unto the river: for I will deliver the inhabitants of the land into your hand; and thou shalt drive them out before thee." (Exodus 23: 31) It is clear that this god plays favorites, and is very far from even-handed in dealing with his children. And indeed this is a god who, far from abjuring wars and the depredations of empire, lends the inevitable carnage his supernatural support, providing that he be praised, offered homage and sacrifice, and obeyed on all counts by his chosen people.

But even this relationship with his chosen people is not on firm ground, for this god finds fault with everyone but himself. "And God saw that the wickedness of man was great in the earth, and that every imagination of the thoughts of his heart was only evil continually. And it repented the Lord that he had made man on the earth, and it grieved him at his heart. And the Lord said, I will destroy man whom I have created from the face of the earth; both man and beast, and the creeping things, and the fowls of the air; for it repenteth me that I have made them." (Genesis 6: 5-7) It is the human who so displeases this god that he contemplates their destruction. All the other creatures of the Earth—innocent as far as we know—are also slated for destruction, just for the hell of it, because (rather like a spoiled child in mid-tantrum) he is in a mood for mayhem.

It seems never to occur to this god that it is the social order that he promotes and underwrites--the patriarchy based on private property; the propensity to overpopulate thanks to agriculture; the unequal distribution of wealth and the extreme social stratification this promotes—are the very cultural institutions that engender the wickedness he so decries. It is the social order--an unjust social order-- that gives rise to acts of desperation among the oppressed and acts of wanton exploitation of the many by the privileged few. If this sounds familiar it is because this model for how to live in the world was established long ago, beginning some six thousand years ago, in a time of abrupt climate change, engendering deep trauma within the social order.** After more than three thousand years of pastoral patriarchy, this way of life was "divinely" sanctioned and codified in the Book of Genesis, to be passed down through our culture of Western civilization, right unto the present day. The wealth inequality we see today, the rise of an international oligarchy, the marginalization of the common man, are all modeled after, and are in a direct line of succession from, this ancient pastoral way of life. The problem is: this way of life is doomed to fail, and fail catastrophically.

The reasons for this have to do with the social ecology of human beings as well as the physical ecology of

---

** See especially The Fall: The Insanity of the Ego in human History and the Dawning of a New Era, (2005) by Steve Taylor, who has this to say: "The Ego Explosion was the most momentous event in the history of the human race. The last 6,000 years of history can only be understood in terms of it. All the different kinds of social and psychic pathology we've looked at—war, patriarchy, social stratification, materialism, the desire for status and power, sexual repression, environmental destruction, as well as the inner discontent and disharmony which afflict us—all of these traits can be traced back to the intensified sense of ego which came into existence in the deserts of Middle East and central Asia 6,000 years ago." (p. 124)

Even more important as a historical resource is the book on which Taylor's efforts are largely based: Saharasia: the 4000 BCE Origins of Child Abuse, Warfare and Social Violence in the Deserts of the Old World (1998, 2006, 2011) by James DeMeo. When the lush world these pastoral people had taken for granted suddenly dried up on them, threatening their very survival, the people were naturally traumatized. Their trauma became institutionalized within their culture, and remains the root of the culture we now recognize as our own—the trauma and dysfunction only amplified over time.

ecosystem-Earth. Beyond these is the larger cosmic order, which has imperatives of its own. One of these might be called the Law of Reciprocity; another, the Principle of Flow.

According to the Principle of Flow--which governs or influences all manner of systems—a dynamic of spreading things around tends to optimize the well-being of the Whole as well as each of its constituent parts (or holons). Within the Gaian ecosystem the cycling and recycling of energy and matter, while spreading it around through networks of interconnection, assures Flow. The water cycle, for instance, which distributes and redistributes this precious substance, passing it from ocean to sky to land and back to ocean again, is just one of the many systems of cycling and recycling our lives depend upon. As close observers of the natural world, many of our wild ancestors, noting the Principle of Flow, modeled their social institutions along these same lines.

Many peoples of cultures other than our own have adapted their economic system to the Principle of Flow. Especially notable is the gift culture, which creates incentives to keep whatever-the-gift-might-be in motion from one person to another to another, and in the process creating trading partners (gift partners) with whom one might have a genuine friendship over long time as part of the exchange. When a gift is given, obligations are created for the recipient to let go of something they have held onto for perhaps too long, and pass that onto someone else. This practice has the effect of loosening one's grip on goods considered as personal belongings, thereby countering the human proclivity for acquiring and hoarding more than one actually needs. At the same time, it encourages entering into and developing reciprocal relationships with others in one's circle or network of interaction.

When wealth inequality becomes established in a society the power-elite, who hold most of the wealth, act as dams and their impoundments, blocking the natural flow of energy and matter, thereby disrupting its natural tendency toward equitable and widespread distribution. When there are lots of rich people, and they are very rich and just sitting on their money, they risk the complete breakdown of their economic system. The reason is, they are weakening the system by defying the Principle of Flow. When flow is blocked, whether by a cultural institution or a dam, pressure builds to the point where something must give. When the breaking point is reached, the results are generally sudden and violent.

The Principle of Flow is closely related to, though no identical with, the Law of Reciprocity. The Law of Reciprocity reflects the requirements of a Life-System to maintain itself--and in maintaining itself also maintaining each of the life-forms it supports. It is a very straightforward law of give-and-take which asks that all living beings give back to the system that gives them life at least as much as the Life-System has given them. And giving back extra is even better, because inevitably there will be free-riders, who take from the system but never give back. All, or virtually all, of the creatures who live by instinct give back to the Life-System as good or better than they get, and this happens more or less automatically by virtue of instinct. It is the cultural animal who is problematical in this regard, and more so all the time, as globalization sweeps away the last remnants of those who have traditionally abided by the Law of Reciprocity.

These days, most of us just take and take and never give back, just as our culture encourages us to do. Defiance of the Law of Reciprocity is foundational to our culture, tying in nicely with the Big Lie of Separation. Cut down a forest, turn it into a town, as in Gilgamesh--and as in six thousand years of Western civilization. Destroy the habitats of the Earth's other creatures, simplifying ecosystems here, there, and everywhere, never giving any of it a second thought. Why should you concern yourself with such things when your culture commands that you take dominion over the Earth and all its creatures? Nor do you have to believe in the divine origin of this command for this notion to have insinuated itself into your consciousness. When everyone around you believes in the Myth of Human Supremacy as well as the Big Lie of Separation, why would you question what everyone else takes for granted? But don't fail to notice that the world is falling apart, or rather, is being dismantled, ecosystem by ecosystem, by the "smartest" but least well-adapted creature on planet Earth. And we are doing all this thanks to a culture that must be understood as pathological—as advancing corruption, addiction to Power, and extreme forms neurosis and psychosis among the people, making us all very unwell.

The ancient Gnostics believed the deity of the Abrahamic religions to be an imposter-god, the Demiurge, who is in fact the lord of the Archons—the very Archons whose mission is to undermine the human project. As we have seen, the god of the Old Testament reveals himself to be a less-than-benevolent spirit of questionable mental health who lends his almighty powers to the furtherance of social division, the ambitions of empire, and the carnage of war. Whether or not the Gnostics accurately identified this god, it is clear that in terms of character traits, Sophia and Yahweh represent radically different sorts of deities. If it were possible to chose the goddess over the god and live in her story instead of his, what might that look like and what might it mean for us personally and for the larger world. (This is the proposition I want to look at next.)

In the book, Animate Earth: Science, Intuition and Gaia (2006) by Stephan Harding, the author seems to want to have it both ways. That is, he seems to believe there is more to Gaia than the complex systems dynamics and feedback loops that can be studied by science, but the case he makes for this is not as strong as one might hope. He can say, for instance, that we need to "recover the ancient view of Gaia as a fully integrated, living being consisting of all her life-forms, air, rocks, oceans, lakes and rivers, if we are ever to halt the latest, and possibly greatest, mass extinction." (p. 222) But notice that there is no suggestion of personhood here, no being independent of the constituent (physical) parts he names. He feels comfortable in granting Gaia a high degree of responsiveness and intelligence, but not in granting her a will and personality, or feelings (sentience) of her own. Somehow, in this view, Earth is considered to be animate but not quite a being in her own right. And I find that to be the chief failing of this book: its trying to split the difference between mechanism and organism, but ultimately coming up with a non-viable hybrid that is both, and therefore, neither.

Of the books surveyed here, most interesting to me is Darwin's Unfinished Business: the Self-Organizing Intelligence of Nature (2012), by Simon G. Powell, for its many original insights. Not a conventional academic scientist, Powell comes at his subject matter from a rather unconventional place: direct experience in nature while under the influence of magic mushrooms. Thanks no doubt to his publisher, the word mushroom never appears in the book; nor are the arguments he makes dependent upon this subjective experience. But this is where the passion and conviction come from, I'm sure. He knows some things, knows them deeply and viscerally, but the case he makes for what he knows is based on science, much of it cutting-edge.

Refreshingly, Powell does not buy the notion of a random chance Universe, and he takes on materialists like Richard Dawkins and Daniel Dennett for the fundamental absurdity of their core assumptions. Instead of randomness, Powell finds a sensible intelligence that gives shape and direction to all evolving beings. "The point of all this is to show that evolution happens if there is sense to be made, and sense can be made only if it is configured into the greater system within which evolution occurs. Once a system has been intelligently configured with sensible rules and laws (i.e., an intelligently configured context is set up in advance), then evolution can happen within the system in response to that original sensibleness." (p.65) When Powell speaks of an "intelligently configured context" he does not mean to imply a Configurer-in-Chief. "Of course this does not necessarily mean that Nature was itself designed by some other intelligence, but rather that Nature is an intelligence unto itself, Nature's fine-tuned laws representing the most primary expression of this intelligence (as I intimated earlier, natural intelligence is the Universe)." (p. 111)

Although he doesn't mention the Big Lie of Separation, Powell sees some of its results. "It is certainly no coincidence that we live in an era in which environmental crises of one sort or another are impressing themselves upon us. The root of the problem lies in a conceptual folly according to which we isolate ourselves from the vast contextual system in which we are rooted." (p.118) Overly focused on ourselves, we miss the big picture. "But if we do acknowledge that life is connected into a sensible weblike matrix or pattern, then it becomes clear that this pattern extends outwards and connects everything, that the entire Universe with its laws and constants is the ultimate systematized environmental context that drives all evolutionary processes. It is surely in harmonious accordance to this larger context that we must strive to live." (p. 119) Of course this holistic view of our larger context should be absolutely undeniable, the evidence is that overwhelming; and yet, because the ideology of materialism rejects this evidence out of hand it, big-gun thinkers like Dennett, Dawkins, and the physicist Lawrence Krause, loudly insist that we do not live in an interconnected, interdependent, ecological Universe, but one based on nothing more than non-teleological random chance.

I once heard Krause, a highly regarded cosmologist and educator, declare that if a third of the Universe should suddenly disappear, the two-thirds that remained wouldn't even notice. And I thought to myself: this is what happens to the human brain after decades of marinating in unsubstantiated ideology. And it happens all the time, because ideology is taught as if it were actual science--and few seem to notice the difference between naked assumption (it's a random-chance Universe) and verifiable fact (the Earth orbits the sun).

Simon Powell makes a strong case for the self-organizing intelligence of Nature, going up against many of the orthodoxies of scientific materialism to make his provocative but solidly argued points. But when it comes down to questioning the most foundational assumption of materialism, his nerve seems to fail him as he goes all orthodox. "If the Universe is seen as a jigsawlike system whose components naturally self-organize into coherent patterns, then the emergence of mind within this cosmic system appears to represent a kind of dynamic meta-pattern. This is because for mind to arise there must perforce be a number of already extant patterns in place, in this case stable biological patterns such as advanced polyneuronal nervous systems. As far as we know, it is only when a biological system has evolved a certain threshold of polyneuronal complexity that conscious minds can arise." (p. 246) Nothing he says here sounds particularly outrageous, as long as one accepts the assumption that matter is primary and that consciousness is secondary. Most people do accept this as an unquestioned truism, but it may not be true. A very strong case can be made that consciousness is fundamental, with matter a derivative of consciousness.

None of the authors surveyed here have considered this possibility, and that, I think, is why none of them can grant Gaia true personhood, sentience, or her own will and volition. This, I think, is why they all hedge in granting her the status of organism (or superorganism), even when they are convinced of her intelligence. It could be that in their conformity to groupthink and materialist ideology, they are actually correct, and the Earth System of Life (Gaia) is really just a glorified (and glorious) machine. But I think it is worth considering that she may be an organism after all, and that this status as willful, feeling, mortal being may have implications for humans as well as for the larger Project of Life that the materialist model cannot offer.

For anyone interested in Simon Powell's work, here is an hour-long Youtube sampling of his thinking. The first 15 minutes are hilarious. https://www.youtube.com/watch?v=AaqoLTqQvyc

Part 4: Myth, Truth, and Meaning

THINKING AND WRITING about the Sophia Myth has encouraged me to probe the depths of the culture we have inherited from the desert peoples of Saharasia, and to examine some of the foundational principles upon which our worldview is based. Many of these principles are highly questionable; some are dead wrong. Since the chaos and destruction we are visiting upon the natural world (and therefore upon ourselves) can be traced quite directly to certain foundational principles that underlie our culture, it is essential that we scrutinize these more-than-mistaken ideas and call them out for what they are-- including their life-destroying effects upon the Gaian system that supports and nurtures the lives of us all. This kind of inquiry is bound to take many out of their comfort zone, because it raises questions about the very nature of reality—a reality that most of us have long taken for granted, thanks to our cultural conditioning. Given what is ultimately at stake here—life on Earth as we know it—I think a little temporary discomfort might well be in order. What do you think?

The Sophia Myth, as interpreted by John Lamb Lash from the writings of the ancient Gnostics, tells the story of a goddess from our galaxy's core who became our very own Earth. The thing about myths is, if you take them seriously you have to trust them for telling some kind of truth, even if that truth is not fully comprehensible given our present understanding of things. The value of a myth lies in its potential to bring the obscure or incomprehensible into some kind of focus, supplying insight (however fleeting or incomplete) into the mystery of life, making sense of the world, and thereby making meaning. Making meaning is not a passive process but requires as much resourcefulness and creativity as any of us can bring to this project. And it is not as if we will ever arrive at any kind of absolute truth, if there even is such a thing. What we are trying to do here is inquire into the possibility of making more sense of the world using this myth rather than the myths that inform our culture now. If we succeed, we may also satisfy the human need to make, or discover, meaning.

The two Master-Narratives that guide the lives of the so-called civilized world are, as I have already suggested, problematical. Making one's only home uninhabitable—as we busily dismantle and poison planet Earth—is indeed problematical. The narratives of monotheistic religion and scientific materialism each sanction and underwrite this wholesale project of mass extinction, an extinction from which we ourselves are not exempt. Given this failure of our cultural narratives, including the myths, lies, and misperceptions on which they are based, it seems urgently appropriate to explore other ways of understanding the world of which we are a part. The Sophia Myth would seem to offer some promise in this direction.

The Nag Hamadi Codices come to us, after sixteen hundred years underground, as mere fragments of a larger narrative. If there ever was a single cohesive and coherent Gnostic storyline, which seems doubtful given the factionalism of our kind, such an "official" narrative is not available to us now. What we have instead are partial outlines of a story along with some rather large gaps. We are told, for instance, that Sophia and her male counterpart, Thelete, designed the human genome while in the galaxy's core (the Pleroma) and, in concert with their fellow Aeons, projected it far out into the galaxy's arm (the Kenoma). The timing of all this is left extremely vague. Our current science tells us that the Earth itself is about 4.5 billion years old, and that life first appeared here about 3.8 billion years ago. By our reckoning, that would make Sophia somewhat older than 4.5 billion years.

The concept of evolution is not part of the Myth as we know it. Science tells us that life began with single-celled (prokaryote) organisms that, over the first couple billion years, became ever more sophisticated at solving various survival issues while also markedly increasing in diversity. From these arose more complex single-celled organism (eukaryotes). Eventually, complexity and diversity showed up as multi-celled organisms, which (through the process of evolution) became ever more complex, diverse, and fine-tuned for survival. Quite far along in this process, mammals, and then primates, appeared on the scene. Humanoids didn't show up until just a very few million years ago. Anatomically modern man has only been around for about 200,000 years. No timeline like this is part of the extant Gnostic writings, and indeed the immense biodiversity that has long characterized the planet (with some upswings and downswings) goes all but unacknowledged. Also unacknowledged is the vital role all these creatures have played in the building of ever more resilient ecosystems over time, and how complexity, diversity, and resilience contribute to the integrity, stability, and beauty of the Gaian (Sophianic) Whole.

The reasons for this glaring omission can likely be traced to the culture out of which the Gnostics arose, which is, basically, our culture—with all its anti-ecological biases. Also glaringly absent is any guidance about how the human ought to interact with our fellow-Earthlings. We aren't told to take dominion over them, but neither are we told to treat them with respect, as was common among indigenous peoples, who spoke with fondness of "all our relations," acknowledging our kinship to all living beings. From the Gnostics--coming as they did out of a settled pastoral/agricultural lifeway--just nothing at all about this vital relationship.

These are not insurmountable omissions. The biological sciences, and especially the very young science of ecology, are telling us what our wild ancestors knew intuitively, by shamanistic insight, and by living close to Nature: the human is part of a larger Gaian Whole; we are an important, but not an exceptional, member of the Community of Life; and we have a role to fulfill within the larger Life-System. Or as the ecological pioneer, Aldo Leopold, once remarked on this subject: "The land ethic simply enlarges the boundaries of the community to include soils, waters, plants, and animals, or collectively: the land...In short, a land ethic changes the role of Homo sapiens from conqueror of the land-community to plain member and citizen of it. It implies respect for his fellow members, and also respect for the community as such." (A Sand County Almanac, p.) When faced with a decision about living ethically within the larger Community of Life, Leopold offers this rather profound insight into how we might think about our ecological responsibilities: "A thing is right when it tends to preserve the integrity, stability, and beauty of the biotic community. It is wrong when it tends otherwise." This is an obvious and sensible guideline for anyone living in an ecologically integrated natural world, as we do. But we also live within a cultural world that promotes and validates the private ownership of the land, along with the use of that land for the purpose of private profit and wealth creation. As long as this cultural overlay remains in place, smothering any possibility of an ecologically sound land ethic, there is no way for the human, as a collective, to behave in ways that enhance, rather than diminish, the biotic community. This is why I call culture a trap.

We are trapped by stories that do not square with the ecological nature of the world, stories that are in direct opposition to the welfare of the biotic community, stories that ultimately diminish us as human beings, denying us the potential that resides deep within our own nature. The intertwined stories of capitalism, industrialism, and consumerism now have global reach, creating a revolution of rising expectations, throwing global exploitation into hyper-drive. Think China and India. Think world-wide deforestation, dying oceans, and irreversible climate chaos. It is obvious that we all need to be living in radically different stories than the ones we are living in now. But there are few alternative stories on offer, and, even if there were, it is not clear how a global population of 7+ billion, trapped in the throes of our (now global) economic stories, could or would jump from an old story into a new one. Some have posited the possibility of a sudden global mind change. While perhaps theoretically possible, this strikes me as highly unlikely given our factional nature and how divided the world is on just about everything. So, is there any hope at all of being saved by a new and different story?

Can't say for sure, but if a new story could save us, it would have to be radically different from our old stories in very particular ways. It would have to be a story that inspired the human to live in harmony with the Community of Life and with Mother Earth herself. All I can say at this point is that the Sophia Myth seems to fit the bill for this better than anything else now on offer.

The Sophia Myth tells us that the Earth is a living being, supernatural but not immortal, not omnipotent, not omniscient, very much a feeling being, self-aware, willful, wondrously creative, a lover of beauty, and super-smart, but temperamental and capable of error. I personally find such a deity to be much more relatable-to than a heavy-handed patriarchal god who chooses to rule by intimidation and fear. I feel compassion for the Aeon Sophia for all she has been through. I can empathize with how she must have felt when she found herself isolated from her fellow Aeons in an alien and hostile-seeming environment far from home. I like the fact that she is a caring being who delights in creating and nurturing life forms and that she has such a profoundly artistic sensibility and love of beauty. I would like to be in relationship with this divine creature, and would love it if she would somehow initiate contact with me. I can't say that has happened yet, but I have attempted to make contact with her: by way of magic mushrooms, last spring.

I was seeking some sort of answer to a question I have come to regard as ever more relevant to the destiny of the human species, and also of great interest to me personally. The question is: is the Earth in fact a living being, or is it simply an autopoetic system of systems that calibrates itself according to natural laws and feedback loops, providing the conditions for life to survive and thrive, but not alive itself? In other words, is Gaia more akin to a finely-tuned machine, or is she an organism much like the rest of us? When you have a question of such significance, where do you go for an answer?

According to Terrence McKenna, Simon Powell, and other cosmic explorers I had consulted, a good place to start might be the magic mushroom. And so it was that I—for the first time in more than thirty years--ingested five grams of blue-stained dried mushrooms, and took the tour. I started out by the pond, where I had set up a chair to take in the sights in my own back yard. The usual visual and perceptual filters that allow us to function as if the world around us were simply ordinary soon fell away and now I could see each tree, lily pad, and flower in its own magical splendor, complete with colors so vibrant, so full of life, that I could not but smile at the wonder of their being. It was also evident that none of the individual plants or birds or dragonflies that caught my eye were lone isolated individuals, but were all part of something larger than themselves--and that that something was coherent and purposeful. I could easily have sat there marveling at the super-reality all around me for a long, long time, more than content to discover this much physical and metaphysical beauty in my own back yard. But the mushroom had other ideas.

Feeling inwardly pushed, I made my way to my trailer and sat down in my chair, then got right back up again and made my way to bed. What followed was three hours of as much intensity as I was able to handle. Early on I got sick to my stomach and puked, with my innards feeling queasy for quite awhile after. But this was nothing to the sensations that were to course through my body in the time that followed. What I was feeling, in every cell of my body, was primal yearning; and, it seemed, every shade of emotion it was possible to feel. I twitched, I screamed, I made faces to match the feelings that were surging through me. What was I supposed to make of all these sensations? I sensed intuitively exactly what it was that

I was being allowed to know. And it didn't come in words; it came by way of feeling: physically, viscerally, engaging all my senses.

As I experienced all this it seemed beyond doubt that my question was being answered in a direct and utterly convincing way. Not only was the Earth a living, intelligent being, it was very much a feeling being, with a range of sentience far beyond the human repertoire of emotions. I was being treated to as many of these feelings as I was able to deal with. The experience was not all pleasant, because life itself is not all pleasant. And yet, even as I made faces and let out yelps at all the raw intensity I was experiencing, I also felt elation. Not ecstasy, not euphoria, but elation that this knowledge was being shared with me. I wanted to know if the Earth was a feeling being, and this was my answer.

I should say that I have never much liked snakes, but I had the sense that the Earth Mother shares some qualities with the serpent, because, as these feelings coursed through me, one upon another upon another, I felt like an undifferentiated being without appendages, but with an enormous capacity for feelings of all kinds. This was Gaia-Sophia, the Earth Mother, whose subterranean being and experience I was permitted to sample for myself.

What I had perceived in the early part of this tour—the psychedelic colors and super-real appearance of all I beheld: the birds and trees and flowers, the flowing water and the living sky—were, individually and collectively, creative manifestations of a relentless surge of yearnings that longed to be expressed in articulate, exquisite detail. Every living being on this earth—the eagle, the spider, the tiger, the snail, the giant redwood, the microscopic bacterium—reflect some constellation of the sensations that course without ceasing through the Mother of us all. We are all expressions of who and what she is, and it is clear that she has a brilliantly practical mind that finds ways to make double and triple use of everything, and in this way defy the so-called laws of entropy. And there can be no doubt that she has a superbly developed aesthetic sensibility, which lends to everything she touches its own radiant beauty.

What I experienced on this magical mystery tour was primarily body knowledge, and many of these sensations seemed to come with their own built-in interpretations. This sort of knowledge is not something that is easily passed on to someone else, even if we were not all trained to be skeptical of trance-based knowledge. Nor am I asking for immediate and total acceptance of this version of reality. Rather, I am just sharing a meaningful experience with someone who might have some sympathy for what I was seeking, and for what I seemed to find. I am looking for a New Story to live in, because the one I inherited no longer works for me. This was, for me, a step in the direction of that New Story.

I took this trip back in May on an especially lovely day. At the time, I felt that some part of the essence of Gaia-Sophia had been visited upon me, but not that the two of us had actually conversed, mind to mind or soul to soul. I am sure that I got all that I was able to handle at the time. It certainly felt that way, but the lack of dialog or sense of interchange left my skeptical side to question how much of this was projection or just chemicals doing their psychedelic thing. I have never doubted what I felt; that was way too intense to question. But my interpretation of its meaning—that I was feeling some part of Sophia's own feelings—has come to feel less certain over time. I guess it is always like this for those who hold to a faith. At some point, doubt creeps in. In any case, I cannot say with certainty that Sophia and our Earth are one and the same, though this is something I would like to believe.

I want to believe that our Earth is a living, conscious,

intelligent being because it is emotionally satisfying to think of her in those terms. As such a being myself, living among other such beings, I can understand and relate to someone, even a divine someone, who shares with me characteristics like: an individuated personality; a highly developed repertoire of emotions and sensations, as well as an aesthetic sensibility that delights in beauty; a mind that can solve practical problems of survival, but one that is also driven by an intense curiosity to know and comprehend the nature of everything, including how and why it works the way it does. Sophia, though supernatural and far more highly developed than her offspring, seems to be just such a creature as myself. And if that is true, what else might be true about other entities and beings within the cosmos, such as, say, our very own sun?

According to the Sophia Myth, our sun chooses sides between Sophia and the Archons, forming a three-body system of sun, Earth, and moon (called trimorphic protenoia) which, in the Gnostic view, is considered as independent of the other planets that orbit the sun. These other planets, the steroma of the Demiurge, are considered to be mechanistic in nature, unlike our Earth, Moon, and Sun, which are by nature organic. In this view, our Sun, like the Earth itself, is gendered as feminine, not masculine, as many Native American groups have believed. But the point is, our Sun is understood to share in all the qualities of personhood, sentience, volition, and intelligence that characterize the Earth Mother herself.

Here I want to explore why the people of our culture are likely to reject the notion that celestial "objects" could possibly be endowed with such qualities, and then suggest how these cultural biases may be mistaken.

Many indigenous peoples throughout history and prehistory have personified the Earth below and the heavens above. Many have revered the Sun as a giver of life, and made a sort of religion out of this relationship. When the Abrahamic religions came on the scene, with the strict injunction that "thou shalt have no other gods above me" (or else!) sun worship fell out of favor. The essence of monotheism is that there is only one god, and no others will be tolerated. Thus, the divinity and personhood of celestial beings like the Sun were stripped away from them, and made to be heresy and blasphemy, punishable even unto death. Under this kind of pressure, is it any wonder that most among the faithful (and many more besides) cannot even consider the Sun as an intelligent and purposeful being?

With the Scientific Revolution coming into its own some three to four hundred years ago, our notions about the nature of reality changed radically. The philosophical theory of atomism, first propounded by early Greeks such as Democratus and Leucuppis came to light with the discovery of a lost manuscript in the early fifteenth century. This was De rerum natura (On the Nature of Things) penned by Lucretius in the first century B.C., a work that was to have ever greater influence on natural philosophy as the 17th century progressed. Atomism posits that the Universe consists of atoms and the void, and nothing else; that atoms are the invisible, indestructible building blocks out of which everything is made. The unavoidable implication of this view is that if it isn't material, it doesn't exist.

The philosophy of materialism is largely built upon the foundation of atomism. "Materialism," according to Wikipedia, "is a form of philosophical monism which holds that Matter is the fundamental substance in nature, and that all things, including mental aspects and consciousness, are results of material interactions." That matter is primary and that consciousness is secondary stands as an unwavering doctrine of scientific materialism even today. But it is only a doctrine, a belief based on unproven assumptions, and may well be wrong. If it is wrong, and the reverse is true—that consciousness is primary and matter secondary—we would find ourselves living in a world transformed.

Among philosophers, the conundrum of consciousness is called the "hard problem." This is because no one has yet offered a satisfactory explanation for how consciousness can arise out of matter. It is the problem of explaining how you get something out of nothing. At what point does matter, assumed to be inert, produce consciousness? And how is this accomplished? Theories abound, but no one knows. Something out of nothing is a hard problem indeed.

Consciousness is something that all human beings share. Awareness is the ground of our being. If you weren't aware you couldn't be reading these words. Indeed, life itself requires consciousness. Some would argue that only creatures with a complex nervous system are conscious—humans, of course; certain primates, maybe; possibly higher mammals, like dogs. But this is a self-centered view of things, and ultimately rather ridiculous. Ever try to swat a fly or mosquito? Did they fail to notice your effort? If so, they paid the price. Every living being is aware, as far as I can tell, and their awareness is appropriate to who and what they are. Amoebas probably don't need a grasp of philosophy or mathematics to live the life of an amoeba, but they need to sense the world around them: to find food; to escape predators; to avoid toxic environments; to find a mate and reproduce. Sensing the world around us is part of what it means to be alive, and sensing requires a sensibility of some sort: sentience, the capacity for awareness. As far as plants and animals go, this should be obvious enough. To be an organism and alive is to possess consciousness at some level or other. But where does consciousness end? What about mountains and rivers? What about a grain of sand, a drop of water?

If consciousness is indeed fundamental to the Universe, then consciousness has been there since the beginning (whenever that might have been), and it goes all the way down. That is to say, consciousness is everywhere, though certainly it is not evenly distributed. The Earth, for example, is consciousness-rich; some places in deep space, where not much seems to be happening, is presumably less so--though some rudiment of consciousness must exist even there (or so logic would seem to demand, given our premise). The view that consciousness pervades the Universe is called by philosophers, panpsychism, translating roughly into everywhere mind. Our wild ancestors understood the world to be filled with spirit in general and with individuated spirits in particular, a worldview that answers to the name of animism.

Though panpsychism and animism have much in common, they are not identical: panpsychism is a philosophical construct which seeks to explain an underlying feature of reality; that is, it is just an idea. By contrast, animism is a way of life based on the conviction that everything is connected to everything else and that each and all are animated by mind and spirit. In this way, animism is panpsychism taken seriously and made integral to the daily life of the people.

From the point of view of a life-form on Earth, consciousness is very much associated with life. It should be noted that no one yet has been able to define exactly what consciousness is; nor can we definitively say what life is. Thus it is not surprising that we cannot explain the relationship between these two, though it appears that consciousness and life somehow go together, and that the complexity of consciousness correlates (at least roughly) with the complexity of the organism. But this commonsense, life-form-limited perspective does not offer much insight into consciousness beyond the realm of organism. The Nag Hamadi Codices speak in passing of an Originator who, in some manner or other, gave rise to the Aeons who inhabit our galaxy's core. What is not at all clear is whether this deity is presumed to be autopoetic or allopoetic in nature, and this is a very important distinction indeed.

Autopoetic means self-generating, self-organizing, self-regulating, in a process that unfolds from within. In this worldview, all is one and continuous.

To be allopoetic means that something is made by a maker, who stands outside and apart from whatever is made—creating a discontinuity between the two, and a split in what can no longer be thought of as a Universe. Nor do we have any insight into who made the maker, and so on, unto infinite regression.

At this point I would invoke Occam's Razor, which states that the most straightforward explanation is probably closer to the truth than one requiring complicated, contorted elaboration. On this basis, I reject the notion that matter is primary and consciousness secondary because something out of nothing makes no sense. I likewise reject the belief that the Universe was created by something outside the Universe—thus defying equally the orthodoxies of scientific materialism and the Abrahamic religions. Instead I propose, in accord with cutting-edge science, that the Universe is self-generating and self-organizing and that consciousness or mind is fundamental to it all. At the very least, I think we should try this out as a thought experiment and see where this, in conjunction with the Sophia Myth, might take us.

As the Gnostics tell it, the Sophia story is confined to our own Milky Way galaxy at a time well beyond the origin of the Universe. The Aeons (the goddesses and gods) who inhabit the galaxy's core are evidently highly developed mental and emotional beings, with no apparent physicality beyond exuding an aura of divine luminosity. Hyper-curious by nature, they take satisfaction in conducting experiments just to see what will happen as their carefully-designed projects progress over time. (How boring it would be for them if they had the foreknowledge of omniscience, with nothing to anticipate but the unfolding of what was already known). By tradition, these divine experiments are designed from within the protected confines of the Pleroma by two oppositely gendered Aeons (such as Sophia and Thelete) and, when ready, are thrust out into one of the galaxy's arms (the Kenoma) to be watched with interest, but not interfered with. When Sophia's curiosity gets the better of her and she wanders from the safety of the galaxy's core, she is breaking from the usual protocol—with results that are anomalous and far-reaching.

The Gnostic material suggests that the Pleroma is the realm of consciousness while the Kenoma is the realm of matter. While the relationship between these two is not spelled out, it would appear that consciousness has priority over matter; that mind orders matter, and not the other way around. In any case, Sophia brings her own powers of consciousness into the Kenoma, which "is composed of dark elementary matter arrays (dema), atomic and subatomic fields, including proto-organic elements, residue of past worlds." (Not in His Image, p. 174) When her own divine luminosity collides and combines with this "residue of past worlds" something anomalous happens: she becomes the living planet Earth, investing gross matter with consciousness. It may have been an accident, a one-off mistake, but it proved to be a fortuitous one for the genesis and evolution of Life on a living planet—the only such planet any of us knows of.

This is our origin story, as told by the Gnostics. And certainly it is different from the other two origin stories we are familiar with. Random chance may be a factor here, as is matter itself, but these play subordinate roles in a galaxy heavily invested with consciousness and the attendant qualities of sentience, intelligence, personhood, and volition.

The consciousness concentrated in the galaxy's core is, by our own lesser lights, considered as supernatural. The Aeons are powerful beings, but they can suffer the frailties of mental and emotional imbalance and are thereby capable of error, as Sophia herself demonstrates. Certainly they lack the powers of omniscience and omnipotence, and are no more immortal than the galaxy itself. And, unlike the deity of the Old Testament, they do not meddle in their experiments, tipping the scales in a preferred direction.

Nonintervention seems to be a rule of theirs, and it is one with implications both positive and negative—at least from our point of view. We civilized humans have made a mess of things here, with ongoing disasters that seems to worsen by the day—to the point that a little divine intervention would be welcomed. According to John Lamb Lash, such an intervention might just be on the way. He calls this possible miracle-in-the-making Sophia's Correction, drawing on hints left in the Nag Hamadi Codices. But just what this correction might consist of remains—for now—shrouded in mystery.

Meanwhile, the Archons are operating on a highly interventionist program to take us down, and seem to be succeeding quite nicely, as we humans get sucked ever more deeply into their world of simulated reality.

Much is at stake in how this all plays out. At this moment, pretty much everything that we know, value, and love in this world is on the line, and the prospects for an outcome that favors life over non-life are looking far from bright. Are we capable of abandoning the dysfunctional stories that are ruining our lives and the life of the planet? Can a New Story, with Sophia at the center, bring us back into some sort of balance with the world and make us whole again? Are truth and meaning still available to us at this late date?

CHAPTER 30

THE TREE, THE HUMAN AND MORALITY

MANY BELIEVE THAT morality is only about humans and their relations with one another; and it is true that our traditional morality, as propounded by Western Religion, has had this very narrow focus. Among those who reject Western Religion but embrace Western Science is the dominant belief that morality is a strictly human construct in a Universe that is absent any sort of moral order. But there is a moral order to the Cosmos, and some of the most conspicuous exemplars of this moral order are trees.

One profound aspect of the tree as moral exemplar is contained in the following words of the Buddhist priest Thich Nhat Hahn:

"I asked the leaf whether it was frightened because it was autumn and the other leaves were falling. The leaf told me, "No. During the whole spring and summer I was completely alive. I worked hard to help nourish the tree, and now much of me is in the tree. I am not limited by this form. I am also the whole tree, and when I go back to the soil, I will continue to nourish the tree. So I don't worry at all. As I leave this branch and float to the ground, I will wave to the tree and tell her, 'I will see you again very soon.'

Suddenly I saw a kind of wisdom very much like the Wisdom contained in the Heart Sutra. You have to *see* life. You should not say, life *of* the leaf, you should only speak of life *in* the leaf and life *in* the tree. My life is just Life, and you can see it in me and in the tree. That day there was a wind blowing and, after a while, I saw the leaf leave the branch and float down to the soil, dancing joyfully, because as it floated it saw itself already there in the tree. It was so happy. I bowed my head, knowing that I have a lot to learn from the leaf because it is not afraid--it knew nothing can be born and nothing can die."

In this instance, a single leaf on a single tree offers an invaluable lesson of life to a single human being—who then passes the lesson on to other humans. There is a moral to this story, having to do with the relationship between the individual (the holon) and the Whole (as embodied by the tree). Also, there is a question of identity here that amounts to a paradox. The human is inclined to see the leaf as an atomistic isolated individual who exists for a time and then withers into nothingness. This is perceived by the human to be a cause for sadness. But the leaf has a different view of things, a Bigger Picture of how things work in the world. It is part of a larger Whole, and IS the Whole at one and the same time. It is not a thing-in-itself but part of an ongoing process: the process of Life. As long as that process continues, the leaf is a part of it. The human--who has been taught to see himself as an isolated individual--struggles with this notion, even while apprehending its deeper truth.

No doubt there are moral implications to this story, mostly having to do with how the individual views his own identity and mortality (or immortality), and how the leaf's Larger View might change the individual human's approach and attitude to life. But the focus remains on the individual, and does not

THE TREE, THE HUMAN AND MORALITY

necessarily invoke a Cosmic moral order. To see the Cosmic moral order, as expressed by trees, you have to look at trees as a collective—indeed, as a community.

Science has learned a lot about the behavior of trees in the last decade or two. Much of this new science has been captured in the 2016 book, *The Hidden Life of Trees: What they feel, How they Communicate*, by Peter Wohlleben. For as long as there have been trees and humans, we have had the aboveground perspective on the nature of trees, understanding little about what goes on belowground. What we see when we look at a stand of trees is fierce competition among individuals for sunlight, nutrients, and water. This competition is real, but is perhaps the least interesting thing about how trees interact with one another. What the new science shows is how mutually helpful, how scrupulously cooperative, how downright social trees are with one another, deep down in the dirt. Strong, healthy trees share nutrients (as well as information) with smaller, weaker trees, based, evidently, upon the principle of all for one and one for all. United we stand, divided we fall.

But trees cannot achieve their impressive level of mutually beneficial symbiosis all on their own; for this they rely upon a symbiotic relationship with an entirely different order of being: the fungus. Fungal threads grow into the soft root hairs of the tree and thereby establish a partnership beneficial to both. "The fungus not only penetrates and envelops the tree's roots, but also allows its web to roam throughout the surrounding forest floor. In so doing, it extends the reach of the tree's own roots as the web grows out toward other trees. Here it connects with other trees' fungal partners and roots. And so a network is created, and now it's easy for the trees to exchange vital nutrients and even information—such as an impending insect attack." (p.51) The forest ecologist, Suzanne Simard, whose pioneering work provides much of the scientific basis for the insights of Wohllben's book, calls this relational network the wood wide web.

As she says in an Afterword to the book: "The wood wide web has been mapped, traced, monitored, and coaxed to reveal the beautiful structures and finely adapted languages of the forest network....These discoveries have transformed our discovery of trees from competitive crusaders of the self to members of a collective, relating, communicating system." (p. 249)

CHAPTER 31

INDIGENOUS FOLKS AND US

THANK YOU, NINA, for recognizing my longtime persistence in this area of inquiry. My interest in indigenous people was piqued in the early 'eighties when I was thinking of writing a book about my great grandfather, who for eight years was an Indian Agent for the Sac and Fox tribes of Iowa. I realized that I didn't know much about Indians, and I was curious to learn more. It just happened about that time that the publications of books by and about Native Americans began to really take off. For three years, I read nothing but books by and about Indians. I guess I was a little bit spellbound by these people who lived close to Nature, and by a wholly different ethic than our own. I did branch out in my reading after this extreme immersion, but have continued to explore the Indigenous Worldview and lifeway on a regular basis ever since. I have formed some rather strong opinions about the differences between "them" and "us," and I don't claim absolute objective detachment on this subject. Like most people, I tended to find what I wanted to find in the material before me. For example, I wanted to believe that other people before us (of the "civilized" world) lived in a way more in balance with human potential and the natural world—and I did find that, again and again and again.

When DeMeo cites the difference between unarmored matrists and armored patrists, he is pointing to the same pattern I had noticed in case after case after case. I think it is fair to speak of an Indigenous Worldview as a generalization that applies to our wild ancestors and other indigenous folks throughout history and pre-history and all around the globe. Most were mobile egalitarian animists who lived by following the ripening of plant foods and the movements of favored animal species. They lived in a world abundant with life forms and spirit beings, and their primary adaptation to this lifeway was to integrate themselves into the Whole. They experienced fat times and lean times in a world in which they were fitted to live. Yet they had luxuries that few of us have ever known, and especially the freedom to be as fully human, and as fully themselves, as they were motivated to become. I am not saying that they lived without constraints. Certainly they did not. But their constraints were very different from ours, and if I had my druthers, I'd rather be living with theirs.

CHAPTER 32

AN IDEOLOGY THAT IS MORALLY, SOCIALLY AND ECOLOGICALLY BANKRUP

CAPITALISM AND ITS pathological offspring, neoliberalism, are morally, socially, and ecologically bankrupt, because they are based on false premises and outright lies. And because these and their supporting systems and institutions are based in untruths, they are inflicting terminal damage not only upon the human social order but upon the biosphere of this planet, creating a literal hell on Earth. Before examining the foundational beliefs of this dangerous ideology, I want first to establish a baseline by which to measure their falsehood.

One way to understand our situation is to recognize that humanity lives and thrives by three distinct but interrelated economies: Nature's economy, the human economy, and the money economy.

The natural economy includes all of the chemical, geological, biological, and ecological features and relationships on this planet, which--in myriad complex interactions--together create the conditions for life to flourish. As a living, evolving planet, the Earth has developed vast webs of interdependent relationships between and among animals, plants, and their habitats. Over the 3.8-billion-year history of life on Earth, these relationships have become ever more complex, diverse, and resilient, and also inspiringly beautiful. The physical beauty of the natural world is an outward manifestation of an exuberantly healthy ecosystem; to behold and experience such exquisite loveliness serves to reward all who participate in the optimal functioning of the Whole. Conversely, whatever diminishes complexity, diversity, resilience, and the Earth's ecological order, creates ugliness (think of an open-pit mine, a river on fire, the Alberta tar sands, a devastating oil spill), and that, too, is a measure of ecosystem health.

The human economy involves every sort of human relationship, from romantic love to friendship to the adversarial relationship of enemies and competitors, engaging, at one time or another, every shade of human emotion and every possible relationship from altruistic to mutualistic to the exploitative. Family and community relationships, in particular, operate in this highly nuanced, dynamic sphere of social networks, and the "glue" that holds these groups together is based in trust, sharing, and cooperation. The human being is a highly social animal who thrives on positive social interactions and relationships within groups of a limited size. To a large extent, we take our identity and sense of well-being from our position within a group, whether that group be our family, our circle of friends, or our immediate community. The transactions that occur within the human economy reflect our nature as a subjective grouping animal possessing a distinct personality, with physical and emotional needs and drives that seek satisfaction in the social sphere—no money involved.

The money economy includes every aspect of resource extraction, manufacture, transportation, distribution,

AN IDEOLOGY THAT IS MORALLY, SOCIALLY, AND ECOLOGICALLY BANKRUPT

consumption, and waste "disposal," as well as all manner of service industries that operate on the basis of dollars changing hands. It serves the purposes of neoliberals to conflate the human economy with the money economy, blurring the distinctions between them. For instance, the concept of society supposes a rich tapestry of interwoven human relationships, informed and directed by culture and based in human social needs, meanings, and satisfactions. When British Prime Minister Margaret Thatcher pronounced back in the 80s that there was no such thing as society, she was operating out of the neoliberal playbook, conflating the human economy and the money economy into a single category, in which everything has its price--thereby reducing the human world to little more than a marketplace.

Indeed, reductionism is key to the neoliberal turn of mind, as this form of oversimplification screens out all manner of subtlety, complexity and nuance that might militate against the advancement of the neoliberal agenda. Nowhere is this reductionism more evident than in its anti-ecological view of Nature. Within the capitalist/neoliberal paradigm, Nature is not only denied the status of intelligence, sentience, selfhood, and volition (all qualities of a living being) but the Earth and its processes are seen as nothing more than a non-living low-status concatenation of "resources" to be exploited at will for human ends. Far from being understood as the source of all life, including human life, and integral to every breath we take, the Earth is regarded as separate from the human, as some sort of alien Other, to be used, abused, and discarded without a second thought.

The discipline of economics, as taught in universities throughout the West and practiced by graduates of these institutions, is as blind to Nature's ecological economy and the human economy of meaningful relationships as it is to the impossibility of infinite growth on a finite planet. According to this view of the world (one that is measured strictly by Gross Domestic Product), if it cannot be calculated in dollars and cents, it is just an externality of no consequence. This is what is known as living in a bubble: a reductionist bubble in which the realities of a living natural world as well as the psychological and other non-material needs of the human organism have no place. Living in this way is living a lie, and it has no viable future.

The same could be said for the paradigm of endless growth on a finite--and ever more degraded—planet: growth unto planetary exhaustion bankrupts the future for all living beings, including human beings.

In many ways, capitalism and neoliberalism are the logical, almost inevitable, extensions of cultural beliefs and values going back centuries and millennia, though now carried to an unhinged extreme. When you consider the tenets of neoliberalism, such as: individualism, self-interest, liberty, freedom of choice, entrepreneurial spirit, economic growth, technical progress, and freedom for corporations to pursue economic advantage without State intervention, all of these points of doctrine have precedent within the culture of civilization, going way back.

Here it is worth recalling that our wild ancestors living in small mobile groups and making their living by hunting and gathering conducted their lives by a belief and value system almost directly antithetical to this one. In their world, survival was all about the group, sharing, and an equitable distribution of resources and power. The conditions of their lives demanded communitarianism, egalitarianism, and group solidarity, if they were to survive and thrive. The kinds of selfishness and stratification enshrined in the dogmas of neoliberalism would have torn these small groups apart, and they knew very well

AN IDEOLOGY THAT IS MORALLY, SOCIALLY, AND ECOLOGICALLY BANKRUPT

that their survival depended upon group cohesion, that none of them would make it as lone, isolated individuals. This was the way humans and humanoids have lived for thousands of generations, and--it is interesting to note--they did not destroy their world in the process.

Against this baseline of proven success, we now have ideologues pushing an agenda based on a wholly different understanding of the world. Individualism, self-interest, "liberty," freedom of choice, and the entrepreneurial spirit, are all based on the assumption that the isolated individual is the fundamental unit of the human species. This way of thinking goes back at least as far as Democritus and the early Greek atomists, who believed that everything is made up of indestructible and irreducible material building blocks called atoms. When applied to people, this way of seeing the world becomes social atomism, which focuses on the individual as the prime social unit and sees society as little more than a collection of autonomous self-interested individuals. John Locke and Thomas Hobbes were early promoters of this social paradigm, and their thinking strongly influenced nascent *laissez faire* capitalism, and continues to this day to provide ideological support for this system.

The rationale for the neoliberal agenda is based on this notion that the human being is not only an isolated individual among other such individuals, but is a self-interested rational actor always looking to maximize financial or other personal gain. The neoliberal model for the social order makes very specific assumptions about what constitutes liberty, freedom of choice, and responsibility. According to this view, everyone is responsible for themselves, and perhaps for their families, but they owe no responsibility to society as a whole (because there "is no society"), and certainly no one owes a responsibility to Mother Earth. When it comes to the Earth, it is all about the rights of humans, and especially property rights; responsibility, or reciprocity, doesn't come into the equation at all.

Liberty, under this model, amounts to freedom from restraint, especially any sort of interference by the State. Thanks to the neoliberal think tanks and a compliant corporate media, the State is portrayed not as the constitutionally-guaranteed representative of the people and the people's interest, but as an out-of-touch, draconian, power-hungry bureaucracy with designs to dominate the lives of citizens and to stifle the vitality of an otherwise vibrant business community. Ignored in this "liberty" meme is the RIGHT of ordinary citizens to breath clan air, drink clean water, be protected from health-destroying industrial poisons and practices, while also preserving some semblance of ecosystem health--allowing other-than-human persons their own right to life.

The neoliberal mantra of "freedom of choice" is little more than code for: you are on your own. It is your choice to succeed or fail, to be mired in poverty or bask in prosperity: it is up to you and you alone to take full responsibility for your condition in life. The presumption behind this point of doctrine is that all individuals have equal footing in the world, that there are no structural components within society that privilege some and disadvantage others. Conveniently overlooked are a myriad of factors--including race, gender, and class--that to a very large degree determine not only where a person starts out in life but just how far their own personal qualities can take them within a highly stratified society. A black boy born in the ghetto without a father present might indeed rise to become a famous brain surgeon, and even seek the presidency of the United States, just as a white boy born into affluence and social standing might leverage those advantages into a fortune, and seek that same high office. But you have to overlook a lot of social, economic, and political realities to believe that both

AN IDEOLOGY THAT IS MORALLY, SOCIALLY, AND ECOLOGICALLY BANKRUPT

these individuals had an equal chance in life, and that it was simply their qualities of character—their freedom of choice--that led them both to national prominence. But this is what neoliberal doctrine specifies, in defiance of social reality. But this sleight of hand only works if you focus solely on the individual and ignore the many-faceted context in which every individual is embedded.

In answer to the moral and social question: am I my brother's keeper? the neoliberal answer is an emphatic NO! There is no society; there is no common good; there is no social contract that requires the individual, or business, or government, to consider the social welfare of the whole, or of its many constituents. There is no obligation even to Life itself, and certainly not if it gets in the way of making money.

The promoters of neoliberalism are also big promoters of the "entrepreneurial spirit." But what exactly is this "spirit" that they so glorify? Certainly, it is based in human creativity, and creativity must surely be seen as one of our most glorious qualities as human beings. But creativity to what end? The neoliberal rationale goes something like this: If, through your creativity, you manage to identify a human want or need, and you come up with a way to satisfy human desire with a marketable product or service, you have demonstrated the entrepreneurial spirit and have thereby earned the right to make as much money off your offering as the market will bear. This sounds perfectly reasonable within the framework of the capitalist system, but is singularly unreasonable upon a trashed out, severely degraded planet possessed of finite resources and nearing ecological collapse.

The wants and needs supplied by the capitalist system are largely artificial, and often supremely superficial. The need for food, water, shelter, warmth, sexual gratification, and companionship are vital factors in human well-being. There are also a number of other, less material, yearnings and needs important to the emotional and psychological health of the human organism, such as love, a strong connection to the natural world, meaningful work, a sense of purpose and of belonging to something larger and more important than the isolated self, and, group recognition of one's best qualities as an individual. What our culture, our society, and our economic system have done is attempt to fill this entire suite of needs and longings with material goods and manufactured experiences that can be bought and sold in a marketplace.

Upon his death, the late Steve Jobs was lionized as a national hero. Why? Because he was an innovator, a creative entrepreneur who delivered the goods to the eager consumer while raking in cash by the truckload for shareholders, and, not incidentally, significantly boosting the tech sector of the American economy. (His adoring fans found it convenient to ignore How Apple has used offshore tax havens to avoid paying U.S. taxes by the billions.)

Embodied within the many peons to this "giant of the tech industry," and the entrepreneurial spirit he represents, are three other related doctrines within the neoliberal faith. These are: the imperative of economic growth; the importance of technological progress; and giving the public what they want.

As I have already more than hinted, the growth imperative built into our economy amounts to blindness born of a death wish. It is impossible to go on endlessly using limited resources on a finite planet. Reality will assert itself and a crash will ensue. In contrast to the mass psychosis that underlies our money economy, Nature's economy works on the principle of reciprocity, renewal, and the recycling of resources. This is a self-sustaining system, and more: since life began on this planet some 3.8 billion years ago the trajectory of biospheric evolution

AN IDEOLOGY THAT IS MORALLY, SOCIALLY, AND ECOLOGICALLY BANKRUPT

has been toward ever-greater complexity, ever-greater diversity, and ever-greater ecosystem resilience. Until recently, Life has more than held its own here; even in the face of serious setbacks and system shocks, it has thrived. By the time agricultural man came on the scene, the biotic community was in prime condition. So much so that it appeared to have no limits to its resilience: it seemed we could take and take, while never giving anything back, and still everything would be just fine. But, no, there are natural limits to everything, except perhaps to the appetites of capitalism—and these limits become ever more apparent as we precipitate mass extinctions and proceed toward resource and ecosystem exhaustion.

While every other species (as well as our own wild ancestors) have lived within the annual solar budget and off the interest of Nature's bounty, the people of our culture have--in the last few millennia, and especially in the last century and a half—spent down not only the interest, but Nature's capital. Nature's capital is the accrued resilience of its ecosystems, which is built upon an evolutionary history of ever-elaborating complexity and diversity—almost four billion years worth. And now that "savings account" is getting very low indeed--and yet we continue in our frenzy of ever-accelerating drawdown. Drawdown is a technical term for mining a resource until there is none left worth the taking.

The growth imperative of capitalism is, in large part, a product of usury. The concept of paying interest on money borrowed implies an ever-expanding supply not only of money but of new people (suckers) entering the game to keep the game going. In other words, usury--with its demands of interest to be paid on debt--is a pyramid or Ponzi scheme, and the entire capitalist system has bought into it. In this way, interest drives growth, and the only way to reverse this juggernaut-to-hell would be to erase all debt and outlaw usury as a crime against Life—which it is. Don't see this happening soon? No, I don't either--and this is exactly the trap we are in.

Related to the growth imperative, and to glorifying the entrepreneurial spirit, is the neoliberal commitment to technological progress. To be fair, capitalists cannot be blamed for humanity's fraught relationship with technology. We as a culture, and even to some extent as a species, have been unable to say No to technology, going way back, because the human being has a decided weakness for Power, and power is something that technology delivers often enough to keep us hooked. When you can't say No to something it is called an addiction, and our kind has been addicted to both Power and technology for quite a long time now.

What capitalism and its hyper-charged spin-off (neoliberalism) have done is provide a rationale and incentive for accelerating the pace of technological innovation. That incentive and rationale is the possibility of making big bucks, thus compounding the power addiction with the lust for riches, and all the trinkets and status symbols that riches promise. When venture capital combines with technical expertise and the creative imagination somebody is bound to make some money somewhere. And of course that is always "good for the economy"-- the money economy, that is.

Apologists for the market system like to claim that capitalists and entrepreneurs are merely providing people with what they want—which is both true and untrue at the same time. Endless in-your-face advertising, based upon cynically strategized marketing campaigns, is in the business of aggressively CREATING, not simply supplying, demand. The relentless drumbeat of buy-buy-buy echoes through the chambers of the mind—carrying the subliminal promise to fulfill your every desire, if only you consume-consume-consume. Buy

AN IDEOLOGY THAT IS MORALLY, SOCIALLY, AND ECOLOGICALLY BANKRUPT

our product: get your instant gratification now! In this huckster-driven game, a person's deepest and most urgent needs—say for love, approval, and in-group status—are played upon in a sleight-of-hand illusion where monetized material "stuff" is projected and perceived as a proxy for the genuine article—or even as love and approval themselves.

Consider, for example, a middle-aged well-to-do white male who is going through what has been culturally identified as a "mid-life crisis"—that is to say, he is feeling strangely insecure about his own identity and what he is doing--or should do--with his life. In a pre-capitalist culture, such a person would likely engage in some form of traditional ritualistic soul searching—some equivalent of the Sun Dance, say, in which physical ordeal is undergone in pursuit of life-changing revelations. In our capitalist Western culture, where all such traditions have been stripped from us, our way of dealing with these psychological/emotional/spiritual issues is to seek solace in the material world. Thus, when faced with such insecurities, a fairly typical response of the "rich" American will be to purchase a big-ticket item, such as an expensive sports car, in the hopes of bolstering self-confidence, burnishing his image among his peers, and advertising his desirability to the opposite sex. This is all very symbolic: substituting a flashy plaything of the marketplace for the deeper qualities of character and behavior that, in the real, human economy are required to earn true self-esteem and the genuine respect of others. But, hey, within the materialistic, superficial world of capitalism such an extravagant purchase is "good for the economy," and there is no higher value than this.

All of the destruction and degradation of Nature's economy that goes into the mining, manufacturing, and transporting of the thousands of components that comprise this single item of conspicuous consumption never earn a mention or a second thought. Nor do we like to think about the unsafe and exploitative working conditions of those toiling in the mines and on the assembly lines. As far as the economists and capitalists are concerned these are externalities not worthy of our attention. If an individual is willing the pay the dollar price for such a purchase, industry, the capitalist system, and society generally, is quite happy that this demand be filled, no questions asked.

But what if the products of industry are doing demonstrable damage not merely to Nature and to strangers we'll never meet but to our own population as a whole--as is the case with junk food? Medical science tells us that obesity, diabetes, and heart problems are directly related to what we eat, and that junk food like candy bars, soda pop, and chips are among the worst things we could possibly put into our bodies. Yet, despite the warnings of science, the junk food industry thrives, even as its consumers languish in ill-health.

In April of 1999, eleven top executives representing the world's largest junk food manufacturers met at the Minneapolis headquarters of Pillsbury to discuss their part in America's obesity epidemic. Or at least that was the main idea of its organizers. In attendance were representatives from Kraft, Nestle, Nabisco, General Mills, Proctor and Gamble, Mars, and Coca-Cola. In an ideal world, this group would have reached a consensus about how they might all start subtracting the salt, sugar, and fat from their various product lines, thereby making a positive contribution to a worsening public health epidemic. But that is not what happened. The C.E.O. of General Mills, Stephen Sanger, said that he, for one, would not jeopardize the sanctity of the recipes that had made his company's products so successful. And that settled that: nobody else in this group was going to take a chance on losing market share for their company all on their own.

In a later interview, Geoffrey Bible, former C.E.O. of Phillip

AN IDEOLOGY THAT IS MORALLY, SOCIALLY, AND ECOLOGICALLY BANKRUPT

Morris-Nabisco explained the industry rationale this way: "People could point to these things and say, 'They've got too much sugar, they've got too much salt. Well, that's what the consumer wants, and we're not putting a gun to their head to eat it. That's what they want. If we give them less, they'll buy less, and the competitor will get our market. So you're sort of trapped." A trap indeed—a trap inherent in the system itself-- and we are all caught in it!

Junk food is scrupulously formulated to reach that sweet spot, known in the industry as the "bliss point," so as to be maximally addictive. The tobacco industry has operated on the same principle, spiking naturally addictive nicotine with chemicals to make it even more addicting. "We're just giving the people what they want," they say—as do the crack dealers. It also happens to be good for business when the addicts are compelled to come back for more.

The principle that compels the junk food industry to incrementally poison the populace is the same one that compels the giant petrochemical industry to systematically poison the planet. The very same principle drives Big-Oil to pollute and endanger the planet with ever more dangerous procedures and theaters of operation. Likewise, the mining industry tears the Earth apart to get at precious treasures, and in the process brings up massive amounts of toxins that poison the biosphere. Agribusiness strip-mines what little is left of the Earth's topsoil, substituting dangerous chemicals for natural biological fertility--chemicals that ultimately drain into bays and oceans, creating marine dead zones where nothing can live. All this looks very like a war against Life; but what is the motive behind this wanton destruction of the biosphere? To a very large degree, it is the profit motive.

Capitalism, as an institution, comes with certain institutional imperatives, and making a profit is right at the heart of them all. The profit motive is taken for granted by just about everybody, but where does this idea come from? Does the profit motive really represent the natural way of the world, as some would insist, or is it instead a perverse and unnatural principle on which to base human interaction? To get at the heart of the matter it might be well to think back to simpler times before money and middlemen.

Imagine that you are born a Karuk Indian who lives in a small village on the lower mid-Klamath River, who fishes for salmon with a dipnet. You and your family together not only construct the dipnet but weave the netting material out of wild iris that grows in your area. This is an extremely painstaking and time-consuming job--first spinning short lengths of iris fibers into reliably strong cording and then weaving this cording into netting material—all of which requires great dexterity and skill. Your downriver neighbors, the Yuroks, are experts at making river-worthy dugout canoes, and this too is a time-consuming painstaking process requiring great skill. You have no redwood trees in your area from which to carve canoes, and this is not a skill that has developed among your people. Yurok country does not produce wild iris as the Karuk country does, and only a few of the more inland Yuroks weave their own nets. Over the generations of living as neighbors, your two peoples have established particular families as trading partners, and when it comes time to trade canoes for dipnets and gill-nets, the trading families get together and work out a trade that is satisfactory to both parties.

Knowing how much work has gone into the fishing gear you and your family have put together, you naturally want to trade away no more than you have to for that perfectly fashioned canoe you are now looking at and aching to get on the water. The incentives in this transaction are to make the best deal you can, but not one that is so lopsided that you alienate

AN IDEOLOGY THAT IS MORALLY, SOCIALLY, AND ECOLOGICALLY BANKRUPT

your trading partner. Next time you or other Karuks are ready to acquire a new canoe, or something else, you want to be able to count on the good will of these people, and that means consistently arriving at deals that are felt to be fair by both parties.

This is trade at its primitive best: straightforward barter with no profit motive and no middle man involved.

It is the middle man who brought the profit motive into trade in the first place, and it is the demand for profit that drives the Earth-destroying juggernaut of endless growth. The middle man comes in three basic forms: the merchant, the investor, and the banker. The merchant buys merchandise at the lowest price he can negotiate and sells his goods at the highest price his customers are willing to pay. The difference between these two figures is his profit margin, and the rationale for exacting this toll involves not only the risk he takes in buying something he might not be able to sell, but his "overhead": the physical space where his goods are on sale, and whatever amenities are required to keep that space desirable to customers and employees, such as heat and light. Employees are of course another more or less "fixed cost" of the business. Many businesses fail, and so whatever profits might accrue to the successful business person are generally considered to be the just rewards for the risks undertaken.

This is the basic business model, and it makes a certain amount of sense if you grant the necessity for middle men in a complex society. But when business goes global and the conditions in poor countries can be exploited for ultra-cheap labor and horrendous working conditions—all to increase the profit margin of the middle man who buys super-cheap and sells at a price slightly lower than his competitors—you end up with something like Walmart, which nationwide has crowded out thousands of small businesses, and made the Walton family among the richest people in the world.

THE CULTURE TRAP

Historically, investors have been persons of wealth, with enough extra money that they could afford to gamble on a project involving some risk. Sometimes projects fail, and in that case their investment might be wholly or partly lost. On the other hand, when a project succeeds it might well reward the investor with spectacular returns. Speculating on projects or sectors of the economy with potential for rapid growth, and with commensurately large returns, has become a way of life within capitalism, spawning a particular class within society: the profit-seeking investor class.

Closely allied to this class of individual is the usurer, who demands that interest be paid on money loaned. Before the Industrial Revolution, the usurer was considered a pariah within society, a predatory parasite. But once the Industrial Revolution opened up a new array of possibilities for making money—in the exploitation of resources, in the manufacture and sale of various products, as well as the acquisition and sale of land itself—the usurer proved useful to industry, as well as to the projects of colonialism and empire, and his status inflated proportionately.

Usurers, venture capitalists, and large scale investors of various stripes (now including certain giant vertically-integrated corporations) are all in the game of making big bucks off what has come to be called Casino Capitalism. Casino capitalism is particularly attractive when it is possible to gamble with other people's money (to include taxpayer bailouts) while diverting all the profits to private accounts—as happens when banks are allowed to combine with investment firms. When, as a mega-money-corporation, you become too big to fail and the taxpayer bailout is guaranteed, there is really no gamble involved at all—especially when the government decision-makers overseeing your industry are your own hand-picked people.

AN IDEOLOGY THAT IS MORALLY, SOCIALLY, AND ECOLOGICALLY BANKRUPT

This financialization of capitalism is a way of making money without having to produce a real product, and should be understood as both predatory and parasitic. But is this blight upon capitalism an aberration of a fundamentally sound system, or is it an inherent and inevitable part of the system itself? I believe the best way to understand this decadent, late stage of capitalism is to look at the cultural beliefs and values that underlie this system, while also recognizing that human beings tend to behave in ways that they are incentivized to behave.

If you grow up within a society where sharing, generosity, and compassion for others are held in high esteem by those around you, while selfishness is looked upon as moral failure--because selfishness undermines group cohesion, posing a threat to group survival—you are likely not only to behave in solidarity with your group, but to feel the conviction of your behavior.

Throughout our evolutionary history, this has been the human (and humanoid) strategy for survival. The group always takes care of its own, because survival is only possible as a group. And a key feature of group dynamics for the hundreds of generations that we were mobile hunter-gatherers has been egalitarianism. Social stratification does not work well within small groups: the resentment it spawns tears those groups apart.

Within larger groups, such as our own American society, social stratification has been structurally built-in to our Constitution and into our capitalist way of life, and it hasn't torn the group apart yet. Not yet, but we are definitely headed in that direction as wealth and power inequality become exponentially more extreme.

Another cultural aberration, and one upon which the edifice of capitalism is built, is private property. To all our wild ancestors, and to indigenous peoples everywhere, the very concept of private property is not only absurd, it is sacrilege. How could you possibly claim ownership to this same Mother Earth that gives you your life? It is true that bands of tribal peoples would lay claim to the rights of usufruct of a territory that they claimed for their group's day-to-day subsistence. In this they were living off the interest of Nature's bounty, and within the annual solar budget (and of course they knew better than to degrade or destroy the source of their livelihood). This notion of "owning" a piece of Mother Earth and thinking you could do whatever you wanted with it--including stripping it of its life forms and life-giving qualities--that is nothing short of insanity. And of course it is ultimately suicidal--but the normalcy bias, which allows us to see what we are accustomed to as being "normal"—blinds us to this obvious reality. So "private property" is taken for granted, allowing the ongoing destruction of our life support system in the name of wealth creation.

The desirability of wealth creation as a cultural institution goes back only a few thousand years, and is based on the pastoral and agricultural way of life. The Old Testament, written some 3,000 years ago, overflows with approval for wealth creation. To become a patriarch upon a large estate with man-servants, maid-servants, extensive herds of cattle and sheep, and many children, stands as a model for the God-fearing man of substance. This social ideal has been with us through the centuries, and is with us still. We still have our patriarchs, our oligarchs, our power-elite, and they, more than anyone else, run the show.

It is for their sake—for the 1% and the one thousandth of 1%--(and incidentally for the sake of their operatives and hangers on) that the most aggressive tenets of neoliberalism are inflicted upon an ever more powerless working- and middle-class. This has been for me personally the hardest of all

AN IDEOLOGY THAT IS MORALLY, SOCIALLY, AND ECOLOGICALLY BANKRUPT

insights to grasp, to penetrate my naive supposition that what appeared to be class warfare must surely be no more than an incidental by-product of the power-elite pursuing their own self-interest. Surely, all of the attacks upon the middle and lower echelons of society that are embodied in the neoliberal agenda—privatization, deregulation, union-busting, slashing the social safety net, and all the rest—were not motivated by malicious intent. Only the most deranged of wetiko monsters would launch such an attack upon their own kind, reducing the quality of life for millions and millions of fellow human beings, just because they could. Just for the sake of exercising raw, compassionless power.

Like everyone else, I have heard it said that power corrupts, and absolute power corrupts absolutely. Somehow, I thought this had mainly to do with dictatorial heads of state and a few others in high places--a tiny minority. What has taken me so long to comprehend is that the human character is extremely fragile in certain ways, extremely vulnerable to corruption, including the corrosion of conscience, when wielding and dealing with power. This is our tragic flaw, and none of us is immune to its dis-integrating effects. Exercising power hollows us out from the inside, eating away at our empathy and integrity, turning us into soulless marionettes. And the more power we exercise over time the more twisted we become. On the outside we look like normal human beings; on the inside we become ever more psychopathic, ever more hollow.

This fragility in the face of power is not a new phenomenon, but a tendency of human nature that goes way back. Egalitarian societies solve the problem of dominating individuals through small-group peer pressure. If that doesn't work, exile or execution can be last resorts. Among more socially stratified, non-egalitarian groups the problem of inequality is solved through various leveling traditions, such as giveaways or feasts sponsored by the over-prosperous individual or family. Great prestige accrues to the fortunate few who share their good fortune with others, while the group itself sheds its built-up resentments at creeping inequality. In this time of feasting and sharing accrued inequality is reversed in an atmosphere of celebration. When things get too far out of balance again, it will be time for another great feast or giveaway.

In these cases, group cohesion has priority over the self-aggrandizement of the individual. This is good for the social order and the general contentment of the group, but redistributing wealth and pulling the rug from under a rigidifying social hierarchy is also good for those at the top, because it protects them from the insidious corrosion of too much wealth and power. In a very real way, it helps to preserve the inner core of their humanity.

The capitalist system, with its glorification of the self-aggrandizing individual, does the reverse. By encouraging selfishness and extreme social stratification, the capitalist ideology undermines group solidarity while at the same time inviting heart-rot into the soul of the self-seeking, self-absorbed individual. Operating out of a value system that defines human success in strictly materialistic terms, and lacking any but the shallowest vision of life's meanings and purposes, or even a mature moral compass, the capitalist ideology functions like a parasite of the heart and mind that feeds upon our humanity—turning us into wetiko monsters.

For all the reasons stated here, and for millions of others left unexplored, capitalism (and its extreme form, neoliberalism) constitute an ideology that is socially, morally, and ecologically bankrupt--and as such is bound to fail, and probably quite soon. The question is: what will be left in its wake? A planet that has been stripped of its wholeness, certainly, as well as the greater part of humanity stripped of its wholeness. Will

AN IDEOLOGY THAT IS MORALLY, SOCIALLY, AND ECOLOGICALLY BANKRUPT

something good arise from this wreckage? Only if all these old cultural lies are left for dead and something true takes their place.

CHAPTER 33

THE MOST DANGEROUS ANIMAL ON EARTH

THERE IS NO question that the human being is the most dangerous animal on Earth. We are a danger to all the other creatures who live here, a danger to the Bio-Systems that support Life here, and are therefore a danger to ourselves as a species. But what exactly is it that makes us so extraordinarily lethal? The usual suspects include our big self-reflective brain, our dexterous opposable thumb, our mastery of fire, and language. I wouldn't discount any of these, and taken together they give us an impressive edge. But I believe it these in conjunction with something else that gives us leverage far beyond the powers of any other species on Earth, and that something else is culture, along with the language that makes culture possible.

For as long as humans have been guided primarily by culture rather than instinct we have passed on stories, values, and memes, and other forms of useful knowledge, from one generation to the next. Certain kinds of shared group knowledge can be picked up through observing others and imitating what they do: monkey see, monkey do. This may be seen as a form of pre-culture, or proto-culture, but not as culture itself. True culture is achieved through the medium of language and is the exclusive domain of humans. (Material culture—the artifacts of a group's technology—is also true culture, but not to the present point.) For countless generations a peoples' culture--as carried by their language—can be been passed on through the group's oral and storytelling traditions. And make no mistake, oral culture has given humans a dramatic competitive advantage over the other creatures of the world, and this advantage has been cumulative—up to a point. Inevitably, there is a limit to how much information a group's oral culture can carry, because there is a limit to how much the human memory can store, retrieve, and bring back to life.

The written word has no such limits, and this is what makes it such a danger to the natural balances of the world, because written language's virtually unlimited capacity to build an edifice of accruing information increases –exponentially--the human competitive advantage over all the living creatures of the Earth— an advantage that our kind seems compelled to exploit to the fullest.

Thus, written language can be seen as a super-adaptation which transforms the human into a super-organism. With the written word, the collective human memory of oral culture is expanded beyond the individual or the small local group to include, in potential, all living human beings around the world. This is a quantum leap in human capacity, one that can be scaled upwards as the human population increases, and as the complexity of the Power Systems with which we interact expands—expanding, of course, in accordance with their own growth imperative.

Since the earliest days of hieroglyphics and stone tablets, some five thousand years ago, the written word has been used as a tool of the State to implement tyranny at home and expand empire abroad. With the much simpler Phoenician alphabet, written on parchment and papyrus, the conquest and subsequent administration of the Assyrian and Persian empires was immeasurably streamlined. When orders, directives, and policies from on-high were written down "in black and white," errors and misunderstandings were reduced to a minimum—and thus the will of Supreme Authority was duly implemented.

The Phoenicians were a trading people, and this newer more portable technology was a boon to commerce. Trade encourages interchanges with disparate peoples and travels to foreign locales, and in this way commerce is expansive, outward-looking, and opportunistic, as is empire. Indeed, commerce and empire have a long history as mutually dependent bedfellows, with the power of the State sanctioning and defending commerce at home and abroad, even as commerce—whether honest or piratical—has fed the coffers of the State with a share of its often ill-acquired booty. The written word, from early on, has been an essential ingredient of this symbiotic relationship between acquisitive commerce and the roving, grasping hand of empire.

Over the centuries, the written word has continued to expedite the agendas of commerce and empire. Empire is initially won by force of arms, but to be held and systematically exploited the conquered colonies require administration—and administration requires the written word. The will of imperial power must reach across space and time, from the homeland to the provinces, with as little ambiguity and as much specificity as possible. This requirement of empire has led to the rise of a particular class of people—those who are well versed in the use and meaning of language, including not only the aristocratic class of administrators, but also a bureaucratic class of scribes and petty officials. In this way, power and privilege was bestowed upon to the literate, and literacy itself was hoarded and guarded by those to whom it gave power.

The social ideal of universal literacy is a fairly recent innovation; for most of the last several millennia, the ability to read the written word was the prerogative of the elite classes, and of the sub-elite classes who served them. In this way, literacy (and its lack) served to perpetuate the class system and keep the common people "in their place."

The State and the Church were competing institutions of Power, and both held power over the people by exercising a monopoly over the written word. The various monastic orders of the Catholic Church had their scribes, who copied surviving documents from the Golden Age of Greece and the Roman Empire, as well as the sacred texts of their own (book) religion. These monastic orders held much of the history of Western civilization in their hands, dispensing or suppressing it according to the edicts of the Holy Order, or to the whims of superiors within the Church's rigid hierarchy.

It was, and still is, all about controlling the narrative.

Then as now, the power-elite maintain their position in the socio-political order by controlling which ideas and pieces of information will see the light of day, and which will not. Censorship can be as blatant as banning particular books or as subtle as ignoring certain subject matter while focusing public attention on something else. If information cannot be totally suppressed, it can at the very least be spun or framed in such a way as to minimize threats to the status quo.

With the rise of the printing press in the 15th century, the power of the written word was magnified, because it could reach more people, and potentially influence events of the day. As more books became available, literacy gradually increased among the common people. With the broader dissemination of information and ideas came a new stirring in society, a flowering forth of the collective imagination with an accompanying new optimism about life's possibilities—a social movement that came to be known as the Renaissance. As part of the Spirit of the Age, the perceived value of the unique individual gained newfound prestige, and with it came a rising democratic impulse.

The Protestant Reformation of the early 16th century, for instance, would have been unthinkable without the printing press and the rise of literacy. With Martin Luther's translation of the bible into German, the word of 'the good book' was taken out of the Latinate monopolizing hands of the priestly class and placed in the hands of the people, to be read and interpreted by and for themselves. This was a revolution in the distribution of power—from autocratic to democratic—and it all hinged on the written word, and its availability to the people.

Of course this revolution was never complete or in any way final-- and indeed in my own time the power-elite have all but strangled democracy, and done so all around the world. Partly, they have done this by controlling the media—print media, yes, but also the various other forms of communication that now partly supplant the written word: radio, television, the Internet. By monopolizing the people's source of information and ideas, they--like the Church and State before them—control the narrative, ensuring that the distribution of power stays on its present course. The longtime and ongoing trajectory has been to concentrate ever more wealth and power into the hands of the few, at the expense of the many. This is what civilization is about, and always has been.

Starting with the first piece of Mother Earth demarcated as "private property" for the purposes of agriculture, civilization has been about social stratification, an authoritarian political order, and the accumulation of wealth and power for the propertied class. As the human population burgeoned, these tendencies only intensified and became more entrenched. With the rise of the city and mass society, hierarchy asserted itself at all levels of social organization, as did the need for rules, laws, and ordinances, along with a bureaucracy to administer and enforce them--all based on the written or printed word.

With the rise of the corporation and the spread of empire across the globe, the written word has been used not only to subjugate people but to exploit every part of the living world for all that our people could take. As our technologies have grown in sophistication, we have been able to take more and more, from both aboveground and below, reaching into every corner of the world with our machines and our all-devouring appetite. All this has generated enormous amounts of paperwork, which continues to multiply exponentially, along with our population and our insatiable hunger for ever more stuff, as we gobble up what is left of the world.

The written (and then the printed) word did not arise in a vacuum, but evolved at a time and place where they served a particular purpose. It is no easy matter to sort out whether supply created demand or whether necessity was the mother of invention. Likely both dynamics came into play. In my own age of extreme complexity, we are unabashedly dependent upon some form or other of the written word to carry on our business. But the world you inherit will be a far different place, and the question is: does the written word have a rightful place in your life, or is it something to be shunned, suppressed, or simply ignored?

I myself am divided on this subject, because while I can see how damaging the written word has been to the living world, I have also experienced some of the many glories that the written word can accomplish, and it would grieve me to see these glories erased from the world.

On a personal level, I find the written word to be a boon to my own quality of life, and something I would not want to do without. In my lifetime, I have read several thousand books, and these have added inestimable richness to my life. In my twenties and thirties I was a literature major, and for nearly a dozen years I read some of the Western world's greatest fiction, and did this as a nearly full-time job. What I found was that each book of fiction represented a different world I was able to live in vicariously, inhabiting for a time the lives of various characters, identifying with them as they interacted with others in their particular time and place. These experiences expanded my geographical and historical horizons, while helping to cultivate in me a sense of empathy for other people and other ways of life. A literary experience, though vicarious, has a whole range of effects on the human organism, evoking feelings and thoughts that are just a real as any other feelings and thoughts drawn from so-called real life. This is why it is so important to be selective about the stories you choose to live in—because some stories enhance your life and well-being while others just bring you down.

Once I got into my forties I started reading mostly non-fiction, much of it slanted toward ecology, anthropology, philosophy, and history. From the time I was a boy, I have had the feeling that there was more to the world than anyone let on—something deeper than ever got talked about. Much of my non-fiction reading has been an attempt to get at what that something deeper might be. That quest has continued into my seventies, because there are always more pieces to the puzzle. The availability of high-quality books in print is a gift of the age I live in, and one that I deeply appreciate. In terms of human history and pre-history, this privilege is rare and recent and not to be taken for granted.

The kinds of books that I most often read are based on scholarship--that is, they are books based on, or influenced by, other books and articles. These other books and articles are in turn based on previous books and articles. A book, in other words, is a kind of intellectual pyramid scheme which combines the thinking of many minds. The book at the top of the pyramid may be the work of a single individual, but one who has been influenced by the work of many minds—and these, in turn, were influenced by untold other minds. This kind of book appeals to me because it concentrates the work of any number of minds and focuses their insights through the sensibility of a single seeker of understanding. This is a powerful magnification of the human intellect, and no other creature on Earth has anything to match it.

As a thinker, I find that writing things down is indispensible to deep, complex thought. Once I get some words down on paper, I don't have to hold that thought in my mind, but can move on to new, related thoughts, all of which are seeking a bigger picture than I can ever hold in my mind at once. Thus, I have learned to value writing as a mode of thinking, a way of coaxing thoughts of the mind and articulating what otherwise would remain as little more than inchoate feelings and impressions. I might have a vague sense of how I felt about a given matter, but fine distinctions would remain inaccessible, because not fully formed, as they become by the act of writing—and even more so by the act of rewriting.

That part of my life which is lived without the written word--as when I am hiking or gardening or fishing—is good, and satisfying in its way. But evidently it does not engage or satisfy every part of my being, because I seem to require the intellectual and emotional stimulation of books in my life. Beyond this, I also require my own written words to know the depth and extent of what--at some level of consciousness--is on my mind. This is writing as discovery, and it serves as an invaluable extension of the human mind.

When I think about your life and the world you have inherited from us, I think, on the one hand, that you will be far better off if you somehow manage to completely escape all the baggage that comes along with Western civilization, including all that is carried in our language, both oral and written. It is bound to be a contaminating influence and could easily lead you down the same wrong paths that we have taken—and that, I believe, would spell an end to our species. On the other hand, I would have you be a booklover just like I am, and take intellectual and emotional nourishment from the best our culture has produced. Also, I am writing this to you because I think it important that you understand what led to the damaged world that has come down to you from your forbearers. So, as you can see, I am conflicted here.

At this point I have to consider that I may be more a product of the culture of civilization than I would choose to be, and a victim of certain mistaken assumptions, particularly in the area of epistemology: in how we know what we know. In my world, and in my own personal experience, the surest path to understanding is through book-learning. Ironically enough, some of my reading tells me that peoples of other cultures followed a different path to the discovery of truth—what might be thought of as a spiritual path. Many disparate peoples over time have believed that the world is filled with spirits, and by communing with these spirits they could achieve deep knowledge about the world. According to the bias of Western culture the world is entirely material, and since spirits cannot be weighed, measured, or verified by science, they must not exist. But this is simply a supposition, an article of faith that is itself unverifiable.

So, if the world is filled with spirits, or there is some other repository of knowledge about the world and how to live here (such as morphic or akashic fields), then I am sure you would be better off to follow that path, and not the path of the written word. If you are living as part of a group of mobile of hunters and foragers, you will not, in any case, be lugging books around with you as you follow the ripening of plants and the movements of your chosen prey animals. Under these conditions, there will be no place in your life for books and reading.

From the perspective of the dominant worldview--inculcated and perpetuated by the culture of civilization--your life, without the benefits of civilization would seem to be most deprived and miserable. But I have come to doubt this view, not least of all because of my reading in anthropology. It seems that people who live in small compatible groups in unspoiled Nature are not only happy in their lives but can also be highly evolved individuals, reaching a stage of human development virtually unknown within the confines of civilization.

The written word is a powerful tool—a super-adaptation that transforms the human into a super-organism. As our history shows, it is far too powerful to be entrusted to the hands of a population of self-centered, insecure, anti-ecological adolescents. We have used the mass-mobilization powers of the printed and electronic word on behalf of Power Systems—our economic system, systems of technology, and the corporation--and the effect has been to dismantle the living world, and to feed it, piece by piece, to the maw of entropy. This ongoing and accelerating accelerating enterprise would not be possible without the printed and electronic word.

Some would say that the word itself is neutral; that it all depends in how it is used. The written, printed, and electronic word all have been used to further the agendas of our Power Systems, but what if they were to serve Bio-Systems instead? What if the human was fully integrated into the Community of Life and living in loyalty the Whole? What if we discovered that living in right relationship with Mother Earth brought us fully into ourselves, and that serving the Project of Life was our natural calling, and brought us our deepest satisfactions? In this case, couldn't the power of the written word be used to enhance Life rather than degrade it?

This strikes me as a lovely ideal, and one I would love to see and experience myself. I would love to believe that such a scenario was possible, that the lion would lie down with the lamb, we humans would have transcended our weakness for Power, and that we would all live happily ever after—just like in a fairytale. All it would take is a transformation of the human personality from self-absorbed, hubristic adolescent into a fully mature, disciplined, humble human being.

The key to a human future with long-term prospects is to live in balance with the Community of Life and to be in right relationship with Mother Earth. I believe this can be done, and has been done, but that such a state of being is scale-dependent, and can be achieved only by living small, simple, and humble. The written and printed word does not share these characteristics, and therefore has no place in such a world. Even without this super-adaptation, we would remain the most dangerous animal on Earth, because we would still have language and culture, mastery of fire, our very adept opposable thumb, and a restless self-reflective brain ever eager to create something new.

One final question remains: Even without the written and printed word and the Power Systems these serve, is the human being so constituted that we can find our proper place here on this living ecological planet? Or are we simply too dangerous to the rest of our family to make this place our home?

Only time will tell.

CHAPTER 34

WHOSE WOODS THESE ARE, I THOUGHT I KNEW

WHENEVER I READ Robert Frost's poem, "Stopping by the woods on a snowy evening," I am jarred by its opening line, and the one that follows: "Whose woods these are I think I know/His house is in the village though." What disconcerts me is the very idea that anyone could "own" a forest. As someone who has spent a lot of time in the woods, I know that a forest belongs to itself and to no one else. This is because a forest lives and breathes as a self-contained whole, with its own ecological integrity and qualities of uniqueness that, to someone like me, is experienced as a being with personhood. To the extent that humans honor this integrity of personhood the spirit of the forest welcomes them, but the human construct of "ownership" is quite foreign to the reality of what a forest actually is. I have always known that my society and culture do not agree with me in this matter, but that doesn't mean that they are right and I am wrong. In any case, I grew up in a world of both private and public forests in which most of the private land was characterized not by trees but by their absence, thanks to unending industrial clearcuts. And even when planted trees started growing back, it was obvious that this was to be a monocultural cropland and would never be a diverse, complex forest again. These stump farms and tree plantations stood in contrast to our public lands, as managed by the U.S Forest Service, which, though partly deforested, managed to leave enough trees standing as to seem forest-like. I thus saw these public lands as kind of a compromise between an ecological understanding of forests and the liquidation mentality of industry—as informed by the driving incentives of capitalism.

When I took my first job with the Forest Service in 1981 I assumed that a strong conservation ethic would be general among my fellow workers, but soon learned that this outfit had a culture of its own, in which conservation played a bit part, but was always subordinate to the starring role of "getting out the cut." Indeed, I arrived just in time to witness the Reagan administration mandating that we triple the cut on our forest—with no regard whatever for the legal requirements of so-called "sustained yield" forestry. What followed was a vast patchwork of clearcuts and a parade of logging trucks barreling down the highway toward mills in town. This was a period known as "logging without laws." Lawsuits were filed by regional and national environmental groups, and a few timber sales were stalled or stopped, but for years the carnage only multiplied. Eventually, under the Clinton administration, law and order was restored with the Northwest Forest Plan—at least in theory.

What follows is a story about an undercover operation of capitalism as it played out over my 22-year career with the Forest Service. At the time, I had no name for the ideology that was controlling events on my district, and on districts all over this nation. Nor did I then suspect its long range agenda. Only now is it clear to me that an extremely intense form of capitalism, called neoliberalism, was at work behind the scenes, and that its ultimate objective was the privatization of this country's public lands.

As it turns out, privatization is one of neoliberalism's key strategies, and its goal is to transfer public lands, public goods, and public services into the hands of the wealthy few, for the sake of private profit and wealth creation. Historically, in frontier America, the transfer of public land into private hands proved to be a surefire formula for amassing great wealth into the hands of a few—and of course it was all done "legally" through land grants and various legislative acts. Best known is the Homestead Act of 1862, which, besides making arable land available to small pioneer farmers, was also manipulated to amass vast tracts of prime land into the hands of sharp operators. Less well-known is the Desert Land Act of 1877, which ended up transferring big chunks of supposedly non-arable land into the hands of land speculation companies. On its heels came the Timber and Stone Act of 1878, by which large swaths of land came into the hands of logging and mining companies—through fraudulent, but semi-legal, double dealing. Similarly, much treaty-guaranteed Indian land has managed to find its way into white ownership over the years, by way of sharp practice and shifty legislation whenever gold, oil, or other valuable resources were discovered on these lands.

Although it is true that this form of privatization has a long history in this country, this part of the neoliberal agenda is not simply a continuation of a time-honored tradition. Along the way, a social and political consensus was reached about certain lands that should be kept in the public domain, as, for instance, a substantial portion of America's remaining forest lands. In 1891, following many decades of unrestrained land clearance and timber harvest (leaving the continued viability of the nation's forestland in doubt) the Forest Reserve Act authorized the withdrawal of land from the public domain to be put into forest reserves. Over time, the National Forest System would come to include 193,000 acres, to be managed by the United States Forest Service. This way of conserving some part of America's geological, biological, and ecological heritage was extended to other landscapes, and entrusted to the care of other governmental agencies, including the Bureau of Land Management, the U.S Fish and Wildlife Service, and the National Park Service. Maintaining some vestige of mostly or partially intact natural landscapes was considered by most Americans to be in the public interest, and--with broad public support--became the law of the land.

Those pushing the neoliberal doctrine of privatization would like to walk this bit of history back, and erase it altogether, if possible. Here I think it is useful to understand what the frontier meant in the history of capitalism and wealth creation. North America, South America, Australia, New Zealand and a few other land masses were very lightly populated and lightly used upon first contact by Europeans—in the 1400s and beyond. What this amounted to was an unprecedented windfall, at a time when Europe was experiencing the effects of overpopulation and the drawdown of natural resources. This frontier condition of abundant resources--available for the taking, especially for the most violent and unscrupulous--was the source of many a fortune, and also of what came to be known as the American Dream. From the neoliberal point of view, and from their freebooting precursors in frontier America and elsewhere, life is a zero-sum game in which there are winners and losers. Either you take what you want, or it is taken from you, in a world of bloody competition. Just as the American Indian was the place-holder and provisional custodian for the Europeans who would supplant them--and who would make maximum use of these resources that had scarcely been touched-- so too now with America's public lands. There is so much more to be gotten from them, once they are exploited to the full, and of course fortunes to be made in the process.

Knowing that the American people are favorably disposed toward their public lands, the think-tanks and politicians who represent the interests of industry pursue their ultimate aim of privatizing America's public lands not by direct assault, but indirectly and by stages. By consistently underfunding the agencies whose mission it is to oversee and manage these lands--forcing cutbacks, consolidations, and downsizing—a strategically stingy Congress can point to failures and inefficiencies, and call into question the very efficacy of publicly managed lands.

In my 22 years as a Forest Service employee, I saw this ploy playing out on my own Ranger District, as two ranger stations were consolidated into one and funding for half of the local workforce withdrawn. This meant not only that scores of people lost their jobs, but that those who remained were forced to take on the tasks of those who had been let go. Morale, which ordinarily ran quite high, was suddenly at an all-time low. A Ranger District can be a very tight-knit community, and one that takes its mission and its day to day work very seriously. When the ax falls suddenly from above--coming from some anonymous authoritarian place that does not, and cannot, appreciate the synergy and camaraderie that has developed within this community--reactions run the gamut around this most unwelcome shake-up of the established local order. Along with anger and resentment there is also grief at the loss of friends and good working relationships--emotions that are tempered by the ongoing insecurity of not knowing where or when the bottom might drop out next. Over time, new working relationships are established and these negative feelings fade into a kind of background static. What remains unabated, however, is the impossibility of one person doing the job of two or three dedicated individuals, and doing the job with a high degree of excellence. There is nothing for it but to do the best you can under the circumstances, but it is difficult to take the kind of pride in your work that you once did when the job required of you was commensurate with the number of hours in the day.

The people affected by this strategy of death-by-slow-starvation will likely never know the hidden agenda behind their miserable working conditions. The long-term goal of transferring ownership of America's public lands into private hands is not the project of a day, or even a single decade. The powers pursuing this end know that such a transformation of the social, economic, political, and physical landscape is going to take finesse and perfect timing. The first phase of this project is to underfund and downsize America's land management agencies, and then when these agencies falter here and there in their respective missions, orchestrate a concerted attack upon them as incompetent and inefficient, repeating again and again that government workers are simply not up to the job. This direct attack is buttressed by a longstanding campaign to discredit government in general—a think tank concocted mantra that has been echoed repeatedly through the auspices of the corporate media. The corollary proposition is that business, as an institution, is infinitely more efficient than government will ever be. The public is supposed to believe that if only corporations were in charge, everything would be much better than the way things are now. And though many do believe this, there is still very little public appetite for selling off what many Americans regard as be their natural birthright—this land that belongs to us all: the commons.

Given how widespread this sentiment is, the forces for privatization recognize that there must be an intermediate step or two before these lands can be privatized and exploited to the full. Accordingly, the next phase of the privatization project is to issue repeated calls for turning these federal lands over to the states, who, so the story goes, know how to manage the lands within their borders far better than a distant federal bureaucracy. This rationale may sound reasonable enough, but is actually more than a little disingenuous.

For one thing, just about every one of this country's fifty states is cash-strapped, and, unlike the federal government, they are constitutionally required to balance their budgets. In my own state of Oregon, it just so happens that over the past thirty years corporations have had their tax bill steadily reduced by a compliant state legislature, transferring that burden onto the people. In general, the average Oregon taxpayer is amenable to supporting most state programs, but at some point the burden is just too heavy to bear, and the taxpayers revolt. Over these same thirty years, many state programs have been pared way down, while others have been axed altogether. Funding for K through 12 and higher education has been severely cut back, leaving Oregon's education system as one of the poorest in the nation. This pattern of cash-strapped state governments struggling to fund the programs required to maintain a decent quality of life for its citizens is shared, to some degree, by every state in the union.

Now, consider what would happen in those states holding a fair amount of federally administered public lands within their borders when that land suddenly became theirs to take care of—even if the land came with (purposely insufficient) block grants to fund forest management for the first few years. As soon as it was legally possible, those lands would start being sold off to the highest bidder. And who would the highest bidder be? Very likely it would be one of the big, deep-pocket timber giants, whose land management policies are guided principally by the profit motive. And that means a lot of trees would fall in a lot of places all at once. As for the concept of multiple-use--including not only recreation for humans, but functional ecosystems and habitat for other species, as well as clean, clear water for all living beings—well, if recent history is any indicator, these would be considered as "amenities, " and not consistent with the corporation's institutional imperative for generating maximum profits for their shareholders.

As I write this in early 2017, the privatization of a public forest here in Oregon is presently on the table. The 82,500 acre Elliott State Forest was created in 1930 to provide ongoing funding for the Common School Fund, an expectation it has fulfilled for many decades. Lately, though, timber harvests have declined-- thanks in part to protections accorded to the spotted owl, Coho salmon, and the marbled murrelet, under the Endangered Species Act—and expected revenues have not been forthcoming. The average annual income over the past decade has been around $5 million, and one year (2013) the forest cost more to maintain than it produced in income. Proponents for the sale of this property have thus included interests besides the usual ideological suspects, especially from the education community. As a spokesperson for the Oregon Education Association has said:"For years the property has been costing the schoolchildren of Oregon money, not making a return. In an effort to protect the forest, our students have therefore been shortchanged." The annual budget for the Common School Fund runs to $1.4 billion. The single bid for this property is for $220.8 million—not nothing, to be sure, but a one-time infusion of cash with no benefits for the future.

Among the opponents of this sale are groups who advocate for preserving public lands for future generations of humans and other-than-humans, not only for all the measurable ecosystem services they provide- when their ecological integrity is kept intact--but for qualities less measurable, yet felt instinctively when humans find themselves in the presence of wholeness.

For Oregonians who have lived through a lifetime of ongoing clear-cuts, one thing is known for sure: Once a natural forest is gone, it is gone for good. Trees planted by industry will eventually grow on the same land to become a single-species tree farm--vulnerable, as all mono-crops are, to pests and disease and fire—but no one walking through such a plantation would ever mistake it for a structurally and biologically diverse natural forest. The Elliot State Forest is a mix of natural and industrial forest, with a strong bias toward timber harvest, but with certain minimal protections in place for wildlife and water quality, as administered by the Oregon Department of Forestry. Historically, and right up to the present day, the rule-making board for this agency has been, and is, dominated by individuals who represent the interests of industry, in a classic case of agency capture. If even more forestlands were to come into the hands of powerful industry giants, it would be reasonable to expect this bias toward industry to only intensify—further enfeebling already weak environmental protections.

One Oregon environmentalist with a clear sense of the privatization agenda has this to say about selling off the Elliott. "Our public lands are under unprecedented attack today by forces that would like to see them privatized and commercialized and abandoned for future generations. It would be a shame to look back and see what got its toehold in Oregon under Governor Brown." To be sure, Oregon has a reputation for its rich natural heritage and for appreciating this gift of Nature, and wanting to conserve some part of it. It would be a bitter irony indeed if Oregon, of all states, were to set a precedent for selling off public lands and start those dominoes (and trees) falling in all directions.

Although the shadow of privatization continues to hang overhead like a dark cloud, appearing ready to break loose upon us at any time, we aren't there quite yet.

Meanwhile, another form of privatization has already insinuated itself into the Forest Service. It may call itself outsourcing or a public-private partnership but what it is in practice is taking public sector jobs away from government employees and turning that work over to private sector businesses. This happened on my ranger district in the mid-1980s when Forest Service campgrounds lost the presence of uniformed Forest Service employees and saw something quite different take their place.

I was a wilderness ranger at the time, which meant that as soon as snow in the mountains permitted I got to spend my work-week in the backcountry. But I was in the same Recreation Department as the crew of locals who worked in Developed Recreation, serving each of the 26 Forest Service campgrounds on the McKenzie River Ranger District. That is a lot of campgrounds for a single ranger district, but then this is a highly desirable area for outdoor recreation, attracting people from far and wide. Occasionally, in the early season, I would go out to work on a special project with the people on this crew, and thereby got a pretty good sense of who they were and how they felt about their job. Almost all were locals who had lived in the area for a number of years, if not all their lives. They liked living here and enjoyed exploring the many features of this mountain and river landscape. And those who had been at it for a while also knew something about the history of the area, and also about the Forest Service. When they were approached by a camper in a campground they were generally able to answer whatever questions were put to them. If not, they always carried a radio and could call someone at the ranger station who might know more than they did. Being able to answer questions and point things out on a map—that is, serving the public—was the highlight of their day. Likewise, I know that the public felt well-served by these kinds of interchanges, both for the congenial quality of the interaction and how the good information they got enhanced their experience of the area.

These employees were good people doing good work, locals in a rural area that has very few quality jobs on offer—and they got the ax. What took their place were individuals from out of the area hired by an out-of-state corporation, and what these outsiders knew about the local scene was exactly zero. And even if some of these strangers to area happened to be friendly with a sincere desire to be helpful, the quality of the interaction between them and the public was somehow different, in a subtle but nonetheless disturbing way. Something about this new system went against the public's deepest expectations, a *zeitgeist* and view of the world that had been in the air since the war years.

In the decades immediately following World War Two, the American people were encouraged to believe they were part of something much larger than themselves: a nation that was a unified and cohesive whole, a proud society in a land of geographical diversity and untold natural wonders. It was in this period--the 50s and 60s--that the interstate highways were being constructed, as were many a Forest Service campground. These campgrounds were promoted as belonging to all Americans, and making use of them was a great way to get to know the hidden treasures of this country. Travel and tourism was good for the economy and both were widely promoted in these days when it was commonly believed that "What is good for General Motors is good for America," and an unending and unproblematic supply of gasoline was taken for granted. These Forest Service campgrounds, along with our state and national parks, and national forests generally, were seen as tangible and desirable public assets. These refuges from city life were one of the few places where citizens could see their taxpayer dollars directly at work, and this public resource was understood to be their natural birthright as Americans.

Every person's sense of identity is tied to who they as individuals are in relation to the people around them, to various social groups, and to societal institutions. For American living through the 50s, 60s, and into the 70s, there was a sense of belonging to a large but very special group of people who had survived a world war and were making a good life for themselves in the boom-times that followed. At that time, the government was seen as a benevolent force for good, and all these beautiful parks and campgrounds were embodiments of that belief. When, in the 1980s, formerly free campgrounds started charging fees, and low-fee campgrounds started getting expensive, this came as a challenge to the by then settled belief that free, or nearly free, access to these special places upon the American landscape was a natural right of citizenship. When those nice campground rangers with their green rigs and radios were replaced by indifferent strangers with no ties to the area, working for a company whose prime motive was the maximization of profit, not public service, the world seemed to shift in a disconcerting direction. Suddenly, and rather abrasively, it was no longer a congenial world where we were all in this together, but rather a place where everything had its price, and the currency of good will and the supposed perquisites of citizenship had lost their value.

My own reaction to this change in policy and mood was equal parts disbelief and outrage, as it shook my sense of what

WHOSE WOODS THESE ARE, I THOUGHT I KNEW

America was and who I now was as an American. Had I been living in a fool's paradise all along, believing that something more than money held us together as a society? Was that a delusion, and now the underlying reality was finally asserting itself? I knew something had changed in the culture of the Forest Service itself, as our "leaders" were no longer talking about us as a public service organization, but as a business. Indeed, this way of thinking was showing up in other unexpected places, including the post office and our local schools. The talk was all about customers and clients and giving them fair return on their investment. Suddenly, the many-faceted complexity of public service in the public interest was reduced to a simple business transaction based on money changing hands. What the hell was going on here?

What it was, was the ideology of neoliberalism working its way, like a contagion, through governmental institutions and society generally. But what exactly is neoliberalism? Where did it come from, where is it going, and what does it mean for the world? These are the questions I have set for myself these many years later, and will attempt to answer in the essays that follow. I will also offer an opinion or two on whose woods these are, and what that might mean for human survival and planetary well-being.

CHAPTER 35

THE MOST DANGEROUS SOCIAL INSTITUTIONS

EVEN THOUGH BY your time this most dangerous of social institutions will likely have destroyed itself, you should know something about the rise of the corporation, because of the lessons its brief history contains. Throughout my own lifetime I have been aware of corporations as a powerful force within American society. For instance, it used to be said that: "What is good for General Motors is good for America." Behind this slogan was the clear implication that what is good for corporate America is good for the country at large. I know that many believed that then, as many still do--despite the fact that corporations are dismantling the living world before our very eyes, even as they undermine what remains of democracy.

But what exactly is a corporation, and how did it become what it is today? Though never actually benign, the corporation began simply enough as a way for merchant adventurers to pool their resources and cover their bets in the early days of colonialism. Among the British, charters of incorporation were granted by the crown, along with rights of exclusivity to particular geographic locations. Thus the East India Company was declared to have a trading monopoly with India, and these monopolies were violently enforced by private armies and police within their designated zone of trade. Indeed, extortion, theft, and piracy were a normal part of doing business for this company of freebooting profiteers, whose own private army of 250,000 could, and did, take what it wanted by force. Chartered in 1600, and operating as a joint-stock company from 1650, this immensely powerful organization would serve as the template upon which subsequent corporations were built—though companies following in its wake would cultivate a public image of greater probity and legitimacy than their nakedly piratical model corporation.

Ironically, the same America that would later come to dominate the corporate scene (claiming 19 of the world's largest 25 corporations as of 2002) was, in colonial times, staunchly anti-corporate. Thus, Thomas Jefferson (an aristocrat himself) spoke for the American people when, in 1816, he said: "I hope we shall crush in its birth the aristocracy of our monied corporations which dare already to challenge our government to a trial of strength, and bid defiance to the laws of our country."

In colonial America anti-corporate sentiment arose from different concerns, according to class. Among the educated elite, like Jefferson and other of the Founding Fathers, the issue was one of power, and the social dynamic that resulted from how power was distributed. Among the merchant class, the issue was more directly economic: the kind of corporate monopoly that the British East India Company threatened in the case of tea and other commodities could easily put their own enterprises out of business. Among the working-class, a memory of ill-treatment by one or both of the corporations then operating in colonial America fueled the people's animosity--with many grievances related to the indentured servitude that brought them or their forbearers to America's shores.

The Virginia Company (1607-1624) was responsible for founding the colony at Jamestown, Virginia. To understand why this company was so despised by the working-class survivors of its policies and practices, and how the deep mistrust of corporations fed into the American Revolution, it helps to know something of the historical context in which this company came into existence. In medieval England, the feudal system had been a highly stratified social and land tenure arrangement, with overlords at the top and the serfs at the bottom. As lopsided and patriarchal as this system was, the people at the bottom still had a place to call home. But in the 1400s and 1500s, the land that had once been shared by the people as a commons--to be used for grazing, the growing of vegetables, or other domestic purposes--was transformed by a series of "enclosure" acts to the private ownership of the aristocratic overlord, often used to pasture sheep. Being forcibly (and legally) removed from the land, the peasant class was left to a life of rural vagabondage or urban destitution. Under Henry VIII (1509-1547) landless vagabonds were treated as criminals, and were whipped, had their ears cut off, or were hanged. Such a marginalized population was preyed upon by press gangs that rounded up able-bodied men to serve on the sailing ships of the East India Company; while women, men, and especially children were pressed into forced servitude in the American colonies, where they were treated, and mistreated, as chattel.

The statistics of the Virginia Company do not reflect well on its American operations. In its seventeen-year existence, 6,000 adults and children had been shipped off to the colony under its auspices. Of these, an estimated 4,800 had died at some point in their servitude—more than 350 at the hands of

THE MOST DANGEROUS SOCIAL INSTITUTIONS

Indians, while the remainder met their end through a combination of overwork, starvation, abuse, torture, and execution, at the hands of the company's representatives.

These were unstable and brutal times for the vulnerable landless poor, who were routinely victimized by those invested with power, including the unrestrained power of the corporation. In seeking a better life across the Atlantic, many found much worse conditions instead; and among those who survived, the memory lingered. Nevertheless, the corporation as an institution continued to flourish—so much so that less than fifty years after Jefferson's anxiety about corporate power, another president would express a similar fear:

> "I see in the near future a crisis approaching that unnerves me and causes me to tremble for the safety of my country. . . . corporations have been enthroned and an era of corruption in high places will follow, and the money power of the country will endeavor to prolong its reign by working upon the prejudices of the people until all wealth is aggregated in a few hands and the Republic is destroyed."
> —U.S. PRESIDENT ABRAHAM LINCOLN, NOV. 21, 1864

As it turned out, both presidents had reason to worry about the growing power of the corporation, and what that would mean for our form of government.

A fundamental organizing principle of the corporation is that shareholders have a right to a reasonable return on their investment. From the point of view of investors, this is a necessary condition to incentivize the gamble of an investment. From the point of view of society at large, this is not always such a good deal, because it legitimizes private profit over the common good, and when these two are in conflict society comes up the loser. That is, the management of any corporation is duty-bound to protect the interests of the shareholders, and this obligation must take priority over the public good. Any corporate leader who reverses these priorities will soon find himself (or herself) replaced by someone who will play the game according to this most stringent of corporate rules.

In light of what a joint-stock company is, this foundational principle--that the shareholders always come first--makes perfect sense. But when multiplied by tens of thousands of corporations and considered cumulatively over time, this corporate imperative has been responsible for much mischief in the world. And this mischief has compounded as the corporation has, over the last century and a half, been granted new powers, exemptions, and privileges.

Through a series of statutory revisions, beginning as early as 1820 and accruing throughout the 19th century, corporate investors gained ever more limited liability for whatever harms their corporation might visit upon the world. That is, no matter how large the damages caused by their company the financial responsibility of the investor class was strictly limited.

Even as the investor garnered new insulation from personal responsibility, the corporation was morphing from a custom chartered entity with a limited lifespan to one of perpetual existence under new laws of general incorporation , beginning with the New Jersey general incorporation law of 1889. Unlike every living being in the world, including all humans, the corporation was now potentially immortal. This, like limited liability and the shareholder-first -imperative, would come to have huge implications for the world at large.

Also, in the final few years of the 19th century the corporation began to redefine itself in other ways--with the help of the American judicial system, including the U.S. Supreme Court—such that by the end of the 20th century corporate power would be nearly absolute. This was accomplished by a series of Supreme Court decisions that interpreted the U.S. Constitution—and especially the Bill of Rights—to grant corporations the rights of personhood, *as if* they were actual human beings, with constitutional rights of equal protection under the law. This legal fiction, which began with the 1886 decision in *Santa Clara v. Southern Pacific*, opened the way for subsequent decisions that expanded the rights of corporations to include: due process under state and federal law (1890,1893); freedom from unreasonable searches (1906); trial by jury in a criminal case (1908); compensation for government takings (1922); freedom from double jeopardy (1962); jury by trial in a civil case (1970); the right to commercial speech (1976); the right to political speech (1978). This latter decision in the 1978 case of *First National Bank of Boston v. Bellotti* would set the stage for ever more corporate influence in matters of State, by setting the precedent that corporate money in politics equals the right to free speech.

Because of the way political campaigns are financed in this country, money can and does buy political influence. Equating money with the freedom of speech in electoral politics means that those who can write big checks to political candidates, or hire lobbyists and lawyers to influence sitting politicians, have a distinct advantage over ordinary citizens who lack such deep pockets. The policies and practices of a sitting administration, as well as the laws of the land, are thus tilted in favor of those who can pay for what they want. Under this new pay-to-play system, a corporation is able to have its in-house lawyers write the laws that govern its own regulation, to be rubberstamped by their paid-for 'lawmakers.'

Whatever modest restraints upon money in politics might have prevailed during the thirty-plus years following the money-equals-speech *Bellotti* decision were obliterated by the

Citizens United Supreme Court decision in 2010—a decision which says in effect: there are no limits to how much an individual can contribute to influence the outcome of an election. What this means in practice is that the very rich (nearly all of whom have corporate ties and corporate interests) have so much political influence that they might—without exaggeration--be said to run the country. There is a name for a society that is governed by a handful of rich and powerful families. It is called an oligarchy, and it differs significantly from the ideal of self-rule implied by a republic or democracy.

It seems that when our 16th president feared for the safety of our country--because 'corporations have been enthroned and an era of corruption in high places will follow, and the money power of the country will endeavor to prolong its reign by working upon the prejudices of the people until all wealth is aggregated in a few hands and the Republic is destroyed'—his fears were justified.

Before exploring how this corporate coup is going global, I want to mention two key strategies that the corporation has used to build its strength. The first is to buy out the competition and consolidate ownership into the hands of the few, a market condition known as oligopoly. When one sector of an economy is owned by a very few, price rigging is a near-inevitable result. This is good for shareholder profits, but not so good for the consumer. To counter the monopolistic tendencies of corporate consolidation, Congress has, over the years, enacted anti-trust legislation. Although there are several high-profile cases where the government has broken up monopolistic super-corporations (Standard Oil, American Tobacco, and AT&T), the general rule has been one of rubberstamping corporate consolidation.

The rationale behind anti-trust legislation has been

threefold: to protect the consumer from monopolistic price-gouging; to protect small businesses from predatory takeovers by bigger ones, and; to limit the political influence of overly large corporations. For the most part, teams of corporate lawyers have managed to frustrate these attempts at preserving the public good.

Another fruitful strategy for the corporation to achieve a bare minimum of governmental oversight and regulation is through what is known as the revolving door. The way this works is, industries looking to get policies or regulations rewritten in their favor offer up to an obliging administration certain of their employees to fill key positions in government. For instance, it would serve the corporate interests of the pharmaceutical industry to have strategically placed 'friends' within the Food and Drug Administration, just as it serves the interests of agribusiness to have allies within the Department of Agriculture. Upon returning to their parent companies after serving their time in government—all the while furthering their company's interests--these loyal corporate shills are amply rewarded for their services with promotions, raises, and bonuses. Virtually every agency of government has been infiltrated by just such corporate stooges, furthering private interests at the expense of the public good—thanks to the revolving door.

Throughout its brief history, but especially in the last century and a half, the corporation has been consolidating its power as an institution within society. Its path to power has been piecemeal but relentless, as it acquired strengthening new attributes with each succeeding court decision. Having established its various rights of 'personhood'-- including its right to free 'speech,' by way of spending nearly unlimited amounts of money to further its aims—this 'person' who never dies, and who owes its primary loyalty to legally sheltered shareholders, has found an even more promising path to absolute hegemony, and at a global scale.

The disarming rubric under which global corporate hegemony is sought is 'free trade.' The structure of the 'free trade' system originated in 1944, when delegates from forty-four countries met in Bretton Woods, New Hampshire, to set up a framework of international accords known as the Bretton Woods System. The International Monetary Fund and the World Bank were constituted at this time, and four years later came the General Agreement on Tariffs and Trade. These institutions and agreements created the necessary conditions for a sister institution that would follow in 1994: The World Trade Organization, a private tribunal with the broad powers of settling international trade disputes in secret and with no public oversight. Under the WTO, one nation can sue another if new laws--such as labor, health and safety, or environmental regulations--reduce the values of a corporation's property or expected future profits.

This new wrinkle in international trade was followed by another under the North American Free Trade Agreement. Under this trade pact between the United States, Mexico, and Canada, not only could one *nation* sue another for harming corporate profits, but now *corporations* could sue a nation, a state, province, county, or city, for passing laws that might harm a company's reasonably expected future profits. Such suits are considered by secret arbitration boards out of sight of the public eye, and a number of such suits have been filed and won by the plaintiffs.

For instance, the waste disposal company MetalClad sued Mexico for $90 million because the government had ordered a geological study to determine the suitability of MetalClad's property as a waste disposal site. When the study determined that the facility was situated over an alluvial stream that might contaminate the local water supply, the government nixed the operation. For this act of protecting the people's drinking water, the NAFTA tribunal awarded MetalClad $16.7 million, which was paid by the Mexican government.

For the past seven years a company called TransCanada has been seeking approval from the US State Department for a pipeline from the Alberta tar sands to the Gulf Coast of Louisiana, called the Keystone XL pipeline. If approved, this pipeline would cross seven states and hundreds of creeks and rivers, not to mention the nation's largest underground aquifer, in order to carry the world's dirtiest and most corrosive oil to a port city where it could be refined and shipped to China. TransCanada has been responsible for a number of large and damaging pipeline failures in the recent past, yet this company would have the legal right of eminent domain, forcing thousands of farmers and homeowners to accept the pipeline on their property, whether they wanted it or not.

Also relevant to this pipeline proposal is the potential long-range damage of this especially dirty oil to Earth's ever-worsening climate crisis. Accordingly, an unusual coalition of climate activists, Midwest landowners, and ordinary citizens young and old--accompanied by mounted contingents of cowboys and Indians--passionately opposed this project in a series of high-profile demonstrations, landing many in jail. Meanwhile, the approval process—once looking to be quickly rubberstamped-- dragged on for years. Finally, with a year left in office, President Obama made one of the few bold moves of his presidency: in November of 2015 he rejected the Keystone XL pipeline, saying it would not serve US interests. Within two months TransCanada had announced that it would be suing the United States for $15 billion under provisions of the Investor-State Dispute Settlement agreement of NAFTA.

NAFTA was the corporate toe testing the waters with a three-nation hemispheric agreement, and evidently corporations found conditions agreeable, because now, two decades later, they have come up with similar "free trade" agreements involving many more potential trading partners. One of these is the Atlantic Trade and Investment Partnership (TTIP), which spells out the conditions of trade between the U.S. and much of Europe, and the Investor-State Dispute Settlement (ISDS) provision seems to be part of this agreement, too. We cannot be absolutely certain, because these trade agreements have been negotiated behind closed doors for the last five or six years. So secret are they that even members of Congress have to go to a special secure room to read them, and are forbidden to discuss what they discover there.

Of more immediate concern to me is the Trans-Pacific Partnership, which could come up for an up or down vote at any time now. This agreement has been fast-tracked, which means that Congress has forfeited its constitutional right and obligation to negotiate, or change in any way, the terms of this document. The TPP, which was also hammered out in secret, amounts to a kind of wish list for some of the world's largest corporations and wealthiest investors. We only know this because parts of this document have been leaked to non-profit organizations, which have helped spread the word. Not surprisingly, corporations are granted the right, under ISDS provisions, to sue governments that pass laws which they deem harmful to their expected profits.

For instance, where I live (in Lane County, Oregon) a large contingent of people is deeply concerned about what has been happening to the bees. These pollinators have been disappearing at a worrisome rate, and the people want to do something about it. It has been scientifically established that a class of pesticides known as neonicotinoids kill bees, and there have

THE MOST DANGEROUS SOCIAL INSTITUTIONS

been local cases where linden trees have been sprayed with this chemical and bees have died by the tens of thousands. So, the people want these chemicals banned, and would be happy to see a federal or state law outlawing their use. Failing that, they will settle for a county ordinance prohibiting its use in Lane County.

Both our state and our county have been cash-strapped for several decades now, due in large part to a series of reductions in the corporate tax rate, thanks to corporate-friendly lawmakers, leaving social programs and education in the lurch and state and county coffers all but empty. If the Trans Pacific Partnership becomes law, Bayer, the giant multinational corporation that makes the bee-killing neonictionoids, would have the right to sue Lane County for passing such an ordinance. Knowing that the county could not afford such a lawsuit—win or lose—our local leadership would weigh the options and reasonably decide not to go there, preemptively smothering the will of the people and leaving the bees to the toxins.

When all of these and other trade agreements become law, corporations will rule the world. They are almost there already, and soon their global hegemony will be complete.

So, as you can see, within its brief history the corporation has shown itself to be an enemy of democracy as well as of the common good. I would go further and say that it has shown itself to be the enemy of Life itself. As it has accrued power to itself, the corporation has become ever more dangerous to what humans hold most dear, including a living planet. This is not due simply, or even primarily, to greed or the evil intent of corporate shareholders and executives. Rather, the corporation has become a threat to all Life, and to the Earth itself, because of the kind of system it is: A Power System.

CHAPTER 36

BIOSYSTEMS, POWER SYSTEMS, AND PEOPLE

BY THIS TIME you may be wondering why I have been going on so about the corporation, possibly questioning its relevance to you and your situation. The reason is: I want you to consider the principles behind the rise of the corporation and recognize the dangers of allowing such a social institution into your life and the lives of your people. But to get a handle on these principles it is essential to understand just exactly what a corporation is, what it does, and what it wants.

To speak of what a non-living entity 'wants' may seem absurd on its face, but bear with me on this, as we try to get at what a corporation actually is. We can begin by stating with some certainty that the anatomy of a corporation would suggest that it is a system that functions within a matrix of other systems. But all systems are not created equal, nor is one system identical to another. The Gaian system is what I would call the Master System of planet Earth, and it is primarily a Biosystem. It has physical, chemical, and geological elements, but the Gaian Biosystem's defining attribute is the creation and nurturing of Life. It is this system that has made possible the entire 3.8-billion-year Project of Life. The biological system that is the human being is a late arrival within this Project, and the corporation a later arrival still.

In one light, the corporation can be seen as a simple human artifact—created by humans for humans. But it is actually not quite so simple as this, and that is because of the kind of system that the corporation is. It is not a life-nurturing Biosystem, but is instead a Power System, and as a Power System has an agenda of its own—an agenda that I would suggest is ultimately anti-Life. Why do I say this? Because of what a Power Systems does.

What the corporation as a Power System has done over the course of its existence is exponentially intensify the spending down of the Earth's natural resources, living and otherwise, creating short term human wealth while amplifying the rush toward planetary entropic exhaustion. Power--with its built-in imperative for ever-expanding growth--has exploited our human vulnerabilities to achieve its ends, using us as interchangeable parts within its machine of Power.

As a Power System, the corporation does not stand alone, but works in synergistic combination with other Power Systems. These include technology, with all its delivery systems and in all its multiplying manifestations, as well as our complex economic system (including the banking and money system), with its myriad tentacles reaching into every part of human life. All of these interrelated Power Systems are driven by an agenda of limitless expansion, and of course this is where they prove so destructive to a living but finite planet. The agenda of each of these systems is to take and take until there is nothing left, in order to feed the system's endless appetite for more.

The brief history of the corporation outlined above demonstrates just how relentless these Power Systems are in pursuit of their power agenda. They don't accomplish hegemony in a day, but they accrue power to themselves over time as they insinuate themselves into the lives of humans, gradually but ceaselessly increasing our dependence on them, to the point that we cannot conceive of living without them—either as individuals or as a people.

What a Power System 'wants' is to grow. What a Power System does is to consume the living world and spit it out as toxic waste. Thus, the Power System can be seen to operate on a different, and opposing, principle than the Bio-System, which recycles everything, and creates ever more complexity, diversity, system resilience, beauty, and abundance out of the building blocks of Life.

It is here that we must inevitably fall back on some sort of metaphysical explanation of these countervailing powers. The disciplines of physics and biology try to explain this dichotomy of creative and destructive forces in terms of entropy and negentropy, these being the terms they use to describe the opposing universal tendencies toward disorder and order. The second law of thermodynamics enshrines entropy, or the tendency toward disorder, as natural law. Negentropy, which is an attribute of living systems, has not been similarly enshrined, even though we see its effects all around us. So, science—still mostly stuck in an outdated model of the world--is behind the curve in this regard, offering only partial insights at best.

Various wisdom traditions have tried to come to terms with the polarities of creation and destruction, chaos and order, life and death. The trickster of Native American tradition embodies a mishmash of qualities both life-affirming and life-negating, combining lust and greed with cleverness and creativity, along with a range of other contradictory character traits, all adding up to a figure of incongruous, yet somehow recognizable, complexity.

The mythological system at the heart of Hinduism nods to

the interplay of opposites with such symbolic figures as Shiva, the destroyer, and Shakti, who represents primordial creativity, fertility, and the Life Force--personifying with these figures what Western science sees in starkly impersonal terms.

The Chinese symbol for yin and yang is yet another way of conceptualizing the complementary polarities that characterize our world: night and day, male and female, matter and mind, as well as creation and destruction. Even though I know little of the philosophical system behind this suggestive symbol, I like it for what it represents to me. What I see is a circle that represents the Whole, and within that unity are two opposing but complementary forces, one black and one white, each in a shape that seems to have both a head and a tail. The black head seems to be chasing the white tail, even as the white head is chasing the black tail, suggesting a dynamic and energetic relationship between the two. Noteworthy, too, is the little dot of white within the black form and a corresponding black dot within the white form, suggesting that no force or condition is pure or absolute, but also contains its opposite.

Significantly, this symbolic representation of the polarities that energize our world show them to be perfectly symmetrical, and thus in perfect balance with one another. This is a stylized and static representation of dynamic processes, and as such prone to smoothing over irregularities and rough edges for the sake of appearance. In the phenomenal world that this symbol attempts to represent, the interaction of opposing forces may not always be this neat. Nevertheless, the sense of proportionality and balance that this image evokes is a vital feature of all systems whose ongoing existence depends upon achieving a dynamic homeostatic balance—one that averages out to a tied score between the opposing forces. This kind of balancing act, depending mostly on negative feedback loops, is how Bio-Systems achieve their actively evolving longevity rather than flaming out in a burst of spectacular but evanescent glory.

Using the yin-yang symbol to represent the interaction of polar opposites, imagine the two contrasting figures not in perfect symmetry but out of balance, the dark figure steadily devouring the white and growing ever larger while the white figure diminishes. The circle could easily represent our planet, and the black and white represent entropy and negentropy--death and life--locked in ferocious battle. The second law of thermodynamics is having its way with the first; Thanatos is ravaging Eros; Death smothering Life. In terms of systems dynamics, the negative feedback loops that once maintained a dynamic homeostatic balance between the complementary polarities of black and white are now overwhelmed by self-reinforcing positive feedback loops, as darkness devours the light. This is the state of the world I live in today.

Power Systems serve entropy, and they do it by consuming Life, by converting the energy that Life engenders into non-life. If the appetite for energy is kept in check, yin and yang remain in balance and their interaction resembles a graceful dance of give-and-take between equals. When driven by the imperative for growth, as all Power Systems are, and with no effective limitation to their insatiable appetite for more and more and more, the dance turns into a murderous feeding frenzy.

Significantly, the Power Systems that are now ravaging the Bio-Systems of planet Earth could not exist in their present form without the complicity of humans. We the people of civilization have always regarded ourselves as exceptional--set apart from (and above) all of our fellow Earthlings—and so we are. Without us to enable them, Power Systems might still exist (at least in potential) but lacking enslaved humans to execute their will, they could not be devouring the living world as they are today. So of course we have every right to be proud.

The Earth is an ecological economy of systems within systems within systems. For more than three and a half billion years it was a growth economy, building complexity, diversity, and system resilience, achieving an economy of overflowing abundance. At some point this growth economy had to slow down in the face of limits--limits of space, of fertility, even limits of possibility--and strive to reach an optimum, if ever-changing, equilibrium. Both negative and positive feedback systems were at work during this creative phase of evolutionary experimentation and compounding growth. During this 3+ billion-year period the yin-yang image would have been the reverse of what it is today, with negentropy (Life) in ascendance, the white within the circle overpowering the darkness of chaos and decay. This was the general shape of things until practical limits began to assert themselves, and the growth mode was largely replaced by the maintenance mode, black and the white moving toward parity. Now, working on the principle of the thermostat, negative feedback systems helped maintain optimum levels of everything that made the Bio-System work.

This is the world our wild ancestors inherited: a mature ecological economy sufficiently endowed to comfortably support an upstart population of capable featherless bipeds. Like all the other creatures on the planet, these wild ancestors of ours lived within the Earth's annual solar budget. That is, they lived off the "interest" of Nature's accumulated capital, lived in the gift of her bounty. As hunter-gatherers they might have been capable of over-harvesting or over-hunting a particular species of plant or animal, upsetting in this way the ideal balance, slightly spending down Nature's capital in their home territory. Seeing that this harmed their ecosystem as well as their own future flourishing in place, they had every incentive to learn from, and correct, their blunder. At that point, Power systems were not in control.

When the first wild ecosystem was stolen from all the creatures who filled it, and was converted to agriculture, this signaled a change in relationship between the human and the natural world. The world itself was unimaginably large then and this violation relatively small--but it did set a precedent. It broke an ancient and sacred bond we had with Nature and set us on a course of theft. Instead of living in humble gratitude for the bounty that Nature provided, we started spending down her capital, at first only by mining the topsoil of converted natural ecosystems, then by mining water, minerals, and other "resources" from aboveground and below. One form of theft led to another as we found new ways spend down nearly four billion years of the Earth's accrued biological and geological wealth. Once we began organizing ourselves into armies of exploitation and building a human economy based upon plundering the Earth for all we could take, we had already surrendered to Power, and to the Power Systems that made it work. When we started building machines to aid us in raiding Nature's stores—powdered first by wood and steam, then by coal, then oil—our theft intensified exponentially, as did our population, and our demands.

Our economic system is based upon large-scale theft: upon spending down the Earth's natural capital. The corporation represents an intensification of organized theft, as do the machines of our ever-expanding technology. These are all Power Systems and they work together synergistically to devour the world--and they take a bigger bite every day. If the Earth and its Community of Life are to be spared utter ecological catastrophe, these partners in crime must somehow be separated--once and for all. But how?

Given the extent of our entanglement with Power Systems, and how they have enticed and extorted us with real wealth and power--including its prospect, and its loss--we complicit humans are not likely to end the relationship voluntarily. So, what other possibilities are left? These systems could somehow fail on their own—as, for instance, in a global economic collapse. Or something drastic exterior to these systems could cause them to fail: a reversal of the Earth's polarities, maybe, or something else that caused the global electrical grid to go down and stay down. Some such miracle from on-high is not impossible, but hardly to be counted on. Much more likely, in my view, is a major population crash, due to one or more of Nature's many options for dealing with population overshoot, including flood, fire, famine, and plague.

Or, we could just take ourselves out with any one of the technologies we have, Prometheus-like, purloined from the gods: runaway self-replicating nanotechnology could turn the once-living world into gray goo; genetically modified trees could destroy Nature's own evolved genomes sending global forests into crash mode; reckless experiments with geoengineering could throw planetary cycles out of whack, or; we could just pursue the promise of mutually assured destruction with an atomic World War Three.

Nobody knows exactly how all this is going to play out—not in the short term, not in the middle term, and not in the long term. Realistically, the next hundred years will likely be bloody ugly, and there is not much we can do about it. Something has got to give, and it will. But after things fall apart, what then?

It would seem to come down to one of two scenarios. One preserves a human presence on the planet, and the other says good riddance to the most destructive evolutionary experiment in the history of the Earth. If humans can live simply and keep their population small while conscientiously integrating themselves into the larger Community of Life, there may be a place for us here. This means creating a culture that rewards shouldering our responsibilities as fully mature human beings and using our special gifts to further the Project of Life: a way of being in the world that I call living in loyalty to the Whole. To achieve this would require an absolute and final divorce between the human and all Power Systems. But Power is a particularly pernicious addiction, and it is one that the human is especially vulnerable to, and the only way to reliably beat it is to go cold turkey—and that means losing one hell of a lot of complexity, and keeping things simple from then on.

Simplicity as an ongoing and long-term way of life does not seem absolutely impossible, because it has been done before. But it is difficult to imagine because all that our people have ever known is complexity—a way of life shaped from early on by the Myth of Progress—a myth that runs especially deep in our culture.

Progress is a phenomenon, and an idea, that cuts two ways, depending on the system it serves. In service to Power Systems, progress is pretty much synonymous with systemic expansion, its growth being facilitated by self-reinforcing positive feedback loops. However veiled their inherent violence, Power Systems inevitably operate on the principle of force, taking down whatever comes in their way.

Progress, when in service to Bio-Systems, is not measured in terms of limitless expansion but rather in terms of system optimization. While Power Systems are oriented outward, in the way of empire, Bio-Systems are inward in orientation, ever seeking to improve the conditions that make Life thrive. Thus, the long historical trajectory of Bio-Systems toward ever

BIOSYSTEMS, POWER SYSTEMS, AND PEOPLE

increasing complexity and diversity of organisms, as well as ever greater resilience of ecosystems, is a progressivism that recognizes the limits of a finite planet, and seeks to make the most of the resources available--and it does this by seeking a balance that optimally serves the Whole. Negative feedback loops and mostly closed systems that recycle, reuse, and repurpose nearly all elements of the system keep these Bio-Systems viable by operating (not toward some maximum extreme, but) at a phase that optimally serves the Whole. Progress within this kind of system comes not so much from outward expansion but with improvement from within. Life, and the Bio-Systems which *are* Life and which *support* Life, are progressive in the same way that evolution is progressive. They are self-organizing, self-regulating, self-healing: in other words, Bio-Systems are self-creating, or, technically, autopoetic. And, since Bio-systems are by nature ecological, they are overwhelmingly cooperative, because while competition may serve individuals and constituent systems, the synergy of cooperation is what best serves the Whole.

There is ample reason to believe that the people of the 21st century will so exhaust all remaining resources that you and the people of your Age will not have the wherewithal to replicate our level of complexity, or become entangled, like we are, with Power Systems. After the inevitable crash of industrial civilization, living conditions for any survivors might still be tolerable, in a downscale kind of way, in a world of broken down, but partially salvageable, artifacts. Several generations of survivors may cling to the detritus of this material culture, even as they try to revive the old ethos of civilization. I do not envy these lost generations whose hopes are pinned on a failed way of life. Some remnant of this after-phase may find its way into the world you inherit, and may influence your own approach to life, which is why I am trying to alert you to the dangers of flirting with Power Systems of any kind. They are very bad news for all Life, including human life. So, please do our species, and all species, a favor, and don't get taken in by the con that has so beguiled your gullible ancestors. And make this choice, if ever it is on offer, knowing why you are choosing humility, simplicity, and engaged connection with the living world over the Power that dines on Life.

CHAPTER 37

RAW CAPITALISM: AN OVERVIEW

FOR WELL OVER a century now we have had a rough and ready two-word description for the particular form of capitalism favored by the rich in this country, and by those who do their bidding. The term, *laissez faire* capitalism, has stood not only for an economic system with minimal governmental interference, but also, vaguely, for the belief system behind this form of capitalism. From the early days of frontier capitalism to the present, our economic system has evolved along particular lines, exposing certain patterns of its internal dynamics. Noting and interpreting these patterns over the years, economists and a few others have come to believe that this complex dynamic system---this tiger we've grabbed by the tail--is subject to human manipulation and is more or less under human control. Even the briefest of glances at our economic history raises questions about how deeply we understand this system, or our place within it. As we look into this matter, I want to employ two distinct historical lenses: one that surveys the surface level of capitalism as it has manifested over the past couple centuries, and; one that probes beneath the surface of culture, looking for the values and perceptions, as well as the ontology and epistemology, that underlie the worldview upon which capitalism is based. For the sake of flow and reading convenience, I will deal with these two separately, and will begin with a brief overview of capitalism as it appears on the surface.

It is a truism, as well as a demonstrable fact, that capitalism devours democracy, and increasingly so in the present age. But what exactly is this formidable beast that goes by the name of capitalism? We hear our economic system variously described as late-stage capitalism, crony capitalism, monopoly capitalism, *laissez faire* capitalism, boom-and-bust capitalism, free-market capitalism, corporate capitalism, casino capitalism, and predatory capitalism. I take it that none of these is mutually exclusive from the others; that each descriptor focuses on one particular aspect of our system, and that all may hold at one and the same time. The term, "late-stage," may hint at its near demise, but certainly implies earlier stages of development, as seen through the retrospective lens of history. And it is through this lens that we may best understand something of the dynamics of this institution which so dominates our lives.

These various qualities of capitalism can be seen as falling into three categories: Late-stage and predatory capitalism are judgments about the system; crony capitalism, boom-and-bust capitalism, corporate capitalism, casino capitalism, and monopoly capitalism are more or less objective observations about tendencies of the system to develop in certain directions: toward consolidation, for instance, as in big businesses eating little businesses (through mergers and acquisitions) and, as giants, dominating their segment of the market--often in the form of cartels or monopoly, and nearly always at the expense of the consumer.

Boom and bust capitalism describes a recurring process of

economic expansion and contraction that tears at the social fabric and tends to leave a lot of people hurting, especially at the low end of the cycle and among the most vulnerable. In America, some of the more pronounced low points of the business cycle were visited upon our ancestors in 1819-20, 1839-43, 1857-60, 1873-78, 1893-97, and 1920-21. Boom times tend to punctuate these periods of bust, and to the extent that prosperity is general among the people, it is approved by all, and taken by most to be the normal way of the world, until the bottom drops out--as it did during the Great Depression of the 1930s.

Crony capitalism has many facets, but in general refers to a good-old-boy network where business people cultivate close personal relationships with each other and with individuals and agencies in government that can either harm or help their business interests. This form of cronyism can take the form of regulatory capture, where the regulators tend to protect the industry they oversee rather than the public interest they are sworn to serve. No-bid contracts, tax breaks, look-the-other-way regulation, favorable legislation, and sweetheart deals of various kinds provide the incentives to pursue this form of cronyism, and the revolving door between business and government provide an excellent opportunity to cultivate these kinds of relationships.

Casino capitalism refers to the financialization of the economy, meaning that Wall Street bankers, hedge fund managers, and speculators in various paper "instruments" have an outsized influence on the economy as whole—on what is often thought of as the "real" economy of goods and services. This "real" economy was once heavily based in the manufacture of material goods, and employed a large well-paid workforce--until those jobs were shipped overseas, thanks to so-called "free-trade" treaties and globalization. Casino capitalism stands in sharp contrast to industrial capitalism in that very little in this world of high-stakes speculation has material substance, but rather is based on esoteric abstractions, schemes for gaming the system, and numbers. The concept of leverage is key to understanding how fortunes can be made and lost based on almost nothing at all. For instance, if a lending institution is legally permitted to lend $100 even though it only has ten in its possession--that is leverage. If this institution buys and sells "instruments" that are leveraged in this same way, the actual collateral behind these pieces of paper grows vanishingly small. This is in essence what precipitated the Great Recession of 2007-2008, and, with the removal of regulatory structures such as Dodd-Frank, is poised to happen again. Casino capitalism is making bets with other people's money, with no accountability and with nothing to lose. The word, "bankster," came into currency as people began to understand how this economic meltdown came into being. Nothing has happened since to diminish the relevance of this term, and of course banksters don't go to jail for their crimes.

    Corporate capitalism, like monopoly capitalism, reflects the growth-and-consolidation imperative endemic to the capitalistic system. While monopoly capitalism undermines and subverts fair competition among suppliers of goods and services, leading to price fixing and price gouging, corporate capitalism tends to undermine and subvert the integrity of the State, and, ultimately, democracy itself. As the corporation has grown in size and power over the past century, and especially in recent decades, it has expanded its reach into nearly every aspect of American political and civil life. Corporate interests set much of the agenda of government, with their lobbyists and lawyers not just influencing lawmaking, but now actually writing the laws themselves. These same interests also control the narrative of civil society through their think-tank-informed corporate media outlets, by framing and highlighting certain issues, while ignoring others that do not accord with the corporate agenda. And with their unceasing barrage of advertising--supersaturating the airwaves with their message of buy, buy, buy--the corporate media not only generates cash flow, but also accomplishes another strategic goal: to reduce potentially well-informed citizens of a democracy into brainwashed, obedient consumers, whose conditioned response to the worsening (and endlessly reported) craziness of the world is: to go shopping.

Also, through a series of strategic U.S. Supreme Court appointments over the years, and predictably favorable decisions, the corporation has managed to gather unto itself all the legal rights of a living human being and citizen, allowing it to leverage these rights into the ability to purchase politicians outright, and to do so more or less legally. In furtherance of their agenda, the corporation can then command their acquiescent politicians to rubberstamp trade agreements drawn up by their own in-house lawyers. Through this means, corporations (now largely multinationals) have found a way to subvert the will of the people at all levels of government, even down to cities, counties, and states. For inserted into treaties such as the North American Free Trade Agreement, and others drawn up since, is a pernicious little item called the Investor-State Dispute Settlement (ISDS) provision, which gives the corporation the right to sue any nation, state, or municipality which passes laws that diminish the projected profits of a corporation. If a city, county, or state tries to protect its quality of life by passing laws against things like GMO crops, Confined Feeding Operations (CAFOs), bee-killing pesticides, or fracking, this ISDS provision gives corporations the right to sue these (invariably cash strapped) representative bodies of the people, suppressing and subverting the constitutional right of local self-governance with entangling and expensive lawsuits, or merely with the threat of such an all-consuming ordeal. All of these aspects of corporate capitalism point in one indisputable direction: the corporation, as a socio-economic institution, is now so huge, so powerful, so far-reaching, as to be out of anyone's control, up to and including that of the corporate-corrupted State.

Free-Market capitalism and *laissez-faire* capitalism are two different ways of describing pretty much the same thing; but these are more than mere descriptors of the system: they represent a set of beliefs--an ideology--about how capitalism works best, and that is with no interference or regulation whatever. This belief is in turn based upon yet another article of faith: that most magical and mysterious of metaphors, the Invisible Hand.

The Invisible Hand was the brainchild of Adam Smith, as presented in his highly influential book, *The Wealth of Nations*, first published in 1776. According to theory, markets are self-organizing, self-regulating entities, and by letting them function without interference they will arrive at an optimum economic and social outcome, as if guided by an invisible hand. This doctrine and article of faith--that markets will self-correct and automatically arrive at optimum outcomes--has guided American capitalism (and proto-capitalism) since the early days of the republic. Over the years, as economic distortions of various stripes have proved to be disruptive to the social order—including stock market crashes, recessions and depressions, runaway inflation, etc.—there has been, and continues to be, much partisan wrangling over the extent to which external controls should or should not be applied by the State.

Proponents of *Laissez Faire* capitalism, aka free-market fundamentalists, advocate for no regulation at all: let the markets decide the shape our society should take. There of course will be winners and there will be losers, but let the all-wise invisible hand sort this out for us, free from human attempts at "social engineering." The word, fundamentalist--with its connotation of religious fervor--aptly describes many who hold this unquestioning belief that the capitalist economic system is inhabited and directed by an infallible and benevolent spirit who knows what is best for us. One notable feature of this particular article of faith is that it privileges one group or class of people over another, greatly amplifying the disparity between the investor/owner class and everyone else. Thus, belief in the free-market must be understood as a cultivated ideology, and one with a particular class bias.

Back in the days of the rampaging robber-barons and on into the Gilded Age, this ideology had the name of liberalism, and it dovetailed nicely with our national program of westward expansion and unrestrained exploitation of resources, known as Manifest Destiny. Under the doctrine of liberalism, individual fortunes were made, to be sure, but the nation as a whole was seen to prosper in the process, and so, in a mood of self-congratulation *laissez faire* capitalism charged full steam ahead through the 19th century and into the 20$^{th.}$ Of course there were periods of boom and bust along the way, but the system continued to more or less prosper, until one day in 1929 when it didn't. Following the stock market crash of 1929 and the ensuing decade-long economic contraction known as the Great Depression, it was hard times all around. Somehow, against all hope and belief, *laissez faire* capitalism had failed.

The New Deal policies instituted by Franklin D. Roosevelt (from 1933 onwards), were based on the economic theories of John Maynard Keynes, and implementing them greatly expanded the role of government within the economic sphere. Although these economic policies did not in themselves reverse all of the effects of the depression—it would take America's entry into World War Two to bring that about—Roosevelt's New Deal programs did improve the lives of many ordinary Americans. For serving the unwashed masses in this way Roosevelt was called by many of his contemporaries "a traitor to his class." Only much later would it be acknowledged that through his judicious use of socialism, Roosevelt had actually saved capitalism from its own self-sabotaging excesses.

For the power-elite, capitalism on welfare might be tolerated during this period of emergency, but they really didn't like the State having this much power over them: to tax their fortunes, regulate their business practices, and redistribute their wealth downward. They preferred to see money flowing upward instead, toward them, and they would make a long-term project out of bringing this flow reversal into being. This project would start out modestly enough, with the 1938 meeting of a handful of economically-oriented European intellectuals, but would gain momentum over the years and decades, to become the dominant economic narrative of the late 20th and early 21st century. The closely held name for this project was neoliberalism, and for decades its doctrines seemed to have no name to bring them into focus. Now the name, and the agenda it represents, is less veiled than ever before, but is still only visible to those who know what to look for.

The term, neoliberalism, suggests that it is a newer form of liberalism: an improved model of an older, but outdated, institution. And so it is seen by its faithful adherents. The raw capitalism of the nineteenth century and the first half of the 20th, as reviewed here, is a product of an older order associated with a worldview known as liberalism. Neoliberalism is based upon many of the same assumptions as liberalism, but much intensified and taken to an extreme—and I would say, a malevolent, pathological extreme.

CHAPTER 38

ONCE WAS WANNABE

THERE HAVE BEEN times in my life when I wished I were an Indian, just as there were times when I wished I had been born into a different Age--before nature had been so overrun by man. From a very young age I craved a life lived within the natural world, simple, direct, and infused with spirit. I first experienced this kind of contact with nature at the age of eight, spending many long hours out in the woods, or out in our rowboat on the lake in front of our house, most often alone. A young person alone in nature has a chance to experience the world directly, and to soak up its sacredness, its spiritual dimension. This I did, and the experience deeply influenced my orientation to life. Once you know that Mother Earth is sacred, once you yourself are filled to overflowing with reverence and respect and awe in the face of this sacredness, that knowledge is within you, and not easily put aside. This early experience, reinforced many times over the years, no doubt figures into the spiritual yearnings I was feeling around the age of fifty, yearnings which led me to become a spiritual seeker and Indian wannabe.

THE CULTURE TRAP

Probably my first thought of wanting to be an Indian came when I was in the fifth grade. Fifth grade was my favorite, because it was there that I first learned about cultures other than my own. I remember taking an interest in the Aztecs and Incas, because they seemed different from 1950s Americans. But not a really deep interest, because they crowded together in cities and lived under harsh authoritarian rule. The people who truly fascinated me were the North American Indians. I liked it that they lived in small groups, close to nature, and made their living directly from the natural world. I liked the way they lived in their world without destroying it, and the way nobody was really boss over anyone else. I thought it was okay that they didn't have a lot of the stuff we have, because they had something more important. I couldn't say exactly what that something was, but I had a strong sense that their lives were closer to the way people ought to live than the lives of the Southern Californians I knew: working jobs they disliked, getting caught in traffic snarls, and caught up in that competitive consumption of time-payment nonessentials that we then called "keeping up with the Jonses." I recall overcoming my natural shyness to speak up in class to say that, to me, the lives of the American Indian looked pretty good. I meant their traditional lives, not their lives on reservations, and I still recall my teacher's response. She assured me that not only did Indians sometimes die of starvation, and suffer innumerable discomforts along the way; the worst thing was that they couldn't choose to be whatever they wanted to be the way we lucky modern Americans could, or develop their own individuality the way we could. I paid attention to what she said, but wasn't then sure how much of it to believe. At that time I was not an Indian wannabe, but only a wannabe in the making.

Later in life, I would take timid further steps in that direction. In graduate school, for instance, I made a special study of the American mountain man, and identified with much of the life he led. Not the trapping part, not the killing and skinning of fur-bearing mammals, but living in big, true wilderness, far away from loathsome cities, testing himself against the many challenges that come with a life of freedom in unspoiled nature. Another side of the mountain man's life that I came eventually to recognize was that he, too, was ultimately a pawn in somebody else's chess game, just a small-time functionary in the resource colony that was then the American mountain West. When the fur trade died out, because gentlemen in Europe had taken to wearing silk rather than beaver hats, the mountain man was faced with some hard choices. Some did choose to take up the settled ways of the farmer, and a few, maybe, were happy in that life. But according to my reading, the ones who died happiest were those who went to live among the Indians, and continued to make their living in the wild country they loved—living the lives of Indians. I knew that if I was in their situation, and those were my choices, I, too, would have elected to live as an Indian. All of this was of course historical speculation in the land of What If.

Years later, I would be just as enthralled as many others were when the movie, *Dances with Wolves,* appeared on the big screen. Lieutenant Dunbar, played by Kevin Kostner, was a sympathetic character with whom I could identify. But what made this film different from the usual Hollywood fare was that the Indians were also cast in a sympathetic light. It was the white soldiers, not the tipi dwellers, who were the brutal savages, and it was easy to see why Dunbar was attracted to a people so in harmony with their world. And of course there was the added attraction of Mary McConnell to help win Dunbar over to joining the tribe. Here again, I would have made the same choice, and elected to become an honorary Indian.

Up to this point I was not truly an Indian wannabe, even if I did show some leanings that way. But my wannabe status was soon about to change, and in kind of an odd way. By the early nineteen eighties some kind of cultural shift had taken place that started to be reflected in the publishing world. Books, by and about Indians, began to appear in my local bookstore. This shift was heralded by an unheard-of event in 1969. The Pulitzer Prize that year was awarded to the Native American writer, N. Scott Momaday, for his novel, *House Made of Dawn.* The following year saw the publication of a groundbreaking history of Indian and white relations, written in a popular style, which turned the majority culture's stereotyped notions upside down. Meticulously documenting his narrative, Dee Brown showed, in case after case, how underhanded, rapacious, and bloodthirsty were (not the Indians, but) the white settlers and soldiers. That book was *Bury my Heart at Wounded Knee,* and it was a bestseller. Also a bestseller was prize-winning and critically acclaimed *Love Medicine,* by Louise Erdrich. That book came out in 1984, and other fiction entries by Native American authors were soon to follow, including one of my favorites, *A Yellow Raft on Blue Water,* by Michael Dorris (1987).

These books, and other fictional entries by such Native writers as D'Arcy McNickle, Leslie Marmon Silko, James Welch, Linda Hogan, and Sherman Alexie, fed a growing interest in this fascinating American sub-culture. Also at this time, the work of some of our most gifted, insightful, and sympathetic anthropologists became widely available, and added depth to our understanding of Indian culture. The two that most influenced me were *Make Prayers to the Raven: A Koyukon View of the Northern Forest* (1983) by Richard Nelson, and *Ishi: Last of His Tribe* by Theodora Kroeber, (not an anthropologist herself but much indebted to the work of her anthropologist husband, Alfred Kroeber, 1973). Other important work by non-natives include Peter Matthiessen's *In the Spirit of Crazy Horse,* which first came out in 1983, but was soon caught up in a ten-year legal tangle, and did not receive a wider audience until the early mid-nineties. I saw this book as an updating of Dee Brown's earlier efforts, detailing, as it does, the ongoing state-sponsored oppression of these beleaguered people.

I began reading books by and about Indians in the mid- to late- nineteen eighties, not just because they were now available, but for reasons of my own. I was thinking then of writing a book that centered around my great grandfather, who had for eight years been the Indian Agent for the Sac and Fox Tribe near Ames, Iowa. I had a cedar chest containing letters, photographs, and newspaper clippings all about this man, Horace Rebok, and his work, as well as a book he had written about his charges. Unlike many other such Agents, Horace was actually an advocate for, and friend to, those people he oversaw. He was a compassionate man as well as a clear and progressive thinker, but he was, after all, a product of his age, and believed that his charges must change their ways and assimilate into the majority culture. I thought him an interesting man, but I thought before I wrote about his life as an Indian Agent I should first learn more about these people he was tending.

That is what started me reading books by and about Indians, which eventually led me into my misguided and abortive status as Indian wannabe. It was actually none of the books mentioned above that sent me in that direction, but two that stand alone in my mind as monuments of a particular kind. Both books were biographical in nature, each focusing on a particular Lakota (Sioux) medicine man. Both were written with the help of a white co-author, and each has its own luminous quality that sets it apart from all others. Yet the two books, both dealing with matters of a profound spiritual nature, could hardly be more different from each other in tone and general import. *Black Elk Speaks,* (first published in 1932 but reprinted several times in the 1980s) is of course a literary classic, and is generally held to be one of the hundred most significant books of the twentieth century. The book is poetic in style and mythopoetic in import. It is also somewhat formal in tone, as seems appropriate to depicting a human being of very high stature. That stature is something of a marvel, considering the horrific experiences of the young Black Elk—including the wholesale slaughter and displacement of his people.

What impressed me most when reading this book were two distinct but related phenomena: One was the vibrancy of the underlying culture that must have existed to produce such a fully developed human being as Black Elk; the other was the potency of the spiritual tradition that lay behind Black Elk's visions. In spite of everything, I found myself longing to claim such a cultural heritage as my own. To understand that reaction, you pretty much have to have read the book.

Impressed as I was with *Black Elk Speaks,* I was even more deeply influenced by a book about a rather different sort of Lakota holy man. In the wonderfully engaging book, *Lame Deer: Seeker of Visions* (1972) by John (Fire) Lame Deer and Richard Erdoes, the central character proves to be more wholly-man than holy-man. And that in fact turns out to be the main thrust of the book, which, with great good humor and irreverence, mixes the sacred with the profane even as it confounds absurdity with profundity. Lame Deer is no cast-in-plaster saint, but is, rather, a shrewd, lusty, rambunctious, fun-loving spirit who seems to encompass the whole of human nature, in all its contradictory complexity, within the compass of a single man. Lame Deer is in this way very much like his culture's perception of the Creator, Wakan Tanka—who is two parts Profane Trickster to three parts Divine Perfection to four parts Inexplicable Mystery.

These two books, taken together, gave me a severe case of

spiritual envy. I felt that I, as an individual, was very much lacking in the fullness of spirit and range of personality that I detected in both these remarkable individuals. I found myself willing to take part of the responsibility for my own arrested development, but not all. My culture, I believed, was also partly responsible. Culture is taken into the individual by a process not unlike osmosis. It is absorbed through the very pores of one's skin, without even being noticed. My culture, it seemed to me, has produced a lot of individuals not unlike myself: full of inhibitions, emotionally stunted, spiritually uptight. These are qualities that a person barely notices about himself and his fellows, until he is exposed to people from a very different culture, such as through international travel. In my case, travel and these two books coincided to make me see the formerly invisible. My culture, it became plain, shaped individuals within its sphere of influence into something like what Sherwood Anderson called grotesques—persons whose emotional and spiritual development has been held in check, to the point of deformity, in much the same way that the Chinese selected for small feet among its women: by imposing constraints upon growth.

Not liking to think of myself as somehow incomplete, I found this a painful revelation; and this, in part, is what motivated me toward my nascent, but intensifying, wannabe status. But more than this, I felt a lack of spirituality in my life. I yearned for a sense of connection to a spiritual tradition that was truly meaningful to me, and it seemed that the belief system of the North American Indian tribes was a better fit for me than any other.

All this came on the heels of three years of reading nothing but books by or about Indians—really steeping myself in the subject. The reading had prompted me to write a novel about Indians, which I decided to set on the Pine Ridge Reservation, in South Dakota, home of the Oglala Sioux. While back there researching the book I had picked up a couple handbooks on Lakota spiritual practice and ritual, and had begun using these as a reference point. I was trying to design my own way of worship, if worship is actually the right word for what I mean. I felt a need not only to attune myself to the cosmos but to express my gratitude and appreciation for the wonders of this world. As someone born and raised in America, I was of course exposed to our nation's predominant religion. Twice in my life—once as a teenager and once at forty—I was for a time a true believer in this book religion of a faraway masculine deity. But what I was looking for now was an Earth-based spiritual practice, one that would connect me spiritually to my own home planet, and to my own chosen place upon it.

I was born a lover of Nature, and seemed to know, from a very young age, that Nature held sway over man, and not--as everyone else seemed to believe--the other way around. Likewise, I have always been more impressed with the works of Nature than with the works of man. I have, for instance, long thought cities an abomination upon the land, and have, accordingly, from an early age, yearned to be near mountains, rivers, and the forest primeval. When there was any choice in the matter at all, I have elected to live near trees and streams, and in the foothills, at least, of serious mountains, as I have for most of my life, and do today. In the latter part of the twentieth century, people started coining terms to describe the kind of person I am—words like biocentric and ecocentric, suggesting a worldview that values the Whole over one's own species. But I am not at all happy to use these terms in relation to myself, and in fact regard these clumsy neologisms as not merely a deficiency of our language, but of our culture. By which I mean that we, as a people, are not possessed of the necessary supporting conceptual framework and value system to give voice, and clear definition, to this idea of putting Nature first. And that, I believe, is because we are an anthropocentric people who have taken as our charge to dominate, control, and—as that "good book" tells us—"take dominion over" Nature.

In this regard, I have always felt alienated from my own culture. I know my people are wrong about Nature, and about the status of the human being within the cosmos, as well as on this, our one and only home planet. I know that we are not the center of it all, but just another among a wondrous cornucopia of other Earth-born species. Yes, we are bright, and have some prodigious talents and proclivities. Yes, we are special in many ways. But every species has qualities that make it special—to itself, and within the context of the larger life community. Myself, I want to celebrate that community. I want to celebrate it in and of itself, to marvel at its intricate complexities and simplicities. And I want to give thanks for having a place within that community. I need an outlet for the gratitude I feel for being alive in such a place and time; an outlet for the awe and deep appreciation that builds up in me when I contemplate, or directly experience, the ways of Nature. That was why, in the early1990s, I was looking into the spiritual practice of America's natives, and began carving a ceremonial pipe, along lines suggested by Lakota spiritual tradition. This pipe would come to serve an important function for me, as will be seen, but not at all the one intended.

In any case, it seemed to me that the Indians felt much the same way about the natural world that I do, and about the place of the human within that world. I knew from my reading that among North America's five hundred tribes no two had identical rituals or spiritual practice. Yet, among them all, and, really, among all tribal peoples everywhere, the basic outlook was essentially the same. As hunter/gatherers—and to some degree or other, nomadic—tribal peoples have always lived in the hands of the gods. Living in the hands of the gods selects toward certain qualities within human societies, including well-developed faculties of perception and a general competence in many tasks related to survival, along with an accompanying pride in keen perception and well-honed skills. But offsetting that pride of competence came also the deep humility of recognizing the place of the human enterprise within the larger scheme of things. The survival of the tribe or band depended not only upon the "balance of Nature" but also the "whims of Nature": an especially cold winter, say, or an especially hot century or two. When your life depends upon the whims and balances in nature, and you recognize this fact of your life, you have some incentive to stay on the good side of the gods, and also to engage in practices that have worked well for your ancestors, and not engage in those that led to failure or collapse.

When a people live in the hands of the gods, they are forced to recognize limits, and to live within those limits. They tend to be appreciative of nature's bounty and alert to her varying moods. They cultivate an appropriately humble respect for both natural law and natural caprice. Every tribe has particular plants and animals that they depend upon for survival, and frequently have special rituals relating to those they rely upon most. But all creatures are recognized as belonging to Earth's community of life. Some tribal people, such as the Koyukon, of the northwest interior of Alaska, have an extensive oral tradition concerning virtually every plant and animal they encounter in their daily lives. Fortunately, much of the tribal lore surrounding these plants and animals has been preserved by the anthropologist Richard Nelson, in his fascinating narrative, *Make Prayers to the Raven: A Koyukon View of the Northern Forest.* The Koyukon, like most tribal people, see themselves as being related to all the other creatures, a concept often expressed, by many tribes, in the phrase "all our relations." According to Nelson, "All animals, some plants, and some elements of the physical environment possess spirits and spiritual power."(p.228) In addition, "Humanity, nature, and the supernatural are all joined within a single moral order." Most Native Americans believe, as do the Koyokon, that they owe specific responsibilities to the natural world. It is their duty, generally, to keep their world healthy, and to care, specifically, for those creatures upon whom they depend for their survival. "Nature is to be petitioned and pacified, not forcibly conquered, because nature holds the ultimate power."(p241)

This regard for the other creatures of the Earth, held to some degree by all tribal people, was another one of those things that prompted me to attempt American Indian spiritual practice. For I too feel a kinship with the other creatures of the planet, and would like to acknowledge this in some ritualistically formal way.

Another aspect of Indian culture that I then found appealing, and still do, is the religious tolerance of the people. Among the Koyukon, for example, religious tolerance is related to a broader acceptance of differences among individuals.

Applicability of rules is contingent on belief. People who do not believe in a rule, or set of rules, or the entire ideology may be exempted from punishment for violations against natural entities. This is an important contributor to individuality or heterogeneity that characterized belief and practice among the Koyukon.(p232)

These people are not ruled by absolutes. If this is moral relativism, it is of a type I can approve.

I very much like the idea that an individual can be himself and still be accepted within the group. As Nelson observes of the Koyukon: "They take a highly individualistic approach to all aspects of life, and religion (both traditional and Christian) is no exception."(p235) Thinking of the strong personalities that arose among the various 19th century American tribes—Red Cloud, Crazy Horse, Geronimo, Cochise, Tecumseh, Chief Seattle, Captain Jack, Chief Joseph—only confirms that individualism was nurtured, rather than suppressed, among the Indians. My fifth grade teacher had gotten it exactly backwards. The Indians cultivated individuality, while my own culture cultivated conformity.

I liked it that the Indians practiced egalitarianism, allowing strong personalities to hold whatever sway they could, but granting them no special institutional support, such as hereditary succession. I liked it that the Indians were communitarian—that is, they took care of their own, orphans, widows, and all. Recognizing their interdependence, and the importance of harmony within the group, they shared what they had with one another, and did not value the accumulation of wealth, the power of riches, or inordinate status. They were, in their own glorious way, uncivilized. All of this appealed to me, but it was their metaphysics that appealed to me most, because, like me, they thought of themselves as creatures of this Earth.

My home, spiritual or otherwise, is not in some far-off place, in some realm invisible to the human eye. My heaven, my home, is here on earth, and I crave a way of acknowledging and expressing my relationship to my own home ground. Any religion that tells me to ignore my home and focus elsewhere does not fulfill this basic need.

Nor am I much enamored with that class of person who identifies himself as of the priesthood. I clearly recognize that other persons may be more spiritually advanced than I am, and that there is much I can learn from such individuals. I even acknowledge that others may be in touch with a spiritual realm not fully accessible to me—especially when they enter this realm by means of trance, sacred plants, or unusual privations. I recognize that the work of a shaman is specialized, and perhaps beyond my own competence. But my reading of history, and especially of European history in medieval times, convinces me that the priesthood, as a class of persons in society, are little better than parasites upon a gullible society. And, apart from anything remotely spiritual, the priesthood, as a class, represents an authoritarian, paternalistic, hierarchical, patriarchal, exploitative form of social organization I find antithetical to my own brand of egalitarianism. I like to see power dispersed among the many, rather than concentrated in the hands of the few. American Indian spirituality also appealed to me on this score. Yes, they did have medicine people who specialized in spiritual healing, and those who performed special rituals. And, yes, these people might have a special prestige within the tribe, because of their unusual gifts. But that is all. Very seldom were they elevated to the role of tyrant.

When as an undergraduate I took a course in comparative religions, I believed for a while that I had finally found the right religion for me. That religion was Taoism, and I was immediately drawn to it because it is a nature-based system of beliefs. The Tao means the Way. To live in the Tao means to resonate in harmony with the cosmos. Or this at least was my interpretation, based upon the Tao Te Ching and what the teacher and textbook had to say. This felt right to me, and I was ready right there and then to become a Taoist. When I began to contemplate how I was going to become a Taoist, I came up against a barrier I could see no way around. Was I going to become a Taoist by assiduously reading the Tao Te Ching? That seemed the only way open to me, but also highly inadequate, not to mention sad and pathetic. To attempt Taoism in that way, as a lone individual going against the grain of my own cultural traditions and society seemed about as anti-Tao as anything

I could think of. To become a Taoist, attuned to the Way and to the cosmos, I realized, a person pretty much had to be born into a Taoist culture, and learn the precepts of Lao Tzu at the knee of one's elders. With that revelation, my short career as a Taoist came to an end. And I was back in limbo again, a lone individual without a community of faith.

When I found myself admiring the spiritual tradition of the American Indian, and yearned for it to be my own, I had conveniently forgotten this insight of some thirty years before. What brought it back to me, and with force, was the breaking of a stone.

That stone was a rosy pink pipestone that had come from a cliff face in northern Minnesota. What I was thinking when I picked it up at a powwow in central Oregon was that I might just carve myself a peace pipe. From what I had been reading, for the Indians of the American plains, a ceremonial pipe of the type I was contemplating was a kind of portable altar. It had power and was sacred. Smoking it in a ceremonial way could connect one to the cosmos. This, I thought, was for me.

The stone I had was about three times too big for the pipe I envisioned. Accordingly, after some trepidation, I ran the rock through my bandsaw, lopping off a blank of just the right dimensions. Both blade and stone survived this strange pairing. Then I drilled out the bowl and the draw hole. I felt like I was cheating, using these power tools, but decided to focus on ends rather than means. I found that a pocket knife worked okay to shape the pipe, but that a wood rasp worked even better. The blank was now beginning to take on a bit of its ultimate shape, though still a bit square in places. I had worked on this hunk of semi-soft rock for about five hours, and figured I must have two or three more to go, when, without warning the pipe broke apart in my hands. I was exerting some pressure on it with the rasp, but no more than I had at other times along the way. But there it was, in two pieces, in the palm of my hand.

Upon close examination I noticed a thin layer of a silica-like substance on the fissure line of each piece. Evidently, this thin layer of impurity had been laid down, perhaps hundreds of thousands of years ago, as the rose-colored stone was formed. Being just a thin, clear line, nobody had noticed it. But that little bit of brittleness had been enough to sabotage my efforts, and now I had to decide what to do about it.

Crazy glue was out of the question. Even if it would work, that was just one falseness too many. I looked over the remaining stone and thought I saw a way to make a pipe from it that would exclude the impurity. But I wouldn't be working on it today. I was still shaken by this piece of bad luck, and thought it best to quit before I got further behind.

In the following days I would have time to think about the pipe, and what its breaking meant to me. I did not, first of all, see it as mere accident. This was a message from the spirit world, and it was up to me to figure out what it meant. As I meditated on the matter, my former insight about Taoism came back to me. What I began to realize is that there is no way I could ever authentically practice someone else's religion. This spiritual practice, using the stone pipe and Lakota ritual, belonged to those who were born to it. It did not belong to me, and never authentically could.

This knowledge saddened me. My own culture's spiritual tradition, with all its improbable and anthropocentric doctrines, was woefully wrong for me. And so, I now realized, was everyone else's. It seemed I was a spiritual orphan, and there was nothing I could do about it. This condition was an anomaly, I was sure. The more normal condition of man, throughout all human prehistory, had surely been to grow up in the spiritual tradition of one's people, and to practice that religion as a matter of course, with all its spiritual satisfactions. I was sad because I could never have that experience.

I have heard it said that religion is an individual thing, and in a way it is. Each of us comes to personal conclusions about our own individual relationship to the cosmos and to the Earth and our fellow creatures. Fair enough. But in another sense, religious practice is very much a group experience. By that I do not mean just a social event, though religious practice is very often certainly that. More fundamentally, religion is a socially agreed upon view of the world, and of man's place in that world. Usually, rituals, taboos, and codes of conduct accompany a creation story that tells us who we are and what we are here for. Back in the days when people lived out their lives pretty much within the confines of their own home territory, a group's religious belief and practice helped to hold that group together, to give it social cohesion. Religion in this case served a vital survival function, and its consequences were mostly all positive.

Small groups of people, tribes and bands all over the globe, each evolved their own creation story and code of conduct. Cultural diversity, and absolute religious freedom, was then the rule. Religion was not then dogmatic or absolutist, it was just a story to live by. Nobody was trying to force their gods upon anybody else. And that lasted right up until the rise of monotheism, when suddenly there was only one true god—though several such arose in different places--and you had better believe in this god, and no other, or else! I'm pretty sure that is what the Crusades were supposed to be about, as was many another "holy war." And this cramming of one's god down the throats of others remains the work of missionaries right up to this very day. Somehow, I find this militancy, this tyranny of the one true god, to be out of harmony with what I think of as spiritualism, or even a decent sort of humanity. And now here we are, in the 21ˢᵗ century, and presumably so advanced, fighting bloody wars of religious ideology.

    Primitivist that I am, Nature lover, and Indian wannabe, I think it makes more sense to embrace the spirit within the tree, the river, the osprey in flight; to find connection with the cosmos in the clear night sky, to touch and be touched by the Earth while picking huckleberries in the mountains, or, while looking up from mushroom picking in the old growth forest and sense a brooding presence all around; or, to sit atop a high mountain, and take in the landscape below, seeing in the curving roundness of Earth a wondrous super-organism known as Gaia, and in that moment of seeing it all whole, relishing one's own part and place, one's own connection to the All. Such spiritual practice does not constitute a religion. It is a solitary and highly personal form of worship, if worship is the word. But it is all that is left to me, and will have to suffice. Since I can't go back in time, and be born into a tribe that loves and respects the natural world, there's not much left to wannabe. Not in this, the only life I know of.

BIBLIOGRAPHY

Bernays, E.L. (1963). *Public Relations.* Norman, OK: University of Oklahoma Press.

Brink, N.E. (2016). *Trance Journeys of the Hunter-Gatherers.* Rochester, VT: Bear & Co.

Brown, D. (1970). *Bury My Heart at Wounded Knee.* New York, NY: Holt, Rinehart & Winston.

DeMeo, J. (2011). *Saharasia: The 4000 BCE Origins of Child Abuse, Sex-Repression, Warfare, and Social Violence in the Deserts of the World.* Ashland, OR: Natural Energy Works.

Dorris, M. (2003). *A Yellow Raft on Blue Water.* London, UK: Picador Press

Erdrich, L. (2016). *Love Medicine.* New York, NY: Harper Perennial

Forbes, J.D. & Jensen, D. (2008). *Columbus and Other Cannibals: The Wetiko Disease of Exploitation, Imperialism and Terrorism.* New York, NY: Seven Stories Press.

Gebser, J. (1985). *The Ever-Present Origin.* Athens, OH: Ohio University Press.

Goodman, F.D. (1992). *Ecstasy, Ritual, and Alternate Reality: Religion in a Pluralistic World.* Bloomington. IN: Indiana University Press.

Jensen, D. (2011). *Dreams.* New York, NY: Seven Stories Press.

Jensen, D., Keith, L. & Wilbert, M. (2021). *Bright Green Lies: How the Environmental Movement Lost Its Way and What We Can Do About It.* Rhinebeck, NY: Monkfish Book Publishing Co.

Kroeber, T. (2011) *Ishi: Last of His Tribe.* Berkeley, CA: University of California Press.

Kroeber, A. (2012) *Handbook of the Indians of California.* New York, NY: Dover Publications.

Kuzhar, L.A. & Sanderson, S.K. (2006). *Studying Societies and Cultures: Marvin Harris's Cultural Materialism and Its Legacy.* New York, NY: Routledge Press

Lame Deer, J & Erdoes, R. (1972) *Lame Deer: Seeker of Visions.* New York, NY: Pocket Books

Lash, J. L. (2006). *Not in His Image: Gnostic Vision, Sacred Ecology, and The Future of Belief.* River Junction, VT: Chelsea Green Publishing.

Liedloff, J. (1986). *The Continuum Concept: In Search of Happiness Lost.* Boston, MA: DeCapo Press.

Matthiesen, P. (1983). *In the Spirit of Crazy Horse.* New York, NY: Viking Press.

Momaday, N. S. (2018). *House Made of Dawn.* New York, NY: Harper Perennial.

Mumford, F. (1971). *Myth of the Machine: Technics and Human Development.* New York, NY: Mariner Books.

Neihardt, J. G. (1972). *Black Elk Speaks.* Albany, NY: State University of New York Press.

Nelson, R. (1983). *Make Prayers to the Raven: A Koyukon View of the Northern Forest.* Chicago, IL: University of Chicago Press.

Sahlins, M. (1972). *Stone Age Economics.* Hawthorne, NY: Aldine Publishing Co.

BIBLIOGRAPHY

Scott, J.C. (2018). *Against the Grain: A Deep History of the Earliest States.* New Haven, CT: Yale University Press.

Simard, S. & Gagliano, M. (2018). *Thus Spoke the Plant: A Remarkable Journey of Groundbreaking Scientific Discoveries and Personal Encounters with Plants.* Berkeley, CA: North Atlantic Books.

Smith, A. (2003). *The Wealth of Nations.* New York, NY: Bantam Classics.

Taylor, S. (2005). *The Fall: The Insanity of the Ego in Human History and the Dawning of a New Age.* Alresford, UK: Iff Books, John Hunt Publishing.

Wells, S. (2011). *Pandora's Seed: Why the Hunter-Gatherer Hold the Key to Our Survival.* New York, NY: Random House.

Wohlleben, P. (2016). *The Hidden Life of Trees: What They Feel, How They Communicate – Discoveries from a Secret World.* Vancouver, British Columbia: Greystone Books.

www.ingramcontent.com/pod-product-compliance
Lightning Source LLC
Chambersburg PA
CBHW031611160426
43196CB00006B/91